OHIO TOWN

OHIO TOWN

Helen Hooven Santmyer

Ohio State University Press
Columbus

Library of Congress Cataloging-in-Publication Data

Santmyer, Helen Hooven, 1895–
    Ohio town / Helen Hooven Santmyer.
        p.   cm.
    Includes bibliographical references.
    ISBN 0-8142-0757-x (alk. paper)
        1. Xenia (Ohio)—History.   I. Title.
F499.X4S3   1998
977.1′74—dc21   97-51223
                                                CIP

Cover design by Gore Studio Inc.
Type set in Fairfield.
Printed by Cushing-Malloy, Inc.

The paper used in this publication meets the minimum requirements of the
American National Standard for Information Sciences—Permanence of Paper
for Printed Library Materials. ANSI Z39.48-1992.

9 8 7 6 5 4 3 2

ACKNOWLEDGMENTS

The following sketches are drawn mostly from memory, mine or my elders'; the passage of time may have colored some events to the detriment of accuracy. In addition to what I remember or have been told, there are on record those reminiscences printed from time to time in our paper, the *Xenia Daily Gazette,* written by staff members or contributed in the form of letters by aging inhabitants or by former residents who look back to the town with affection. To these editors, reporters, and correspondents, I gratefully acknowledge my indebtedness.

For information about the town's beginnings I have used these books:

BLACK, ROBERT L. *The Little Miami Railroad.* Cincinnati: No publisher, n.d. [1940].

BROADSTONE, M. A. *History of Greene County, Ohio.* 2 vols. Indianapolis: B. F. Bowen Co., n.d. [1919].

DILLS, R. S. *History of Greene County.* Dayton, O.: Odell and Mayer, 1881.

Greene County, 1803–1908, edited by a Committee of the Homecoming Association. Xenia, O.: Aldine Publishing Co., 1908.

HOWE, HENRY. *Historical Collections of Ohio.* 3 vols. Columbus, O.: Henry Howe and Sons, 1890.

Out of the Wilderness: An Account of Events in Greene County, Ohio, edited by the History Committee of the Greene County Sesquicentennial Organization. Ann Arbor, Mich.: Edwards Brothers, 1953.

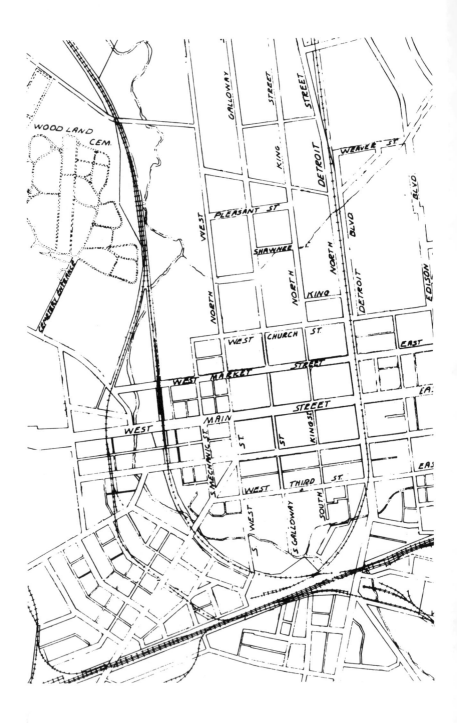

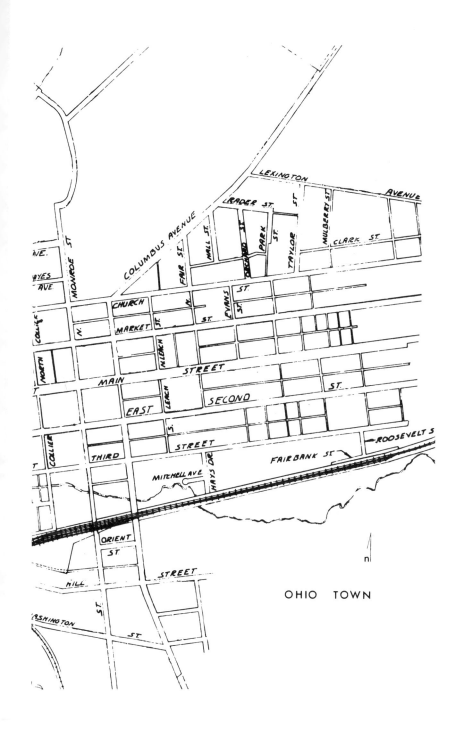

OHIO TOWN

CONTENTS

1. The Courthouse

THE COURTHOUSE SQUARE is the heart of the town. A truth that hardly needs stating, were it not indeed so obvious as never to have been stated, in one's own mind, until the moment comes for remembering and recording. Strangers—tourists following route numbers down Main or Detroit Street—must hardly give the courthouse a conscious thought, its bulk and bad architecture half-hidden as they are behind the trees. County towns are strung along all middle western roads at intervals of twenty or thirty miles, and few courthouses are worth a second glance. But the native cannot be quite so unaware of ours while he is in its neighborhood. Along with the state of the weather and the time of day, there has always been in his mind a background consciousness of the tower with its four-faced clock, the goose-girl drinking fountain on the Main Street curb, the spread of lawn, and the trees in the square whose crests are stirred by winds higher than the roof. For decades there was little change from year to year in any item of the catalogue. Season succeeded to season, and each restored the trees to what they had been before, and did not make of them anything new or different. They were

3

too old to have increased their stature within the memory of anyone there to see them. They were older by several lifetimes than the courthouse; some were more than saplings when space was cleared among them for the first one-room hut of hewn logs that served as the seat of justice.

Now most of the curbside elms have died and been cut down, and the new young trees on the lawn give little promise of attaining the old overarching lift and fall of sunlit branches. And the goose-girl fountain with flowing water on three levels for horse, man, and dog, has been removed as an unnecessary and hideous obstruction. The native who has stayed at home may possibly carry this changed picture in his mind's eye even when it is not before him, but he who has departed to seek his fortune elsewhere sees the courthouse still as an unchanging backdrop for the scenes of his childhood.

In whatever distant place you may be, if you step across a gutter piled with sooty snow, you remember the north side of the square, the hitching bars, and the naked sycamore trees as they were on winter noons when you walked home from school on that side of Market Street because there you could throw snowballs without endangering windows or passers-by. Or, seeing a bandstand on some village green, empty but for blown autumn leaves, you remember concerts by the Sons of Veterans' Band on slowly darkening summer evenings, when you played a kind of surreptitious hide-and-seek around the platform on the Greene Street side of the square, between scattered camp chairs on the grass, in and out among the couples strolling beneath the trees.

And Saturday night in any town will forever recall the Saturday-night excitement of the past, when the curb in front of the courthouse was the center of noise and light and crowded movement. All day long the Negro draymen had lined Greene Street, waiting for customers, their sleepy horses nodding between the shafts of ramshackle drays; all day long every inch of the Main Street curb had been occupied by farmers who had brought their wares to market and spread them on trestle tables on the grass: corn, watermelons, cantaloupes, eggs, and poultry. But after supper draymen and farmers were gone, their places taken by medicine men, mesmerists, phrenologists, painless pullers-of-teeth, strong men in tights, competing against each other with strident voices and powerful lungs, under flaring acetylene lights, while the singing of the Salvation Army from some nearby corner served as raucous accompaniment. Many were frequent and familiar visitors: Rattlesnake Pete, selling rattlesnake oil as a cure-all; Madame Sari, the Hindu snake charmer with her boa constrictor coiling itself around her neck; and Montana Mose, whose corn cure, "once used by Napoleon's army," was sold in pauses between Wild West stories as tall as Paul Bunyan. "Once upon a time," when Montana Mose was caught beyond hope of flight by the stampede of a buffalo herd three miles long and a mile wide, he escaped by leaping from his saddle to the back of a bull, and so, jumping from buffalo to buffalo, let the whole herd pass beneath him . . . "And remember, gentlemen, your corns will never bother you again. . . ."

When you are not reminded—when you are simply remembering in idle revery the town of your childhood—the first vision to flash upon the inward eye is still a vision of the courthouse: the courthouse as it was on quiet summer afternoons, when nothing moved in the length and breadth of the sun-blazing streets, and only a few persons were to be seen in open shop doors or on the benches under the elms; when the trees themselves were limp, unstirring; when the tiled roof was red-hot against the sky, and the hands of the clock in the tower stood motionless at "ten to three."

It is this kind of revery that moved the old men who left the town long ago, and made or did not make their fortunes, who retired and had little to think of but what they remembered; they wrote long nostalgic letters which they mailed to the home newspaper for printing—and now even those clippings which I saved because they so pleased me are yellowed and brittle, and the correspondents themselves returned to dust.

"I remember how the old town looked. . . . The courthouse square was surrounded by an iron fence about seven feet high, surmounted by sharp-pointed iron pickets. Gates opened from all the streets. . . . Each gate was swung shut by weighted chains, for there were several valuable head of livestock which were allowed to pasture on the grass which grew in the park: deer, which had been captured by some of the mighty hunters of that day. . . ."

Among the hunters mentioned is Captain Benoni Nesbitt. My own memory responds to the name. I never saw the iron fence with its gates—I never saw the deer—but my mother knew the Captain, although to her he was "old Benoni Nesbitt." He was the grandfather of friends of hers, and had a tennis court for their pleasure in his yard at the edge of town. He was an old man in her girlhood, heavily bearded and gray, like his sheep dog. And on a hot summer day while the girls and boys played tennis, old Benoni would sit on his porch fanning, and his sheep dog would lie in the tub of water that caught the drip from the spout of the well pump, only his nose up for air. For seventy-five years Mother remembered the old gray man, and the sheep dog in the tub, and that is the picture she handed down to us; it is no wonder then that I can hardly imagine Captain Benoni Nesbitt as a man young enough to go hunting in the north woods.

The letter to the newspaper does not tell how the live deer were caught and transported, but only that the hunters "brought home a live buck and a doe and several fawns, which they presented to the county. . . . Billy and Nancy and the children were great favorites for several years. As they grew older and became more accustomed to people, they were allowed to stray out of the park. They wandered all over town, and being much teased by children, Billy became rather dangerous. Then one morning poor Billy was found impaled on the iron fence." So the story had a sorrowful ending, but it shows the late 1860's or early '70's as an idyllic time when deer could wander unendangered in our streets.

It is the old brick courthouse that these letters recall. Ohio's first courthouses were built of logs, put up hurriedly for the recording of deeds to a promised land. The pioneers, whose stretches of forest had to be transformed by their own labor into pasture and plowland, had no time to spare for cutting down one more tree than was necessary; the scraps of county domain around and about the new courthouse were not immediately cleared. When the four paths that bounded our public square became the first streets of a backwoods settlement, then the edge of the square was defined by a rail fence. The door of the courthouse, back among the trees, looked toward the south; the street on that side in time became Main Street, and there, opposite the door, the rail fence was crossed by a stile. The fence is written into the records, but there is no explanation as to why it was needed—within were the trees, and without, the rudimentary streets where half-wild hogs rooted in the mud. A courthouse attracts loafers as molasses does flies; perhaps the stile was to give them somewhere to congregate. Today's whittler, in blue jeans and hunting jacket, was no doubt preceded by an ancestor in linsey-woolsey, with a coonskin cap, who whiled away long mornings in rifle practice, with squirrels for targets. The stile and the fence remained after the disorderly profusion of trees had been thinned out and a series of courthouses, each larger if not nobler than the last, had followed the first log hut. It was only when the logs gave way to brick that the rail fence was replaced by one of wooden pickets, firmly embedded in the earth and less accessible than the loose rails to brawlers in search of weapons.

The county built its first brick courthouse in the Greek-revival era: four straight walls, two long and two short, high on a stone foundation, and over them a roof that slanted east and west from the ridgepole. In the long walls small-paned windows alternated with shallow pilasters, and above the eaves were the double chimneys, four in a row on each side. From the ridgepole the clock tower ascended in diminishing blocks, with a tall weather vane on the highest and least of them. At the south end the wide gable made a triangular pediment; it was supported on four great Ionic columns, cut from granite. A flight of stone steps, broad enough for comfortable lounging, led to the brick-floored portico and the entrance to the building, and a broad stone-flagged plaza lay between the steps and the Main Street sidewalk.

On this side of the square most of the trees were cut down, and the townsfolk could enjoy again, after years spent in the twilight of the forest, a wide sweep of green sunlit grass. Still a little homesick, remembering the orderliness they had left behind them, they planted along the western curb a straight line of young elm trees to grow up and shade the tavern across the way on summer mornings, and the stagecoach starting out on the post road to Detroit. At first the austerity of the new building was relieved only by the moving shadow on its walls of the big sycamores that towered above the ridgepole, but in time the brick mellowed and the white stone darkened in the air. A brick pavement was laid down in herringbone pattern around the square, and in the middle of the century an iron fence was put up in place of the pickets.

In those days, the stone-flagged plaza at the foot of the steps was the center of community life. There in the decades after the Civil War reuning regiments were photographed; there itinerant preachers shouted their messages, and there the courthouse hangers-on loafed on the steps. Frequently, the court bailiff would appear at the window looking down upon these steps to call for some attorney or witness who might be wanted in the court. Once a Millerite preacher had reached a climax, and was ranting "Which of you will be damned? Which of you will be damned?" just in time to be answered by the bailiff shouting from the window the name of the town's most brilliant but hardest-drinking lawyer. . . . Anyone having business in the courthouse had to run the gauntlet of this crowd. The same memoir-writer who remembered the deer that lived in the square told in another letter how his fellow citizens watched every morning for the arrival of a certain judge—a judge so enormously fat that his struggle up the steps was a town spectacle. The author admitted that he could not recall the judge's name. I thought when I read the item: How sad—to have lived a decent life, to have risen to be judge, to have administered law and justice, to be deserving of recollection . . . and then to be forgotten: everything—even your name—except how fat you were. But I was wrong—not, perhaps, to be sad—but to think that no one lived still to remember that long-ago judge. For an answer to the article soon appeared in the paper's letter column:

"Judge Sexton was a huge man presiding over the Common Pleas court. In no circumstances would he tell his weight, and there was curiosity about it. It was agreed to try a ruse. Lester Arnold had a grain elevator. . . . A man with a buggy accosted Judge Sexton and suggested that he get in and they would drive over town . . . then the driver said he wanted to speak to Lester Arnold a minute—and stopped the buggy right on the scales. Lester came to the door and chatted briefly. The buggy drove on and circled through the streets. Then Judge Sexton got out, the buggy was driven back to the scales, weighed, and the difference taken. I don't remember what it was, but I do remember that later at Judge Sexton's funeral they had to call for extra help to carry the coffin. . . ."

By mid-nineteenth century, every county seat in our corner of the state had a courthouse much like that lost one of ours which is so lovingly remembered. Almost all of them are gone. The multiplication of records made the quarters too cramped, and most of them were replaced in those decades when provincial architecture was at its worst. A few remain. There is one in Dayton, and the city is forever contending with the county commissioners in an effort to preserve it. Another stands in the little country town of Hillsboro—one of time-worn yellow brick, with white pillars. There survives at Georgetown the white courthouse that Grant knew as a boy, and at Lebanon is one of red brick, without a portico, but with an entrance beneath the gable, at the top of wide stone steps, and small-paned windows in the long walls, with brick pilasters between them. Within, a staircase rises at either side and sweeps back in a curve to meet the balcony that crosses above the door. The building may be dingy, crowded, and inconvenient, but it is the pious hope of all who do not have to use it that the county will continue to be too poor to replace it.

9

If we had it to do over again, it is unlikely that we should condemn our old courthouse. It was torn down at the end of the nineteenth century, and even at that date there was lamentation. I can remember, with an effort, when the present building was new and the subject of every conversation; I can almost see again the ravaged earth in which it stood, before the lawns were graded and sown and marked with signs: DON'T WALK ON THE GRASS. I can remember the general outcry against its hideousness, and how I remained unconvinced. I thought it magnificent, from the cavernous arched entrances to the vividly red roof and the tower that soared above the elm trees.

Any doubts I may have entertained were banished—and it must have been a long while after the building was finished, since I remember the time so clearly—when a glassy cement sidewalk was put down where the old higgledy-piggledy brick path had been. We had our skates on almost before the barriers had been carried away. The courthouse walks were always crowded on Saturdays, when farmers hitched their horses to the racks along Market Street and sold their garden truck from wagons backed up to the Main Street curb. On other days the square was almost deserted: everyone walked on the other side of the surrounding streets, past banks, offices, and stores. Consequently, we skated around the courthouse—or, perhaps, it should be said "we skated there, consequently everyone. . . ." That possibility never occurred to us then. On weekday afternoons after school, or day-long in the summertime, we skated to our hearts' content. With an accompanying whir of roller bearings and crash of steel on concrete, we swept round and round the square, or puffed up the slight incline to the Main Street steps and swooped down again, with a last-minute right-angled swing to avoid a ducking in the fountain. I think that ours was the only generation to make a rink of those sidewalks. Before we were grown-up and ready to put our skates away, the cement was cracked in every direction and shattered at the corners, and there were gaps in it too wide to be jumped. After a number of years it was replaced, but by that time a new lot of children had come along who had other things to do than skating around the public square.

The "new" courthouse has aged and darkened, and has about it today an air of long-accustomedness. There has never been a fence around it. After the grass was worn away at the corners, they were planted with barberry bushes. Barelegged boys sit astride the Civil War cannon at the southwest corner, and skin the cat from its muzzle. They are entirely irreverent, but may be forgiven since there are no longer hitching racks. The lawn toward the south is still an unbroken stretch of green, except for the line of rose bushes down each side of the path—we have never fallen victim to the rage for canna beds—but the angles between step and foundation have been planted with shrubs. The steps are not so immaculate as they once were: loafers squat there, having no fence rail to lean on—and loafers have, to put it mildly, untidy habits.

Most of all, the clock in the tower has become an essential part of our lives. I suppose that there is no one of us who does not instinctively consult it when, in his daily walk uptown, he reaches the point where it first comes into view. On almost every street there are chinks between roofs and chimneys where a glimpse of its face may be caught as one passes, and every child who was ever afraid of being late to school grows up knowing where they are. From a distance great enough to reduce other buildings to their true proportions, there is an uninterrupted view of the courthouse tower: from the country— our flattish, rolling country—the clock can be read from as far as your eyes can see. Clustering treetops hide all domestic roofs, but the tower rides above their green billows as a lighthouse above the surf. If your ears are better than your eyes, you can hear it strike the hour when you can no longer distinguish the hands. It strikes with a deliberation in tune with the unhurried lives we led when it was new, the second note following the first only when the last vibrations have died away on the somnolent summer air.

Once upon a time the clock was lighted only until twelve

o'clock. (Now we keep later hours.) There was a queer mixture of impressions on the mind when, out of doors late at night, a first glance toward it showed the courthouse tower wiped out, and a black hollow in the sky in its stead: blank surprise followed by the scuttling, frightened whisper down old paths in the brain: "it's late—awfully late," and then by a sense of exhilaration at one's audacity—all in an instant, before maturity could assert itself against those echoes. This was a reaction doubtless unknown to those who grew up after our time, but it was always felt by us whose first parties-with-boys were held in the years when midnight was the ultimate hour. There was a party in the country once which broke up unceremoniously when the farmer's clock struck twelve and sent us whipping the horses back to town. I remember our mixed amazement, relief, and chagrin when we reached the end of Main Street and saw the clock still lighted. . . . The farmer of course lived by sun-time . . . we might have stayed half an hour longer . . . but perhaps it was as well we hadn't . . . . For us, *lateness* had entity, known in a negative: nothing, where there should have been a lighted clock face hanging against a dark night sky.

When we were children, it was not only the exterior of the courthouse that was familiar to us as bread and butter. We came to associate with the building a lingering if faint redolence of used spittoons. Its marble halls echoed to our footsteps as we carried messages to whatever friend's father happened to be in office at the time. Our first experiments with the typewriter were made in the auditor's office, and his adding machine fortified a conviction that one needn't really agonize over arithmetic. More than once I have stood outside the door of a crowded courtroom, a pair of roller skates slung over one arm, while I waited with the Judge's pigtailed daughters for an adjournment that would give them a chance to wheedle from him a permission not likely to be granted at home. We grew up with a first-hand if limited acquaintance with the mysteries of government. When we found the hall downstairs crowded with farmers in muddy boots, overalls, and mackinaws, we said "Sheriff's sale," with no more than the vaguest notion as to what the term implied; and we passed indifferently between groups of men around the cuspidors, who discussed soil and stock and implements while they chewed, spat, and waited. We knew and took advantage of the pre-election atmosphere, when no office-holder could be too friendly, even to children, and we made ourselves scarce during those weeks in the winter when taxes were due, and an air of strain spread from the Treasurer's Office and permeated the whole building.

Only once in a year did we push through the heavy door beneath the arch with anything like a feeling of awe. Memorial Day morning, when we carried to the courthouse all the seasonable plunder from the garden, had emotions all its own, which changed even those empty corridors from their everyday aspect. Below, in the cool cryptlike basement, members of the Woman's Relief Corps, preparing for the afternoon's parade to the cemetary, stood behind trestle tables and tied up bouquets, one after another, and set them in splint baskets. On other days these women were ordinary neighbors and the mothers of schoolmates, but on Memorial Day they were sanctified by their occupation. Almost timidly we laid down our flowers. Sometimes there was syringa, the twigs heavy-laden and sweet, the pollen dusting with gold everything that touched it. Sometimes there were a few last purple flags, or long plumes of wisteria. If summer had not come too early, there were still old-fashioned single yellow roses, and peonies, pink and red and white, their stout polished leaves creaking in our hot hands when we released them. Almost always there were mounds of greenish snowballs; if they had passed their prime, they dropped at a touch like some worn-out garland from an old hat, not petal after petal, but flower after flower—five flat petals cut out in one piece, with a hole in the center. But however many the blossoms, the priestesses behind the tables pursed their lips and shook their heads; even above a heaped profusion of peonies and snowballs, they sighed: there were so many graves to mark, and more every year. . . . Certainly the bouquets they contrived were sad enough, and pinched-looking, when one saw them later in the parade: in every basket swinging at an old soldier's knee there would be half a dozen of them, each composed of a spray of syringa, a bruised and broken iris, a wisp of garden heliotrope, a wilting but still conspicuous peony.

In this country the grandchildren of the men who fought the Civil War must feel until they die an especial response to certain words, certain phrases, and certain names that is denied to everyone else. When the children of the middle generation were growing up, their fathers who had been soldiers so recently were busy carrying their everyday world on their shoulders—too busy to talk about the war. Or perhaps its horrors had not sunk far enough beneath the surface of their memories. Twenty years later, or twenty-five, they had more leisure for storytelling; they had forgotten their sufferings, or time had made them glamorous; and they had been called heroes so often that they had come to believe it, if not of themselves, of their comrades and their generals. The Civil War was a romantic war, as wars go; for us it was more certainly pure romance because it had really happened, and was not make-believe, because it had happened a long while ago, and was all over and done with when those old men who carried the baskets of stingy bouquets on Memorial Day were hardly more than boys.

They seemed very old to us then, our grandfathers—as old as their faded and moth-eaten uniforms—although the veterans on horseback still rode like soldiers, and those on foot could march in time to the music, shoulders back. To see the parade properly, we did not go to the courthouse: there was too likely to be a disenchanting difficulty in the formation of the lines. We stood instead two or three blocks down Main Street in the shade of the maple trees in front of the doctor's office, or skinned the cat on his hitching rack until the first notes of fife and drum stiffened our backs and stood us up like ramrods on the edge of the curb. I could never watch a Memorial Day parade without a shiver down my spine.

It was this susceptibility to certain emotions that made us regard with fanatic pride the trophy that hung on the wall of the main corridor of the courthouse: a great silken banner, gold-fringed, barred red, white, and blue, with gold letters in the white central band: a banner that had been sent to Ohio from Washington, because in proportion to her population the state had sent the most volunteers to the Union army. From Columbus the banner had been sent to our county because it had been first among our eighty-eight counties, proportionately, in the number of volunteers. A few years ago, happening to be in the courthouse, I remembered that banner and went to see it again. It was not there. When I wondered what had become of it, blank looks were my only answer, until I began to think it had existed only in a dream. But others remembered too, and as the centenary of the war approached, it was recovered from the Ohio State Museum and restored to us, and placed in our own county museum. It is as I had remembered it: fifteen feet long and six feet wide at the base; and on one side the gold letters say, "Ohio true to the Union" and on the other, "Ohio has sent 291,952 of her gallant sons to the field." More children, possibly, will see it in our museum than ever saw it in the courthouse, but they will not behold it with the moist-eyed pride of those of us whose grandfathers were among the 291,000.

Another banner, glass-encased, has taken its place in the courthouse: an older relic but a much later acquisition, having been given to the county in 1928 by the aged recluse daughters of the Whig who had kept it after his party won in the 1840 "Tippecanoe and Tyler too" election. Once its ground was white, but it has grown dingy with the years; its black letters are rusty but still emphatic:

TOM   TIP   TYLER

GREENE

We bear one soldier's gallant name
And prize another's living fame
Not alone to honor the man but to save the

REPUBLIC

"Tom" was Tom Corwin, then well on his way to an honorable career, and in 1840 to be elected governor of Ohio. Greene

County had been named, like so many others in the state, for a
Revolutionary general, and "Tip" was honored in all the Middle
West for his victory over Indians and British. On the reverse of
the banner—to be spelled out through the white, backwards, or
read from the card in the case—was the Whigs' warning and
their promise—which might well have been revived by the Republicans in any of their years of eclipse:

> The Government will take care of itself only.
> We will take care of the Government.

If as school children we learned anything about the election
of 1840, it made no impression on us; it meant nothing to us—
and yet for the old Northwest Territory, which had until that
year voted Democratic, it marked the end of an epoch. Our own
county had been Whig from the party's beginning—nor have we
yet been persuaded to revoke our loyalties: when Whigs turned
Republican, so did we, and Republican we remain. But although the 1840 contest did not pass even here without tur-
bulence, children are not interested in elections unless wars are
precipitated by them. Only maturity would look twice at that
faded banner, or care that the log-cabin campaign was the cause
of feuds between old friends and fist fights between strangers, of
savage brawls in the courthouse square, when rioters (among
them the progenitors of two of our most decorous families) tore
rails from the fence and used them as weapons, with considerable effect, judging from the size of their fines.

Curious little fragments of history, like this, are written in the
books of the clerk of courts. That is one office which we never
entered as children. Few even of adult inquirers into the past
trouble to consult these records, and even the clerk himself may
not know all that is in them. It is a number of years since I have
had reason to climb the stairs to that office. I used to go when
Harvey Elam was clerk; he was my favorite of county officers
whom I have known. He possessed the two prime qualifications
for office: he was a Republican and somewhat disabled physically. Our electorate has an amiable weakness for cripples: if

a man can no longer earn his living otherwise he has a good chance of being voted into the courthouse. Our most exciting contest for the office of auditor was between an arthritic incumbent and a railroad man whose leg had been amputated after an accident. The brakeman was elected. My friend the clerk of courts was bent double with rheumatism; that he was also a man of integrity, intelligence, and imagination was a matter simply of good luck. He was slight and withered, but alert with nervous energy; he had a dry wit and humorous blue eyes. His manner was friendly, as is necessary in a politician, but he was shy and unobtrusive; when encountered on the street, he was not dawdling from cigar shop to barber ship, hobnobbing with his cronies, but walking down the outer edge of the sidewalk with a market basket on his arm. His time was divided between his office and the reading room of the public library; his sources of material were limited, but no musty scholar in the British Museum had a finer enthusiasm for the records of a vanished day. This he proved when anyone asked him for information, or a chance to search through the books for it. He might spread them out on the counter if he were not sure of his visitor's interest; he was more apt to open the gate and offer a chair beside his desk. From this chair you could look out either of two windows: toward the west, into the branches of the elm trees, where the blackbirds assembled behind the thick foliage, their chatter raucous above the guttural lamentation of the pigeons on the roof; or toward the north, and the Opera House across Market Street, beyond the sycamores, beyond the curb where the hitching rack used to be, and continued to be, in your mind, until the something missing from the scene could be named, and you remembered that it had been gone for years.

The oldest of the books on the clerk's shelves bears the date of the county's establishment; its leaves are brittle and its ink faded. The pages are written close, some in scholarly copperplate, some in a hand angular and abrupt but legible enough, and some in an illiterate scrawl, where the pen in awkward fingers scratched and clawed the paper and scattered its ink over the lines. The clerk had deciphered even these; he knew everything that was written in his books. With an engaging twinkle he would point out the recorded downfall of another founder of a first family, who was arrested, tried, and convicted of the "ungodly crime" of playing cards for money, and pocketing the tenpence won. Not only the facts were given: the book contained also the Judge's sermon, delivered when he named the fine, and some paragraphs of moralizing on the part of the then clerk. I am not sure the clerk who showed it to me, himself something of a puritan, did not see in this incident a genuine blot on a family scutcheon; or perhaps he saw it as I did: very funny, and a light on the past—a strange light, thrust in as it is among pages confirming the tradition that life in frontier towns was untrammeled, immoral, and uncouth. Historians of the Northwest Territory have long since put in their books all that happened here that had any effect on the nation as a whole; it is time now that someone seek out the absurd incidents told in the records of scores of courthouses—a collection of them would enliven for us the dead past, restore a warm humanity to ancestors long since forgotten, and color with shadow and high lights a landscape that seems sometimes too exposed, too clear, too sharp in all its edges.

These shelves contain a thousand and one tales of men's misdeeds and errors in their relations with each other. The history of their dealings with the land is kept downstairs, in the books of the recorder. In that office there is none of the leisured quiet that reigns upstairs. The windows face Main Street, but no one turns to look out through them. The floors are crowded with elbow-high desks, where ledgers lie open and lawyers and their clerks and the recorder's helpful young assistants lean on their elbows to study them, or impatiently copy their contents. Their intent earnestness persuades the beholder that here is the heart of the courthouse. You may have believed that the land itself is what matters, that men may come and go, and their names be unimportant—that one may sow an acre where another reaps, and the change be nothing, since it is the same acre, and the wheat or the corn is wheat or corn, whoever the plowman or the reaper.

Farmers, so far as history knows, are stripped of their personal idiosyncrasies; in all that makes them essential to the nation, they are alike. You may have believed this—but the activity in these rooms proves that it is man's relation to the land, whether he be its owner or its slave, that is important to him and to the society he has created here in the shadow of the courthouse.

In the recorder's books there is not the difference found upstairs between late and early, between now and long ago. The landscape may have changed, the pioneer who cleared a certain quarter-section might not recognize his acres could he see them today—but so far as the books know there has been no alteration. So long as a farm is not divided anew, or resurveyed in settlement of some dispute, when it changes hands it is described in the terms used in the first deed granted.

A very little reading in the archives of the American colonies is enough to show that the surveyors of virgin land knew no "monuments" but the trees among which they worked. There were no stones set up by them at the corners of a man's land; with their axes they marked the chosen trees. They had a touching faith in the endurance of vegetable life—or a cynical disbelief in man's persistence in his endeavor to tame the forest, and in the necessity for anything like permanence in their work.

When the first surveyors went into the Ohio country, they followed what had been the practice in the older East. A share in the wilderness bought in 1810 by my great-great-grandfather from his father-in-law, a part of "fraction number 28 in the 2nd township and 5th range west of the Little Miami River," is described as "beginning on the bank of said river at a bunch of redbuds." Redbuds! Lovely in the spring, in full bloom, their queer, exotic, almost Persian, ashes-of-roses color; lovely against the April green of the roofing forest, but so insubstantial, so quick to die—not a mark that would make that river bank not only yours, but your children's children's. Another corner was to be known by a white oak, twenty inches in diameter, the next by a maple eighteen inches in diameter, and the last by another oak tree. Even oaks and maples change in girth, grow old, are blown down in storms, or are sacrificed to the plow. How could any man bear to depend on them for the identification of what was in those days the achieved desire of his heart?

Acres which have been surveyed again lately have been marked with stones at boundary corners, but more often the old descriptions have still to serve, and the first surveyors' terms are printed again in advertisements of sheriff's sales. "Being part of Military Survey No. 5863 . . ." from an elm to an ash, from the ash, "crossing a branch," to the middle of Lick Run, "thence with the meanders of Lick Run" to an oak tree, then, "passing through said tree," back to the original elm. Another description is almost a catalogue of the indigenous forest: it names a sugar tree, a black walnut, two blue ashes and a white elm, a red oak and ironwood (ironwood gone), a large black walnut, a mulberry, two ironwoods, a stake ash and hickory and white walnut (hickory gone), a sugar tree and small blue ash, a burr oak and white walnut. By the parentheses one is forced to conclude that the rest of the trees singled out by the original surveyor are still there—or were, the last time the lines were run. The farmer would of course respect his landmarks, but it is hard to believe that time and nature can have shown any such partiality. It would be interesting to verify the conclusion: to follow the farmer's fences and note the trees and see what more than a hundred years of growth and change have done to them. And as one walked through the weeds that grow today in all fence corners, the imagination could be exercised by picturing how the first surveyor, after struggling through the crowded forest, crashing among saplings with his instruments, hacking down the wild grapevines that twisted about his shoulders—how he found these particular trees at the end of the line he had traced with so much difficulty, and marked them, triumphantly, with his axe. In our earliest surveys, at the end of each boundary measured, occurs the qualification "plus the throw of the axe." The beguiling phrase seems to be peculiar to this region, and is one which sometimes causes trouble for later surveyors trying to settle the boundary lines of quarrelsome neighbors. Our lawyers can only explain it by the guess that if the surveyor found no tree at the exact end of his line, there was sure to be one that could be blazed with his mark within the throw of the axe. And by the vagueness of his measurements he could save himself from later accusations of inexactness. (Later surveyors achieve the same end by the conventional qualification added to the sum of the acreage bounded: "be the same more or less.")

Who were these early surveyors, buckskin-clad, with coonskin caps, and rifles as well as instruments under their arms? We remember Nathaniel Massie, who surveyed Virginia Military Lands, because his name is preserved in Massie's Creek that runs north of town past the old Covenanter church and burying ground. Others have been forgotten, their names as lost as the forest that must have seemed when they stood in its shadow as everlasting as the hills.

The surveyors are gone, the pioneers are gone, the land remains. In the hundred and fifty years that have followed the recording of the first deeds, the deed books have been transferred from courthouse to new courthouse to serve as the ultimate authority in any question as to the ownership of the land. To settle such disputes our foremost lawyers come here to the recorder's office and bend in frowning concentration above their notes. A city may forget the courthouse that stands on one of its corners, but a town like ours would have no excuse for being were it not the county seat; the courthouse justifies its existence. There has been little fundamental change in our position since the days when the four paths that outlined the public square first became streets. Convinced of at least that one constant in an unstable world, you go out through the arched entrance, past the loafers on the steps, and down toward Main Street on pavements whose every crack is familiar, remembered by feet which have skated over them so innumerably many times.

The scene has altered since those days. It was many years ago that the automobiles first began to pass where the horses used to clatter by, but they were usually splashed with mud, just as the buggies had been; they were crowded with farmers' children, flaxen-haired, sunburned, outlandishly garbed. Today both curbs of Main Street are parked solid; cars stream east and west between them, driven, many of them, by the strangers who came to live among us during the last war, or by those coming since. Along the Detroit Street curb, where the beautiful row of elms had stood since long before anyone now living can remember —along that curb, there is the bare expanse where dead trees have been cut down and only two still stand, thin-leaved, dying, for the elms have got the blight and must inevitably go.

But these are superficial alterations. The strangers will go away again, or those who stay will be accepted finally as a part of the town. New trees have been planted—they will not in our lifetime be as lovely as the elms, but someday they will arch their boughs over the street and over the lawn. So long as the farmers go on about their business up and down the steps you have just left behind you, just so long will the courthouse be the heart of the town. In the tower overhead the clock strikes the hour. The slow tranquility of its notes is a reassurance of immutability; while you listen, time seems to be standing still, and change impossible.

2. *Detroit Street and Main*

However fervent his patriotism, no native of a middle western town would ever claim for its business section beauty or dignity or charm, but unless he is asked he does not think of appraising it in such terms. To him who for a lifetime has walked in the shade of certain walls or dodged the raindrops falling from certain eaves, whose thumbs have pressed the same latches, whose palms have turned the same doorknobs, whose feet have crossed the same thresholds times beyond number—to him, mass and line, texture of brick and stone, the movement of the sun across a wall, are so familiar as to be noted with an abstracted eye, and accepted without question.

Only the young and rebellious really see when they look at them the few blocks around the courthouse square: those who are beginning to grow up, beginning to fear now and again the unthinkable chance that the days of their years must be lived out here and not in some distant promised land. They cry out for a little while against the bleak ugliness of sidewalk, shop, and street. As children they had not noticed it. A child goes about his errands absent-mindedly, viewing the scene from the aloof vantage point of one who will be here only temporarily, whose destiny it is to play some part in distant scenes of grandeur and moment. So long as these streets which briefly hold him are friendly and kind, a child moves in them happily; he is indifferent to ugliness; he is blind even to such elements of the picturesque as may exist, since it does not any of it concern him—the *real* him, whom the world will some day know.

Or, perhaps, a child does not recognize the picturesque because he cannot foresee what is doomed to vanish. Growing old, you protest when some new indecency is committed—some new garish sign hung over a new moving-picture theater, some new chain-store front plastered over old bricks. Convinced that with each change the town grows more hideous, you remember with regret the streets as you can see them still, in your mind, their ugliness at least not a standardized ugliness. Those narrow streets parallel to Detroit: to the west they were mainly backyards and stables, but here and there stood a blacksmith's or a cobbler's shop; to the east they were lined with saloons and livery stables, and women and children were afraid to walk there after dark. Now that the livery stables are garages and the saloons are gone, "alleys" are no doubt safe enough, but habit takes you by other ways. East Second Street, too, had its saloons and livery stables. You went that way to buy hot roasted peanuts in the little warm fragrant cubbyhole where old "Uncle John" Winters, a one-armed veteran of the Civil War, was tucked away in a tiny shop around the corner of Whiteman Street, next to the harness-maker's. Sometimes you went with your grandmother to her dressmaker's for a fitting. Mrs. Ryan lived over one of the saloons, but you ducked up her entry stairs before you came to the swinging shutters that men slipped through so furtively, or before you needed to close your nose to the sickening smell, repellent yet fascinating with the fascination of evil. The livery stables reeked, too, particularly in hot weather, but that smell was without the appeal of wickedness. As you crossed the ramp that led from the gutter to a black cavernous interior, you peered in past the shirt-sleeved loafers chewing straws; you could not see much, but you could hear: cheerful whistling, Negro voices, water running, the bored, indolent stamp of a hoof on the floor.

Still with regret, you remember our most metropolitan blocks, in the neighborhood of the courthouse, as they were fifty, fifty-five years ago. As in the Middle Ages, the signs of craftsmen and merchants swung overhead or stood on the sidewalk: the jeweler's watch, set forever at twenty minutes past eight; the Cyclopean eye of the oculist's sign; the barber's red and white pole; buggy whips in a stand, and harness swung from hooks in the door frame of the hardware store (and once upon a time, I think, a horse to wear that harness—a dapple gray, with fiery nostrils and one front foot lifted as if to paw the earth—but this may be a dream compounded of all the merry-go-round horses of my childhood); a glass case of photographs hung at right angles to the wall at the foot of the stairs that led to the "studio"; and the tobacconist's Indian. Our Indian was a maiden in kilts, with laced buskins like Diana's, and a warrior's feather bonnet; she strode forward on her pedestal, offering to the passers-by a handful of cigars. Now, all these obstructions to traffic are gone, and on a Saturday night, the throngs flow unimpeded except by each other's children in and out of the ten-cent stores, the dress shops, and the gents' furnishings.

But if by taking thought you can restore to the heart of the town the picturesqueness of the gone and forgotten, you can never see it as having been in your time beautiful or dignified or charming. And an honest reading of the old stories will prove that picturesqueness is the most that can ever have been claimed for those few blocks around the courthouse. They were never beautiful or dignified, and charm is an adventitious quality which exists in the mind of the beholder. In the beginning were trees—the beautiful hardwood trees of the primeval forest—but where the streets were marked out, the trees were blazed and died, or were cut down and the stumps left until they rotted. In 1809, we're told, Main Street was a stagnant pool of water, a rendezvous for geese, ducks, and hogs. That same year cider was sold (twelve and one-half cents a quart) in front of the courthouse beside a large stump standing in Main Street; the backwoods salesman built a fire against the stump, where he might heat the iron rods to mull the cider for his customers. Somehow these details are less suggestive of Adam's Eden than of Martin Chuzzlewit's.

As children we learned the old stories of the founding of the town as we modeled our salt-and-water relief maps of the county and marked with a cross the cabin where the first court session was held. It was three miles from what was to be the town. In the days when Ohio was part of the Northwest Territory, scattered log cabins and even embryo settlements lay within what were to be the boundaries of our county. In 1803, when the state became a state and the county a county, court was appointed to be held at a log tavern, where a smokehouse nearby could be used as a jury room, and where two small blockhouses afforded protection in case of need. In our youth the electric interurban line passed within view of this site; we used to press our noses against the window as we came near the ancient and dignified farmhouse that had replaced the tavern, in a vain attempt to see the reputed hollow in the turf where that first tavern courthouse had stood. All that we ever saw was the dark brick of a house behind the trees, behind the wide, deeply green, deeply shaded lawn, where a few sheep wandered between the fences, keeping the grass nibbled short. We could only imagine the blockhouses, the tavern, the backwoodsmen and their rifles, and Colonel John Paul on his knees studying the map where the forks of the Shawnee were marked.

Later we came to know the books where the story was written: the fat county histories on the shelf under the window in the reference room of the library. Those books were sturdily rebound in thick brown cloth; their coated-paper pages were thick with grime. They were illustrated with reproductions of old drawings and engravings, and the photographs of bearded leading citizens. They taught us, when we were old enough to read what was actually written without any romantic embellishment by our imaginations, that the establishment of law in the county and the founding of a county seat were attended by humor at least, if not by the beauty of the poetic. All who dwelt in the county assembled for the first holding of court, to make holiday and to see the grand jury in action. In the morning an exhibition of justice at work was denied them, as there were no cases to be presented—but so lustily was the holiday-making carried on that before the day's end the grand jury retired to the smokehouse to draw up indictments against nineteen drunken brawlers, charged with assault and battery, and mayhem.

One of the first duties of the newly elected county officials was the choice of a location for the county seat. Every settler had his own idea as to whose acres should be selected. On that first day of court, two disputants argued the question under the trees outside the log tavern. One was a surveyor; the other was the recently appointed clerk of courts, Colonel John Paul, who owned many hundreds of acres around and about, and naturally wanted the county seat located on his land. The surveyor, to convince him of the futility of his hopes, spread at their feet a map of Ohio and dropped his riding whip across it so that the butt lay on the river at Cincinnati, the tip on Lake Erie's shore. Where the whip crossed the forks of Shawnee Creek he placed his finger. "There will be the county seat." He supported his statement with the explanation that county seats across the state would naturally be on thoroughfares (Indian trails, they were then) from points on the Ohio to points on the lake. He persuaded John Paul. That astute Scot said nothing more, but within a few days journeyed to Cincinnati and entered all the land surrounding the forks of Shawnee. In the autumn of the same year the county seat was laid out on this land, and Colonel Paul, who donated to the county the public square for the courthouse, receives credit in the histories for the founding of the town.

The phrase "forks of Shawnee" caught at our imaginations when we were children because the creek had apparently been so completely forgotten by grownups, yet was so large a part of our world; it was as if we and we alone could understand John Paul and the surveyor. The stream has had no real influence on the development of the town, but it is important that children have had those banks to play on, those waters to fish in. The south fork comes in alongside the railroad track from the east, flows under Detroit Street close by the overhead bridge, and winds through the "Bottoms" between the hill where the station stands and the street where we lived. There the creek banks are lined with willows, and the water runs shallow over a limestone bed. When we played there refuse and rubbish lay under the willows, weeds grew rank in the sun, the water was slightly noisome all the way along. We did not mind; we waded in it, and went seining for minnows and tadpoles every spring. From the Bottoms, the creek flows on into the West End, turns at an angle somewhere along those crooked streets past the old empty ropewalk on Market Street. Here there is a dam: perhaps the mill machinery was once turned by water power; later the pool's banks were landscaped, and weeping-willow trees brush their leaves across its surface. Beyond the dam the creek is out of town and in the country again, and in the pasture at the foot of the hill where we coasted in the winter it is joined by the fork which has crossed the north end of town. Streets going north slope downhill for a couple of long blocks to the creek bed. When we were children the stream oozed through a swamp east of Detroit Street and north of Church, then flowed westward under bridged streets and across weedy low stretches. Now the swamp has been drained and made a park, and the creek disappears into a ten-foot culvert under the railroad track, not to be released again until it has passed beneath three streets and the blocks between. Long ago, enterprising builders filled in the vacant stretches of land, buried the creek, and above it built houses whose cellars are always damp. But though hidden, the stream is not lost to small boys of the north end, who explore the culverts which carry it under their houses. To follow the creek from the park to the far side of Galloway Street is a kind of tribal ordeal which every boy in the neighborhood is dared to undertake from the day he starts to school: an ordeal which could be truly awful if you feared Stygian darkness, enclosed places, flowing water underfoot, and slimy creatures on the walls—but one which convention seems to require belittling, once it has been accomplished.

Halfway between the two branches of the creek is the public square; the business section of the town reaches only half a block beyond it to the north on Detroit Street, but runs all the way south to the railroad station, and east and west on Main Street for two or three blocks. The town as laid out in 1803 by its first surveyor embraced 270 acres, "more or less," of Colonel John Paul's land. At first, so few were the cabins and so heavy the forest, it was necessary to blaze trails to guide strangers from one log house to the next. Two streets were laid out generously, even lavishly, wide; when the trees were cut down, one of these streets, where the riding whip had lain, became part of the post road to Detroit. At the crossroads where it met the east-west trail from Chillicothe, the public square was marked off, and this other street, at first "Chillicothe," was later called "Main." On it the building of the town began. In 1804, there was rivalry in the construction of "two good log houses," one across from the public square to be the new settlement's first tavern; the other, half a block west, to be the house of the Methodist parson. Feeling ran high: two elements of pioneer society strove mightily to outdo each other—but in spite of our early and enduring reputation for godliness, the tavern-builders won. Until the first log courthouse was put up in the square, this tavern was the center of county affairs: here court was held and here was the first general election.

But after the brick Collier House was built on Detroit Street, in the middle of the block facing the public square, the old log tavern could not compete with its spaciousness and elegance, and fell from its position as the center of town life to be a stopping place for wagoners and cattle drovers. The Collier House was the scene of the first public ball to be held in a community which from its founding had a relish for society. During the War of 1812, the inn was made recruiting headquarters for the district, no doubt so chosen because of the ease with which, in the bar, wavering backwoodsmen could be brought to an enlisting frame of mind. The parlors became the stage for other scenes from military life; there were held courts-martial and courts of inquiry. For a while the Collier House was the stopping place of a British officer and his servant, paroled prisoners of war. He was a fine and haughty gentleman in dazzling regimentals, an object

31

of gaping curiosity to folk who had seen their own men go off to fight in fringed shirts and coonskin caps.

When peace came and the way to Detroit was open, the inn was made a stagecoach stop, where travelers were fed and bedded, and horses were changed. Finally, the Collier House in its turn languished and was lost when the Ewing House was opened; there has never been a hotel since in the spot where it stood on Detroit Street. But on the Main Street corner a block east of the square, where the new hotel was built, little has changed since the day of its erection, except its name, its façade, and the nature of its clientele. In mid-century times the Ewing House entertained whatever distinguished guests came to town; in the nineties when it had become "the Grand Hotel" it was rather the resort of local young men than of travelers. Of its character, in my childhood and since, I have known nothing; feminine acquaintance with it was limited to running the gauntlet of its front windows, but I remember how once a group of us approached it by way of the kitchen. We had blackberries to sell; briar-scratched and stained, we offered our full pails to the cook. The cook fetched the manager, who struck a bargain with us. I have forgotten what we needed money for, but I remember the waves of heat and odor floating out through the kitchen door, the unsavory appearance of the cook, undressed to his undershirt, our own torture-by-chiggers—and the limiting of our discomfort to those merely physical details by the surprising circumstance that both cook and manager proved to be amiable men, who liked buying wild blackberries from anonymous schoolgirls.

Around the corner of Detroit Street, and a little south, is another hotel site. Here in the old days was the Hivling House. John Hivling owned most of the two blocks south of the courthouse: on the west side of Detroit Street stood his wool warehouse, on the east side his bank and hotel. He influenced the terms of the franchise given the first railroad, by which it was required to lay its tracks close to the gutter before his hotel. Trains halted there, and legend has it that before there were proper sidewalks he built a platform from the track to his hotel desk, so that anyone alighting from the cars found himself face to face with the hotel clerk. The old Hivling House was later the European Hotel. In the early years of this century, the eastern was so definitely the wrong side of Detroit Street that its proprietor permitted the publication, in a book about the town, of a photograph of the hotel which showed prominently in the foreground the garbage cans and the beer kegs piled at the edge of the sidewalk. Since then the newspaper has built offices and a pressroom along there, and what is left of the space that was once a hotel is now a loan company.

One more hotel we had, and have—the Florence it was called when we were young. It was first advertised in 1831: A House of Entertainment . . . at the sign of the COACH AND FOUR. In the cut which heads the advertisement, the building looks exactly as it does today: sitting square on the corner, three stories high, windows regularly spaced, those on the Market Street side ornamented with wrought-iron balconies. Nor has it altered within; it was built spaciously, with a vast cool lobby, and a wide staircase leading to a balcony off which opened bedrooms on two sides and a ballroom on the third. When we were young, the Florence was the home of a few lone spinsters, a few old men without families who spent their days smoking cigars in the lobby, and a handful of married couples the female halves of which were "too lazy," by the town's verdict, to keep house. Now, tourists stop at this hotel overnight, and the cars at the curb show the license plates of a dozen states. It has been saved from decline by its proprietor's good sense in keeping it as it was in the beginning; there is nothing artificial about its "quaintness"—the small tiles in the floor are uneven and nubbly to walk on, the dark counter and staircase are worn and battered, and perfectly at home on the lobby walls are the Civil War enlistment posters, the exclamatory announcements, with cuts, of races to be run at the county fair, and the advertisements for runaway apprentices and slaves.

The first storekeeper, given his license in 1806, put up on Greene Street his log cabin with its mud-and-stick chimney. That narrow street, one block long, facing the square, has since been the location of various small shops, most of them long-enduring in an unobtrusive and humble fashion. James Gowdy, the first merchant, soon had competition: an early census lists all house-holders and their occupations: carpenter, tavern-keeper, lawyer, tailor, schoolteacher, blacksmith, wheelwright, tanner, tanner, hatter, doctor, merchant, tanner, lawyer, merchant, surveyor, merchant, carpenter, joiner. Merchants outnumber all except tanners, who it is to be hoped had their places of business on the edge of town. The stores must have been across from the courthouse square on Detroit Street or Main: that is where our largest and most important shops have always been.

The earliest dry-goods store still to be remembered was that of the Puterbaughs, on Main Street above Greene. It won enduring fame as the scene of what our normally bloodthirsty town liked to believe was a murder. One of the clerks slept on the premises, in a room at the rear, presumably to guard against robbers. In the middle of one night a fire broke out: all the efforts of the bucket brigade failed to save the store; when everything had been re-duced to ashes and charred lumber, the body of the clerk was found, still in bed, burned to a crisp. It was hard to believe that he could have slept until the fire reached him: it was more ex-citing to think that he had been murdered, preferably with a hatchet (I am sure that a hatchet came into the story somehow), and that the store had been set on fire to hide the crime.

After the Puterbaugh store came that of Allison and Towns-ley, on Main Street across from the courthouse. A great-uncle of mine could describe this store as it had been before the Civil War, in the days when the Scotch Presbyterians along the fron-tier had not yet been persuaded of the evils of drink. At the rear of their center aisle, Messrs. Allison and Townsley kept a keg of whiskey on a stand, with a tin cup tied to the spigot. Any cus-tomer who so desired could refresh himself as freely as if the keg were filled with water.

Allison and Townsley were in business still when my mother was a girl. In my time they had been superseded by another pair of Presbyterians, brothers in this case, whose department store was almost cosmopolitan: here even shoes were sold, and hats, and here overhead wires were first installed for carrying money to the cashier and the change back again: the clerk at your end hung up her little brass box and pulled a wire, and away it sped, clicking. Later, this same store was the first to change from wires to pneumatic tubes, which worked mysteriously out of sight: you could hear the brass cylinder coming, and turn in time to see it fall, *kerchunk,* into the basket.

Much as we were impressed by this store when we were children, the family shopping was not done there except as a last resort. We went to Hutchison and Gibney's, across on Detroit Street, opposite the courthouse entrance, because Miss Fanny Allison was one of its clerks. She and her sister Carrie were across-the-street neighbors of ours, she was a devoted friend of Grandma's, and she expected Grandma's children and grandchildren to trade at Hutchison's and to buy from her. As a matter of justice, she had a right to expect it, since we made ourselves at home with Miss Carrie at any hour of the day, eating her cookies, looking through her stereopticon, even (one of my cousins) rolling in her petunia bed because it "smelled so nice."

Carrie was always kind, and saw humor in everything, in spite of the rheumatism which was slowly crippling her; Fanny, the practical breadwinner, the business woman, could be tart upon occasion, and let what displeasure she felt be known. And there was no evading her eye. Hutchison's carried neither shoes nor hats, and so no questions were asked when you wore new ones—but a sash or hair ribbon or string of beads or pair of gloves that she hadn't sold you was remarked with a lifted eyebrow and a "Where did you get that?" If you could say that an out-of-town aunt had sent you a present, you were lucky. Not that she made any comment if you admitted "Dayton," but her sallow skin turned yellower, her white pompadour stiffened, the air was chilled, and all your pleasure in the new hair ribbon ebbed away.

It was not enough to go to Hutchison's; however busy Fanny was, we had to wait until she was free to attend to our wants. And she was a popular clerk. I have devoted many a summer morning to the purchase of a spool of thread. It was next to

impossible to persuade a friend to go with me to that store; sometimes I fumed with impatience, myself, when I had something
definite in mind to do; sometimes I even sneaked into the other
store, if I were after some trifle from the notion counter. But the
door of one shop was clearly visible from the other, across the
courthouse square, and the back of my knees had a queer exposed feeling, as if Fanny must be watching. Most times,
though, I think I didn't mind sitting on one of Hutchison's
hinged stools, swinging in a semicircle from the counter, listening to the gossip of idle clerks while I waited: I was fond of
Fanny and liked her to be in a good humor; I knew everyone in
the store, and could visit until she was free to look after me.

Remembering—seeing the store again as it was—I realize that
the Hutchison and Gibney's of my childhood was unique. Not
that it looked any different from other prosperous stores of the
time: Mr. Hutchison and Mr. Gibney were then old men—they
had founded their store in the 1860's—but so far as setting the
stage was concerned, they were thoroughly up to date. The
rooms in the early 1900's were cool and airy, with wide aisles and
handsome showcases. A staircase against the wall and a lurching
elevator led to the second floor, where coats, suits, dresses, corsets, and underwear were sold, and carpets and things of that
sort. Downstairs were notions and stockings and gloves (scores
of boxes of gloves and a special counter for trying them on, and
pretty Miss Lida to fit them for you, after you had bought them
from Fanny) and yard goods of every kind: in the winter, serges
and broadcloths, silks, satins, and velvets; in the summer, bolt
after bolt of cottons. (Today, in the spring, in a city department
store, you sometimes catch a hint of that fresh-from-the-loom
scent, and are carried back to that earlier time.) Spread entranc-
ingly on the counter, swept up into a pile, were flowered lawns
and barred dimities and dotted swisses, bright ginghams and
pastel voiles, and sober galateas, which wore so well, and which
we were dressed in for summer-everyday.

Not in these things, nor in anything of outward aspect, was
Hutchison's out of the ordinary, but in its atmosphere. No doubt
each clerk had a special charge: Miss Emma Hutchison at the

notions counter, one of the men at yard goods, others upstairs with the carpets. . . . But there was not one of them except Miss Julia in the cashier's cage who did not roam from counter to counter, from floor to floor, his own private customers in tow. Perhaps the personnel of the store was not always the happy family it seemed; if not, it gave a convincing performance. And it was in part truly family: among the clerks were the cousin, young and pretty, and the son of one partner; the sister, elderly and hunchbacked, and the brother-in-law of the other partner. The other clerks had worked there all their lives. The town knew them by their first names, as they knew each other: Miss Kate, and George and Elmer and two Miss Emmas. . . . They were paid what would seem today pitiful wages, but could earn commissions besides, which accounted for the eagerness of each to hold on to his "regular customers." But any jealousy they felt was suppressed—indeed, so easygoing was the atmosphere of the store it is difficult to believe it existed. Any time you entered the doors you found such clerks as were idle chatting together as comfortably and as eagerly as if they were at a Ladies' Aid meeting in someone's parlor. Only on Saturday nights were the aisles crowded, and everyone busy; then even men came there, with their families. Hutchison's was the accustomed rendezvous of farmers' wives in town for the evening, market baskets on their arms, towheaded children clinging to their skirts. They gossiped interminably with each other and the clerks, while streams of town shoppers eddied and flowed impatiently round them. On such an evening, only upstairs among cloaks and suits, carpets and corsets, was there comparative peace. Over the ready-made clothes presided Miss Emma Haverstick, pencil over her ear. At the corset counter was Rose Berry, svelte and modish as to figure, with all the curves then stylish—Irish as her name in face and coloring. All the Irish clerks in town, as I remember them now, seem to have had red hair, sandy or titian or auburn. Every store had one Irish clerk: not saucy, curly-headed girls, but buxom, middle-aged, good-natured women: there was Kate Langan at Mrs. Sinz's millinery, Mary Golden in the drugstore and her sister Rose at the Bee Hive, Rose Berry at Hutchison's.

My first corset was bought of Fanny Allison, but was fitted by Rose. I remember the solemnity of the occasion. The usual procedure was followed: we sought Fanny downstairs, waited while she explained to some colleague where she was going, waited longer while she hunted for the Negro man-of-all-work who ran the elevator, then went into it with her and creaked slowly to the second floor. There she entered into consultation with Rose, who selected a handful of corsets and led Mother, Fanny, and me into the cubbyhole she called a fitting room. Here my pantywaist was removed and the corsets tried on, to the accompaniment of kind but hardly flattering comments on my lack of figure. I was old enough to have developed one; since I hadn't, the new corset would have to effect at least a waistline. Rose tugged at the strings, while I held my breath. She did all the work and Fanny got credit for the sale: a fair enough arrangement, since Rose's West End friends came to her for anything they wanted from any counter in the store.

A photograph survives of Hutchison and Gibney's as it was in those days: an exterior view which is so familiar that one thinks of it as being so still. Because you knew them so well and so long, it is possible to identify the tiny figures of the clerks grouped in the two wide doors: the women with their high pompadours, dressed in long full black skirts, stiff white shirtwaists, and frilly white aprons; the men in stiff collars and hard straw hats; white-bearded little Mr. Hutchison, square-shouldered little Mr. Gibney, standing apart.

The old Hutchison's survived until the 1920's, but it was never quite the same after the fire. That fire was famous in our annals because it brought painfully to our attention the state of our fire department. So many years had passed since our last serious conflagration that we had failed to notice the superannuation of our firemen. Our equipment was modern enough, but there wasn't a fireman able to climb the ladders once they were in place. As the fire gained headway, a call for volunteers was telephoned to the high school: the response was so immediate and so unanimous that school was dismissed, and the boys raced downstreet to save Hutchison's.

The store was rebuilt, but its note of restrained elegance was unsuited to the kind of competition it had to meet. Long before the struggle was given up, however, many of the old known-forever figures had disappeared. Fanny, who as she aged had still walked erect and brisk as a girl, began to die lingeringly and painfully of cancer of the hip. Her sister Carrie, whom she had cherished and petted all the days of her life, lived on alone for a decade, half-starved but independent, in a room in the Florence Hotel.

During those same years when the local department stores flourished, there were several millinery shops in town, and two particularly that were patronized by my mother and grandmother and their friends: one, a widow's, on Main Street, just around the corner from Detroit; the other, a spinster's, on Greene Street, downstairs in the building that held the library.

Millinery seasons did not change unobtrusively and months ahead of time. The milliners held much-heralded Fall and Spring Openings, and everyone turned out at the same time on a Saturday afternoon and evening to go the rounds, trying on the new styles. In 1905, "Toques, Turbans of various kinds, and large hats of leghorn in the lingerie effect" were advertised. An interior view of Mrs. Sinz's taken in 1908 shows wide brims, high crowns, stiff bows, and wreaths of flowers; on their stands the hats almost conceal the potted palms, mirrors, and rocking chairs which furnished the room. Across the back wall runs a glass counter which you remember full of bright feathers and jeweled hatpins; a shelf above at one end is piled with bolts of wide ribbon.

This room was not a large one, and on an Opening Day was crowded with women trying on and with husbands standing stiffly at attention. We never particularly cared about going with Mother on such occasions. She had a weakness for milli-nery that amounted to a passion: it was her one reckless ex-travagance, but she could not be recklessly extravagant until she had tried on every hat in both her favorite shops. We let her go with Grandma, and then with a few chosen friends followed after, taking care to go first to whichever place she intended

leaving till last. We enjoyed the openings in our own way, trying on whatever struck our fancy, unsupervised except for an
occasional benevolent glance from Miss Kate or a sharper one
from Mrs. Sinz. We were as clean-handed as children could be,
and always dignified and proper, yet we must have been an unmitigated nuisance to milliners who knew that we could not buy,
but who forebore restraining us for fear of offending our mothers. One of those Spring Openings I particularly remember, because I found a perfect hat at Mrs. Sinz's. I must have been
eight or nine that year, and it was the sort of hat nine-year-olds
dreamed of: white lace straw, the brim wide at the front, nar-
rowing behind where the white streamers hung—a flat crown,
not more than an inch high, and on each side, over the ribbon,
slanting from crown to brim, a wreath of tiny velvet forget-me-
nots. I tried it on, looked at the price, tried it on again. . . . At
dinner that evening I said, "I saw a hat today I liked." Mother
cut me short. "I saw one, too, that might suit you. We'll go look
at it tonight." My heart sank. I might have coaxed Mother into
buying me an expensive hat by showing her how beautiful it
looked on me, but if she had chosen already, she would never
see me in the forget-me-not—wreathed straw. Resigned but dis-
consolate, I stalked back with her to Mrs. Sinz's.

Inside she asked Mrs. Sinz for the hat which she had requested her to lay aside. Kate, smiling over her shoulder at me,
bent over a drawer, brought it out, and held it up. *It was the
very same hat.* My heart rose in me and sang; I was nigh to
bursting with joy and love of my mother, in whom I should have
had faith. Never in my life have I had an article of clothing so
much cherished as that white lace straw, with the ribbons and
forget-me-nots. Even now I cannot laugh at an old "blueprint"
which amuses my friends, although it shows the hat sitting flat
as a pancake on top of my hair ribbon, high above and unrelated
to my Sunday-solemn face.

Scattered along these same blocks were several jewelers, a furniture store, two or three men's clothiers, and a couple of shoe-
stores. There were three drugstores with whose interiors we
were familiar: one on the corner of Second and Detroit streets,

where we went for most of our sodas, because it was the closest to our house; one farther along, near the Main Street corner, which was still called "Fleming's," although no Fleming had owned it in my memory; and Galloway's, up on the corner of Main and Greene streets. Mr. Galloway operated his drugstore for pleasure, not profit: it was the evening gathering place of my father's friends, where they told their best stories and settled the destinies of local Republican politicians. Daytimes, the store was mostly empty except for children. Mr. Galloway would take no trouble for a casual customer: often he would claim to be out of something which was plainly visible on the shelf behind him. In February he set up tables down the length of the store and piled them with valentines, romantic and comic. These he sold more cheaply than anyone else in town, and stood by listening while we poked through them. He felt himself rewarded when the little girl who lived next door to us—seven years old, golden-haired, blue-eyed, angelic of expression—turned to him and said, with vindictive emphasis, "I want a *noogly* one for my teacher!"

We had also two cheap stores long before Kresge's and Wool-worth's came to town: the Bee-Hive, up on Main Street, where red-haired Rose Golden worked, and the Famous Cheap Store, on Detroit between Second and Main. The Famous was closer to our house, and we went there oftener, on Grandma's errands and our own; it was owned by a notoriously miserly couple, and it looked like a miser's den: a narrow, dark little hole, with a squeezed aisle between counters heaped with household necessities. Above the counters were overloaded shelves, supported by flimsy posts, with pots and pans swinging from nails driven in their edges—if you were grown-up you could see the storekeepers behind them only piecemeal and fragmentarily. But we liked the store because toward the back was a whole counter of tiny dolls from which we could recruit our doll-house families: the prettiest of them had curled wigs and eyes that opened and closed; they cost fifty cents, and made acceptable birthday presents.

The place of the The Famous and the Bee-Hive in our economy was filled in time by the five-and-ten-cent stores, but any demands met by the Woman's Exchange and West's Book Store have since gone unsatisfied. The Woman's Exchange was on Greene Street, next to the milliner: it was run by three spinster sisters, the Misses Melissa, Amanda, and Cora Horne. They were Grandma's age, or older, and friends of hers, and so we bought there whatever we could. Their room was all white woodwork and glass-topped counters: it was as immaculate as their own parlor. They sold pies and homemade bread, cookies and tall, thick-iced cakes—and they offered for sale hand-painted calendars and place cards, hemstitching and embroideries of different kinds; they took orders for any kind of handicraft wrought for pin money by the wives and spinsters of the town. Miss Melissa, the oldest, was tall, grave and handsome; Miss Amanda was middle-sized, fluttery, and of a giggling habit; Miss Cora, the youngest, was short and timid. Miss Cora was too dependent on Miss Melissa to do anything foolish; it was Amanda who disgraced herself in her old age (in her sisters' eyes, and Grandma's, at any rate) by marrying a senile widower, whose only fortune was his pension and only recommendation his crippled condition. He had lost a leg in the service of his country in the Civil War, and needed a nurse and breadwinner more than Miss Melissa did.

West's Book Store was across Main Street from the courthouse. Little Mr. and Mrs. West had no clerks except occasionally when Mrs. West's sister, on a visit, helped out. There were no books, so far as I can remember, except a few leather-backed gift books and diaries. The back room was given over to wallpaper; in front were tables of bric-a-brac: lamps, china, pottery; and on the side walls, pictures and samples of picture moldings. Oddly, perhaps, the Wests had excellent taste, and made a comfortable living by framing pictures, providing wallpaper for our big old houses, and selling expensive wedding and Christmas presents. As children we made (with some assistance) all our Christmas gifts except Mother's, which was "boughten," usually at the Book Store. We told Mrs. West how much we had to spend, and she showed us everything in the shop that came within our means. Generally we ended by buying a Rookwood vase or pitcher, having assured ourselves of its genuineness by surreptitiously upending it to check the potter's mark. Mrs. West would hand over the wrapped package, beaming as happily as if she herself were giving the present. It was really Mr. West who knew most about Rookwood and things like that, but he was a cross, thin little man with fierce white mustachios, and we avoided him in the store when we could. They were a very quiet, conservative pair; nevertheless, Mr. West bought one of the first automobiles in our town: a high, insubstantial electric, so exactly like a buggy that the Wests, sitting erect behind the dashboard, seemed fantastically exposed without a good stout horse in front of them.

A little farther south on Detroit Street, and east and west on Main, were the grocers and butchers. Their fathers, most of them Germans, had been saloon-keepers or market gardeners and hucksters; the second generation had achieved the more profitable and respectable status of shopkeepers. Not that their fathers' saloons had been anything but respectable: they were beer gardens, really, without the gardens—family institutions, where the daughters of the house filled the tankards and served them. Before I was born, all these had gone: there was only one German saloon in town, kept by a newcomer, a self-proclaimed anarchist; we sidled past his windows as if we suspected that the kegs piled there in pyramids were full of dynamite and might blow up if passers-by did not walk softly. The other saloons of my childhood, owned by Irishmen, had windows discreetly curtained with faded green rep, and swinging shutters for doors.

The Germans of that earlier day, the market gardeners and the saloon-keepers, were all connected, in one way or another, and so in my childhood were butcher and grocer. Two brothers whose father had been a huckster owned the finest grocery in the town; their sister was the wife of an East Main Street butcher; the wife of one of them was sister to the wife of the other leading grocer. Grandma as a young married woman had bought vegetables from the huckster-father when the sons were barefoot gardener's boys just learning English; when I used to go to their store with her, when she was growing old and they were middle-aged, they treated her with a courtly consideration that was charming to witness. One of them was tall and thin, with a black mustache; the other was short and heavier, and hung his glasses over his ear to keep them out of his way. Both were neat and spruce in navy blue serge or black alpaca jackets, and they never, never wore aprons. That grocery was then, and continued to be, until the son-and-nephew retired a number of years ago and there was no one to take it over, a most beautiful and fascinating place, holding on its shelves the rare and costly fruits of the seven seas and all their islands. Above the candy counter there were tall glass jars, shaped like Grecian urns, full of multicolored drops, and silver shot for icing cakes, and pale green mints and salted nuts. On the other side were jars of pickled fish curled around on themselves, pickled onions, and anchovies and caviar. Across the front of the store, behind the windows, the fruits were piled: even Malaga grapes were taken out of the barrel and heaped there, bits of cork still clinging to the stems. And always the fragrance of roasting coffee filled the air. Every housewife in those days ground her own coffee: I remember Grandma's invariable order: half Mocha, half Java, mixed. (Even to the end, in the days of packaged coffee, the old familiar warm fragrance whiffed out at you from the basement grills as you passed that corner.) Fetz's store had never many customers in it, but the telephone was always busy; basketed orders would be ranged in the space around the potbellied stove, ready for delivery: a sign of the trust that was placed in the owners by the town's housekeepers.

The grocery of the brother-in-law, half a block north, was a different kind of place. A wooden awning was supported by posts at the curb. Beneath it, stands were loaded; bushel baskets of peaches and tomatoes snagged your petticoats as you passed. Watermelons were piled where there was room for them, and empty crates were stacked one on another in the gutter. All day long, in the summer, the Negro handy man watered the vegetables from a sprinkling can; in the fall, high-school boys on the way home to lunch seized handfuls of cranberries as they passed, and threw them at each other the rest of the way down the block. Inside, the narrow store was crowded with burlap sacks of potatoes; and barrels of sour pickles and of salted fish stood open, and the scent of brine was thick in your nose. The grocer was a big man with a paunch, who went in his shirt sleeves, a straw hat pushed to the back of his head. He would bear watching when he selected potatoes for you, if you were a child running errands. And he was a power in local Republican politics.

Next to this grocery was "our" butcher. It seems not altogether odd to me to see that, in an old carnival program, he once advertised "kind treatment"—I remember too well how often he gave us each a wiener before he took Mother's order. These we ate uncooked, on the street going home or farther uptown, trailing behind Mother a yard or so because she preferred in the circumstances to pretend we did not belong to her. The wife of this butcher was a sister of the four men who owned a meat store up on Main Street. The youngest of these brothers was a hunter, who went every fall to Maine or Canada with his cronies; for a while after he returned, deer and bear hung from the hooks where we were accustomed to seeing the carcasses of hogs dripping into the sawdust.

When I was little, the process of huckster-into-storekeeper began again with the advent of two Russian-Jewish brothers who came to our door with fruits and vegetables as soon as they could make change, before they could speak English. Later, in the years when I was growing up, each one of them had his own fruitstore, and Mother, because she had been one of their first customers, received the same favored treatment there that Grandma had been given at Fetz's. By that time we had forgotten they had not always been here. They were followed by two or three other Jewish families who set up little clothing stores, and a shoe-repair shop to take the place of the older cobblers, and a junkshop, and a tire-and-auto accessories store where Ed Hunt's bicycle shop used to be, down on Main Street. Ed Hunt was the especial dependence of all the children in town because he re-

45

paired bicycles and roller skates again and again, with no hint that such jobs as we had for him were too trifling to be welcome.

After the Jews, or about the same time, came the Greeks, to start an ice-cream parlor on Main Street, a restaurant on Detroit. One of the stocky, swarthy, unintelligible confectioners went home in 1917 to lead an army: he was, it seemed, a general. After the war he returned, with additional brothers and sisters, nieces and nephews, and put on his confectioner's apron again. Of the few foreigners who have come to our town, only the Greeks have continued the use of their own tongue; consequently, a smattering of Greek—a word here, a phrase there— is acquired by our children who play with theirs, at home and at school.

I believe that our present motion-picture theater is also owned by a Greek—an out-of-town Greek. The older theaters were the ventures of our native citizens: first, the old nickelodeon, squeezed into a roofed-over passageway between buildings, on Detroit Street; then the Orpheum, up on Main, on the corner across the street from the hotel, which small boys called "The Bucket of Blood," and crowded into on Saturday afternoons because it gave them the fare they loved; and the more respectable Bijou, on Greene Street.

In all these years our business district has not changed greatly in extent: it has spread hardly at all, except for scattered filling stations, used-car and parking lots where old houses have been torn down to make way for them. It still includes the four blocks around the courthouse, a few additional blocks east and west on Main Street, two blocks east on Market and Second, and the long stretch of Detroit Street south to the railroad station, which beyond Third Street becomes a succession of lumber yard, coalyard, filling station and automobile salesroom, and grain elevator, with here and there a derelict boarding house or a Holy Roller tabernacle. This part of Detroit Street once dropped so steeply downhill that the sidewalk was interrupted by a flight of wooden steps, with a handrail; remembering that, you remember too that in those days the streets were unpaved. Even Main and

Detroit were mud and dust, holes and ruts, until after the new courthouse was built and the town fathers felt impelled to live up to the county commissioners. A photograph survives which proves the need for paving: it shows the corner where the two streets cross, with a derisive sign on a post struck in a mud puddle: NO BOATING ALLOWED. When dray-horses' hooves, and the wheels of coal wagons and ice wagons, for the first time clashed and rang on brick, it was a new sound in our streets, which had never heard worse than a squeaking wheel and the soft clop-clop of a horse walking in the dust.

The streets are quieter again, now that the horses are gone, although they are much busier: automobiles surge past in a never ceasing flow; there are few of those long-houred afternoons when nothing stirs in the great width of the two main streets. In truth, we have forgotten how empty Main Street used to be on a hot summer day, until we see an old photograph; we have grown used to the traffic.

But we never became reconciled to the blatancy of chain-store fronts, red and green and yellow. Then, just as it seemed there were more and more of these moving in, making of the town one ugliness, our native businesses—banks, building and loan companies, furniture stores—either built anew or rebuilt their façades, so that it is perhaps true to say that our business section has never been so dignified or handsome, nor looked so prosperous. But occasionally, when we lift our eyes, we notice how few there are of these, really, and how many roofs and chimneys above new windows and new signs are exactly as they have always been. The three buildings on the corners of Main and Detroit rise highest and bulk most solidly against the blue. On the northwest corner stands a stone store-and-office building, the tallest of them all, lifting its pinnacles and the heavy dormer windows built like stepped gables high into the air. Across Main Street, Mr. John Allen once upon a time conducted his bank in the front parlors of his house; when he moved his family to the new mansion up on Second Street, he put up the Allen Building here. Here it has since stood unchanged: red brick, three stories tall, severely plain, with a flat overhanging roof and windows in rows with dentists' names on them, and oculists' and lawyers'. At the southeast corner is the old bank building, home for many decades of the bank John Hivling had started in 1835 in the house at the south end of the same block, and that went through various changes as banking laws were passed. In 1845, it became a branch of the Ohio State Bank; in 1863, a national bank. Four years after this last increase in prestige, the building at the corner was erected: Victorian Gothic in limestone, even the pointed windows in the mansard roof adorned with archivolt and corbel. Side and front wall meet in a curve instead of a right angle, and here was the bank entrance: a high Gothic-arched door at the top of curving iron-railed steps. Now the bank has moved up on Main Street into a Williamsburg-Colonial building, and the old one is most unsuitably occupied: not all the chrome trimming along the front and around the curve can make it seem appropriate for a quick-order cheap restaurant.

Away from these corners—west and north, east and south— roof line, eave, ridgepole, and chimney notch the sky at the same height, in the same shape, as they have always done. Seeing them so, you see also for a blurred instant the streets themselves as they were fifty or sixty years ago; you see them as you do when you think of them in absence, with the eyes of a child. The child you were, on an ordinary day, around five-thirty in the evening, going home—south on Detroit Street—from some last-minute errand for the cook. On the Main Street corner you crossed the current of eastward-bound hands from the ropewalk, smelling of tar. At Second you met the Negro women from the stemmery, reeking of raw tobacco. On the corner there, across the street, lived friends of yours, so that you poised waiting, on the curb, briefly, for shouted salute or challenge. Theirs was the fine old Greek-revival house that had been John Hivling's first bank, with the cashier's flat upstairs; it stands even with the pavement, but on a high foundation, and steps, railed with wrought iron, lead to the pillared front door. In your youth, it was a doctor's office and home. Across Second Street from that house was the uptown railroad station, and you had friends there, too: the children of the stationmaster, who lived up-stairs.

Beyond Second Street, you passed Fetz Brothers' Grocery and a jewelry store, another grocery and a saloon. The saloon was noteworthy only because it occupied what had been in its beginning the house of one of our famous families. Henry Mc-Cracken built it when he came from Pennsylvania in 1836. His descendants—scholars, college presidents—returned in later times to the East; only Miss Anna stayed on in her house out on King Street, and the first home, with its adze-hewn joists and rafters, its small-paned windows upstairs, dropped down the scale from grocery to restaurant to saloon.

You passed the saloon, the end of a back alley, and a boarding house before you came to Hanigers', startling in that dingy block because it was so immaculate in its white paint, set back in a velvety lawn behind catalpa trees. A long while before, in the days when men went west to seek their fortunes, the youngest Haniger had been appointed to stay home, run the family saloon, and take care of his mother and sister, while the older brothers went forth to try their luck. In Arizona they set up a saloon and lodging house, fed, bedded, and outfitted prospectors, accepting mining shares as pay. Some of the shares proved worthless, others beyond price. The Hanigers became millionaires. The older brothers returned from Arizona only for brief visits; the women would not leave their old home, and so the youngest son stayed on with them, clerking—incongruously, for he looked like a bartender all his life—in a jeweler's store, spending what he could of his share of the fortune on the ugly frame house, subscribing lavishly to every charity in town, finding his pleasure in the drugstore foregatherings of his friends. Everything about the Hanigers was so odd and fascinating that you passed the house slowly, peering through the floor-length windows where sometimes, behind the lace curtains, you saw the old lady or Minnie—built alike, slight and small, very German in their shawls and aprons, not knowing in the least how millionaires should behave.

49

Beyond, you came to the unpainted frame building on the corner which housed on the Haniger side a Chinese laundry: you were sent there sometimes for shirts or collars, and so you knew its damp, warm, Oriental smell; you knew the Chinaman, pigtailed, black-bloused, sandaled, who stood behind the counter and handed you the laundry. In the other half of the building was a doctor's office downstairs, and upstairs one family after another, all of them with too many children.

You passed the doctor's office, and were at the corner of your own street, where you turned west, and saw the trees arched against a glowing sky. Perhaps you went toward them thinking of nothing much, comfortably aware that you were nearly home. Perhaps, if the skies were gray, if it were winter and the pavements were streaked with soot, and lumps of black snow filled the gutter, you were even remarking how ugly the town was, and how drab and dull. If the skies were clear, you almost certainly paused at the gate, with a hand on the latch, to search for the first star in the west, to wish for escape and a brilliant future far, far away—and yet at the same instant you were aware of the iron of the gate beneath your hand, and were storing away the memory of how it felt. Thus the unfastidious heart makes up its magpie hoard, heedless of the protesting intelligence. Valentines in a drugstore window, the smell of roasting coffee, sawdust on the butcher's floor—there comes a time in middle age when even the critical mind is almost ready to admit that these are as good to have known and remembered, associated as they are with friendliness between man and man, between man and child, as fair streets and singing towers and classic arcades.

3. Streets and Houses

Like other county seats in the older Middle West, ours is a town of rather narrow, quiet streets, deeply shaded, and of big brick houses, half-hidden by the trees. In any strange place one may guess when wealth was most abundantly produced there by noting the prevailing style of domestic architecture. In certain towns in our state the great houses were built long before the Civil War: in Marietta and Gallipolis, in Lancaster and Chillicothe; the communities where prosperity came later cannot hope to rival them in beauty. Nevertheless, we too have evidence of early and comfortable fortunes in the square brick houses in the big yards that go back to ante bellum days, and of later Gilded-Age successes in the elaborate Victorian villas that are scattered along our residential streets, or stand on corners that were once at the edge of town.

A stranger driving through does not really see our houses, except here and there, in glimpses: the maples are too thick, the branches hang too low. But it comes as something of a shock to the mind to realize, when you begin to describe them, that you are in almost the same position: not since you grew up have you walked the length of any but the home streets, or seen any except your friends' houses, and those briefly between curb and doorstep. Your range was wider, too, as a child, when you were at home in the front yards of most of your schoolfellows. Now you feel how the years have circumscribed your round: there are no more than a score of houses you know so well that you need not, on entering, search for the umbrella rack. You are aware that the streets have not altered much in the years between: mass and weight and chiaroscuro are right and familiar, and any change calls attention to itself, but to describe the houses more definitely you must go back in your memory to the days when you went on foot, and peered through a long succession of iron fences as you passed, or turned away in embarrassment from windows at your eye level, in walls that edged the sidewalk.

These houses without front yards once lined our oldest blocks. When they were built the town was bounded on the north by Church Street and on the south by Third, where back yards ran down to the banks of the creek; east and west, it spread not more than a few blocks each way from Detroit Street. In this compact rectangle are those few survivors of the earliest houses, built by Marylanders and Pennsylvanians in the manner to which they were accustomed: flush with the sidewalk, in one corner of the lot, all the yard behind and to one side—some of them on such narrow lots that they were separated only by brick paths where the eaves dripped, the sun never fell, and moss grew thick in the shadow.

It is true that the acres surveyed and the streets laid out for the town were a part of the Virginia Military Lands, and it is equally true that the majority of early settlers in the county were Virginians who had come directly thence, or by way of Kentucky; but those pioneers were landholders, not townsmen: they took up their grants in the forest and became in time middle western farmers. Only here and there in the older part of town, a one-story house, set back among trees, built high above the ground, with wide steps to a galleried porch, suggests Virginia as its origin. So strong in the town has the Pennsylvania influence been that within my memory the word "square" was equally in use with "block." (I have not heard the old word "square" for many years. But we retain—against all logic—the same prepositions used in the same way to indicate location, or direction of movement. Every town, I suppose, develops its own traditional usage, which no dictionary could ever explain. Here, when we are going east we go *up,* and going west, *down:* perhaps because, here abruptly and there imperceptibly, the land does rise toward the east. We go *out* to the north end and the south end, and come *in* again, whatever the slope of the streets. But anyone who lives on an east-west street, either above or below Detroit Street—and *above* is east of it and *below,* west—goes *over* to any block of a parallel street that is on his side of Detroit. It was always, and still would be: "Run *up* to Fetz's [on Detroit Street] and get a dozen eggs," or "Go *over* to the bakery [on Main Street below Detroit] for a loaf of bread." Anyone who lives east of Detroit Street goes "downtown"— west, "uptown." But any shop or house west of Detroit is *down* on whatever street it may be, if it is only half a block from the courthouse, and any building to the east is *up.*)

The pattern of the oldest houses in town varies but little. They are L-shaped, the base of the L against the sidewalk; the stem, running the length of the yard or against the sidewalk of a cross street, is a narrower wing. The recessed front door stands back from the stone step that encroaches on the sidewalk; one or two windows on each side, upstairs and down, overlook the street. The outer wall of the long side of the L may be broken by windows, or it may be a continuing blank stretch of brick. The front door opens on the stair hall; on either side are the "company" rooms: parlor and parlor bedroom. The long wing, but one room wide, contains the family rooms: dining room or sitting room and kitchen; along its inner side is a two-storied porch, with slim posts upstairs and down, and upstairs a railing to keep the children from falling off. A door from the end of the stair hall opens on this porch, another from the sitting room; and upstairs, doors from the bedrooms give access to it.

Later, more stately and larger houses were built according to the same plan, except that a second wing was added at the top

55

of the L, parallel to the street front, so that the porch was enclosed on three sides. The foundations of these houses are higher: the front door must be approached by a flight of granite steps, set sideways against the house front so as to leave a little of the sidewalk for passers-by; the steps have wrought-iron handrails. The windows, unlike those in the older houses, are well above the heads of inquisitive neighbors. The street fronts are severely restrained: in the center, a recessed door with side lights; on its either side, two windows; above, another row of windows under horizontal eaves: the ridgepole is parallel to the street, and gables and chimneys are in the side walls. Rooms in even these larger houses are small compared to those of later times, and ceilings are low; nevertheless, all these old dwellings have their own dignity: they are simple and austere, but they have been lived in for a long, long time, and that has mellowed them. . . . They can be catalogued; who built them could be discovered, and who lives in them now would be easy to find out. But there is a pleasure in keeping to what can be remembered, or what has always been known, or what was told so long ago that the clash and climax of a story have faded from memory, leaving only irrelevant details, vague as echoes in the mind.

On our street one of these very old houses still stands, a couple of blocks below us; it is renovated now, and gleaming with new paint, but in our childhood a sodden grimy place whose porch and yard were a litter of washtubs and broken toys. It was hard to believe it had been a good house once, where in Mother's day had lived the family of one of her aunts-by-marriage. The first log cabin in the stretch of forest which was later to become the town was in this neighborhood, not far from the road to Cincinnati. The young couple who built it possessed both a baby and a tame bear, which they had raised from a cub and which they chained to a staple in the log wall when they left the cabin. One day the mother came in from hoeing the corn to find not only the bear missing—the staple pulled out of the log—but the baby, too, utterly vanished. Thinking frantically of Indians, she ran for her husband, who was clearing ground some distance away; together they followed the bank of

Shawnee, up past what was later the Seminary tennis courts and the Bottoms between our block and the railroad station. They found no trace of Indians, and finally returned home in despair— where they found both bear and baby: the baby warm in the bear's embrace, the two of them sound asleep under the bunk in the corner. We used to think, kicking our heels on the bridge over Shawnee, that we could invent a better, more exciting end to that story, but we liked to imagine searching the weeds and willows beside the stream for the prints of moccasin and bear paw.

In my mother's childhood the Edwards house and tannery lay at the west end of Third Street, lost, both of them, in a wilderness of trees. The family still lived in their house then, but the tannery had lapsed into disuse. When Mother went there with other children, creeping on it through the weeds between the trees on moonlit nights, it was a broken-windowed haunt of bats and owls: the kind of place to run from, helter-skelter, at the scrape of a tree bough, the movement of a shadow, the scrabble of a rat's feet. The tannery had gone before it was our turn to play hide-and-seek up and down Third Street: when the only Edwardses left were women, the husband of one of the daughters somehow got possession of the property; the tannery was torn down and all the land sold off in building lots. The once-beautiful old house is still there, but in all my lifetime it has been hidden behind the nondescript dwellings put up where the tannery yard used to be: you can find it only by poking down West Street toward its dead end at the railroad track. The inner side of the L is toward this street, the two-story porch with its slender columns recessed between the two wings. It was restored a number of years ago by one of the town's antique-lovers, but its location is a handicap, and it is falling to pieces again now, in need of paint, shutters hanging, and over all an air of neglect.

Houses of this Maryland-Pennsylvania type are scattered here and there over the central blocks of the town. There is one on Detroit Street, a hundred feet or so north of Church, almost forgotten, overshadowed as it is by the Victorian house on the corner, with its iron fence and its brick stable back on Church Street that is itself larger than many a contemporary "model" home.

On Church Street, as on Third, only one house of this type still stands—or, for all I know, ever stood: it is next to the old schoolyard, and at recesstime, day after day, we played our games in the shadow of its long blank outside wall. Second, Main, and Market were older streets; they may once have been lined close by houses of this earliest date; enough are left to remind us of how the town once looked. East on Second Street are two: one on the corner of Whiteman and one a little further up the hill where the Charterses lived. The last Charters generation in town grew up with us, and so we knew well that particular parlor, with its windows at eye level against the sidewalk, and the deep narrow side yard, and the porch enclosed on three sides against the rain. The girls married men "from away," and for the first time in more than a hundred years no children of that name played jackstones on the side-porch step in the spring. The first Charters in this country came from Scotland to New York in 1784; his son was there apprenticed to a piano-maker. Grown-up, the son came west to Cincinnati to practice his trade: the first piano made this side the Alleghanies was made by him. One must suppose that there was a market for pianos in the Cincinnati of those days: certainly there could not have been in the forest wilderness seventy miles north. But there was no Associate Reformed Presbyterian church in Cincinnati, and so the piano-maker moved to where there was one, and became the first of a long line of Charterses in our town. In the beginning he made whatever furniture was needed; then, when there was a demand for them, he returned to pianos. Not too many years ago a few of these instruments still stood in our parlors: great square pianos of dark polished rosewood, inlaid above the yellowed keyboard with morning-glory vines in mother-of-pearl.

The house on the corner below, red brick and green-shuttered, like others of its kind set flush with both sidewalks, was in my childhood the home of a solitary old maid who had inherited the house and its dignified cherry furniture from an otherwise vanished family. She was always "Babe" Rader, but she was so old, and had been alone so long, that the nickname had no meaning: no one ever smiled when it was spoken, or remembered that once she must have been the pet of a large household.

Just west of Detroit on Second Street are two of the more stately versions of these houses, with high foundations, double flights of iron-railed steps, and fanlights over their doors. To one I went long ago, as little Red Ridinghood, for my first Halloween masquerade; to the other, longer ago, went my mother and aunt when they were little girls, to call on Old Cousin Julia Dubois. Which of their grandparents she was cousin to, Mother had long forgotten: she retained only a shadowy memory, entitling her to a sense of lifelong familiarity with the house—a faint memory of a fragile aged lady, to whom she could put a name.

One more very old house farther down the street, like all the others of its type, stands as it was built by the first of the Allisons to come from Pennsylvania. Here the Allison sons grew up: the father of Carrie and Fannie, who died young and never grew rich; and Mr. Matt Allison, who in the middle of the century built the big square pillared house up on Market Street; and Mr. Sam Allison, who was younger and built his house a little later —the brick Victorian mansion across the street on the corner, with its porches and peaks and bay windows, and its brick stable back on King Street.

On Market Street at Whiteman is the most uncompromising of these houses, the severest and least comely. Whether or not the spinsters who dwelt there in my youth were the granddaughters of its builder I have no idea; if not, they should have been. The house seems to embody all the more forbidding traits of the Covenanters who came from Pennsylvania: its bricks are a dark gloomy red; on two sides, its walls edge the sidewalks; its painted steps imperil the passer-by; its front windows are heavily curtained and the side ones shuttered; the recessed porch is enclosed by lattices, upstairs and down. From its back door, for many years, one of the sisters slipped down the back alley to the school building, a black shawl clutched at her chin, her bony face too like a death's-head for first-graders, however amiable she might be.

Across the street most of the original houses have been torn down: houses that stood in so solid a row that you could hop and skip, up and down and up again, from doorstep to doorstep. One was torn down because it was a "cancer house," and no one would rent it; two made way for commerce. The corner house was the one where a long while ago there lived a member of one of our most pious, one of our very strictest Associate Reformed Presbyterian families, who for some unaccountable reason never legally married his wife. It was all right, in a way: no one ever questioned her title to "Mrs."; she lived with him a lifetime, and there were no children. But it seemed odd—odd even in those days when there was more tolerance of eccentricity than there is now, and when the Reformed Presbyterians were still refusing to have any part in a government whose Constitution made no mention of God.

On the same side of Market, near that corner, is the sheriff's house, with the county jail attached to it. The house was built in 1860, and is as simple and dignified as others of that date, but its bricks are painted a gray so cold the sheriff's family must feel the prison atmosphere creeping through their walls. (And sometimes prisoners creep through the walls in the other direction: a jail that is a hundred years old is by no means impregnable.)

Across the street, between the Baptist church—itself a hundred years old, its faded pinkish bricks crumbling a little at the corners—and the newish yellow-pressed-brick supermarket, is an old stone house, its front wall in line with the sidewalk. That house is and always has been an undertaker's establishment, with family quarters upstairs; a brick house that stood next to it, exactly like it in plan and as old, was torn down recently to make way for the grocery; it had belonged for many years to a rival undertaker. Two of a long succession of competitors are memorable. The one who built the brick house was the first, or nearly the first, of his trade in town, and lived long enough to boast of having buried more people than any undertaker in the state. He owned ground all the way through to Church Street; when his daughter married he built a house for her there: a square, dignified, early Victorian house, behind an iron fence. His son-in-law followed him in his business, and in time he too built a house for a daughter: a little frame house, torn down now, tucked in between her grandfather's place and the stone house of his competitor.

One of these competitors, of a later date, was an antiquarian, scholarly enough to write the history of the county, but he will be longest remembered as the source of some of our best stories: he was not only a wit himself, but the cause of wit in others. He was also a politician, and he came to know, as did that earlier, greater Ohioan, "Black Tom" Corwin, the handicap that a quick and ready tongue can be to a man seeking office. Once, when he was running for re-election to his position in the courthouse, he arrived tardily at a Republican rally where he was to have spoken. He failed to resist the opening offered when the chairman asked where he had been. "I've been in the East End," he said, "black-buryin'." His white audience may have enjoyed the pun, but it cost him the election.

Market Street west of Detroit was once upon a time solidly Scotch-Irish Presbyterian: Armstrong, Bigger, Watt, Anderson —and their brick houses, at the sidewalk's edge, were built to endure. One still stands against the back wall of the Florence Hotel; one, where our doctor lived, is across the side street from the Presbyterian church. Two doors farther along is the house built by the first Bigger to come north from Kentucky. The old lady known to the whole church and most of the town as "Gran'ma Bigger" must have been his daughter-in-law. I remember her, through those years of childhood that seem as long as forever, sitting in the parlor window not two feet from you as you passed by on the way home from school, quiet as an image in her stiff black taffeta, her lace kerchief, and cap. All that life meant to her then was the adding of one year to another—and already I have forgotten whether or not she achieved her triumph and celebrated her hundredth birthday. Tucked back in the shadow between her house and the doctor's is the small

OHIO TOWN

frame cottage built in her side yard for her daughter when she married; but in the years when we used to see Gran'ma Bigger in her window, she had long outlived that daughter, her son, and grandson.

Main Street, of course, was the first street to have houses on it, and I do not doubt that some of those still standing were there when it was still "Chillicothe Street"—a wide spot in the trail from Chillicothe west. Just west of Detroit Street, and across from and east of the public square, a number of them have been turned into shops, and at street level they are little different from the newer business buildings. But from the opposite curb they are unmistakable, with their steep-pitched roofs, the ridgepole parallel to the street; the wide double chimneys at either end; and (two or three of them) stepped gables.

Beyond the first block of Main Street, west as far as the railroad crossing, there are few shops, but the houses are coming down one by one, and the trees—the tall maples and the great-girthed sycamores—by the half-dozen at a time, to make way for parking and used-car lots and filling stations. (Any native still averts his eyes from what has been done to Main Street beyond the railroad crossing, where the new four-lane highway to Dayton begins: every tree sacrificed; a bleak, barren stretch of houses with no front yards, where once shade lay solid, and inside the fences cottages were hidden behind lilacs and sweet-shrub bushes.) Defying progress, a few houses survive, and are as old as any in town. They stand tight against one another, their thresholds not six inches from the sidewalk. Some are brick, but the oldest are frame, and sometimes when one is torn down, we discover that there are logs beneath the clapboards. I never knew who lived along that stretch of Main Street, except one crotchety humpbacked dressmaker whom I visited with my bosom friend for her tryings-on; from the talk of my elders I did know who had lived in them in earlier times: the Knoxes, who, in the beginning of my memory, still had the harness shop further up on Main Street; and, across the street, "the three most beautiful girls who ever grew up here," and one of them married my great-aunt Florence's brother, and went to New York, and one of them married a St. Louis millionaire, and the third no one ever knew about, or remembered what became of her.

Only one house of this type is left on East Main Street. Sometime in the last century it became the home of one of the German newcomers, who built his butcher shop beside it, on the corner; now the house has become a bus station and restaurant. On the slope of Main Street hill, in that same block, the Puterbaugh house was replaced a decade ago by the new telephone exchange. Built after the Puterbaugh store had made the family prosperous, it was the most beautiful of all the very old houses in town. It stood midway of the hill; the sidewalk sloped down past the foundation, which rose so high that the door was above your head as you passed. A double flight of steps, railed with wrought iron, led to a square stone landing outside the front door. The recessed entrance was square, too, with slender Ionic pillars between the door and the side lights. The yard was wide and full of fruit trees; from the street you could look between their blossoming boughs to the recessed porch with its white railing and delicate square posts. The house was handed down by the widower of the last of the Puterbaugh daughters to the retired schoolteacher who had been her close friend and who took care of him in his old age. She was not the sort of person one thinks of as a nurse for the aged, but an intellectual whose eighty-year-old eyes could sparkle over the most abstruse mathematical proposition. She loved the house, guarded it as the apple of her eye, and kept it in the state of paint and polish it deserved. But her heirs lived elsewhere; they were willing to sell it to the telephone company.

Workmen who razed the house found a letter under the upper floor of the porch, written and hidden there a half-century before by Mrs. Mary Puterbaugh Moore. The letter was deservedly printed in our newspaper; it was read with some astonishment by this one at least of her fellow citizens: I remembered Mrs. Moore as she had been in my childhood: a big heavy-boned woman, black-browed and stern-looking—intimidating to the young. But apparently her looks had belied her: she had not been without sentiment. The letter was addressed "To Whom it

May Concern in Years to Come"; the date, 1899: "The old porch that was built with this house in 1845 was replaced with a new one this day. The associations of the old porch floor bring up many memories of childhood days as I have played by the hour with many friends and it has in all those years been a floor that many a loved one has walked over. Sorry to part with the good old oak floor but for memory's sake I write these loving words.

"I do not know who of this household will see another floor as I am the only one of the family left. . . . We do not know who will take up this floor nor the circumstances, but if it is occupied by another than either of us I defy them to say they are any happier than George and Mary E. Moore."

Perhaps Mary Puterbaugh Moore would have preferred that the house be torn down rather than allowed to deteriorate. Being torn down, it stands now in our mind's eye as it was in its perfection, beautiful and gracious, and for a long while will be remembered so. It may be that all the men and women of all the generations who dwelt in these houses would have felt the same way; if so, we should lament only the town's loss of dignity and of its air of venerable age when one comes down, instead of feeling sad that a house should so long outlast the possessive love of a family that there was no one left to preserve it.

Among and between these oldest of our houses, on these same blocks, are others, more varied in style, that have been there for nearly as many decades; you almost forget they are there until you begin to walk the streets in your imagination, your memory. . . . At the top of the East Church Street hill across from the old Female College stands the little one-and-a-half-story brick cottage where a one-time superintendent of the schools lived with his wife; they were characters for someone to put into a book some day. The town's stories about them are legion. He made the schools what they had never been before his day—so good that all children went to them, and the private day schools dwindled and died—but he was a cross-grained bigot, almost always in a temper. And she was a constant warning to young men not to marry "literary women." Of an evening the Professor would go downstreet mumbling complaints to whatever neighbors were taking the air at their gateposts—complaints that his supper had been bread and jelly set out on a newspaper laid across the corner of the kitchen table. I do not know how his wife had attained her "literary" reputation, except by belonging to the Woman's Club, but her parsimony was a byword: it was told of her that she would stop the newsboy on his afternoon rounds and ask for the loan of a paper long enough to see whether there was anything in its columns to make it worth buying; on the boy's return she would refold it and hand it back to him, shaking her head.

From my youthful point of view the most notable thing about them was their staunch, unmitigated Presbyterianism. Their children had grown up by that time and gone: the boys had vanished into the world, and were never heard of by the town; one daughter had rebelled—she had refused to conform to convention and had long since disappeared; the other was a model wife and mother of twelve children, whom she brought home for summer holidays. The brick cottage was large enough for her parents, who were thin-boned, wraithlike and tiny; but she was big and bouncing, and we wondered how she and her twelve managed to squeeze into it. Each of the older children was responsible for a younger one, and performed the duty conscientiously: they would come to Sunday school two by two, neat and clean as pins, scrubbed and shiny. It is no wonder that they were well behaved. Their mother, instead of reacting against her parents' strictness, practised it even more thoroughly on her own children: the oldest son was one time confined to his upstairs, dormer-windowed room for three hot summer weeks; he was given a stove and made to do all his own cooking, even to baking his bread.

When her mother died, the erring daughter came home. She rouged the cheeks of the corpse in the coffin. That was long before undertakers rouged their corpses as part of a grisly routine: the horrified, indignant righteous sister washed her mother's face. The wicked sister put the rouge on again; the good sister washed it off. Finally, the old professor had to be called in to arbitrate. . . . It is small wonder that to this day the town holds this family in loving remembrance: few of our citizens have given us so much pleasure.

At the foot of the hill is another old house where long ago a playmate of my mother's lived, in the days when she went to private school in the Female College up the hill. An older sister died—of tuberculosis, Mother thought, remembering her pallor and emaciation—and all the children on their way to school called to see the corpse. To an amazing extent Mother associated houses with the bodies that lay in state in their parlors: here a stillborn child, there a drowned schoolmate, or an old soldier who had never recovered from his imprisonment at Andersonville. One can imagine those little girls of the 1870's, in plaid frocks and pantalettes, eyes wide beneath their bangs, ringing a doorbell and taking their places in a line of callers (surely without their parents' knowledge or consent); but one can only wonder, as Mother herself did, all the rest of her life, at the morbid curiosity whose satisfaction left such undying memories.

On Church Street across from the library is one of the houses built by a Virginian, set back from the street and high above the ground with shrubbery to conceal the lattice under its wide veranda. The yard once extended to the corner; another house has been put up in that space. However, the persimmon tree was left between them, and on late fall afternoons children still linger on their way home from school to gather up the persimmons that have fallen into the drift of golden leaves from neighboring maple trees.

A little way out on North Detroit Street one of the most gracious of the mid-century houses stands deep in its yard, behind a surviving iron fence: a brick house painted white, a recessed door with iron handrails to guard its steps, wooden Ionic pilasters at the corners, a one-story wing stretching out to the side. This was the Millen house—Dave Millen's, after his brother Eli built the baronial villa on King Street; next to it is the more elaborate, less beautiful frame house Dave Millen built in his yard, after the fashion of the time, for his daughter when she married. That same daughter, when I had grown up, had become one of the wise elders of the Woman's Club. I have spent many a winter afternoon in her parlor, noting with youthful delight and condescension its pure Victorianism while I listened to an essay. The old house next door had in the meantime descended to Dave Millen's grandson, whose children romped in its yard while their mother, aunt, and grandaunt entertained The Club.

On West Church Street most of the Greek-revival or early-Victorian houses were replaced in the 1860's and 70's. A few survive, notably the one that had been Hugh Carey's and his forebears', and was his married daughter's when we were children. She was an invalid, the victim of prostrating headaches, and appeared but seldom, in a carriage, swathed in veils. We overheard our elders (who were a little skeptical of her illnesses, but who admitted, when she died, that there must have been *something* . . .) telling how the doctors were going to bore holes through from her nose to her forehead: sinus trouble, by that name, was unknown, at least to children, and so were the tortures devised for its cure; the tales curdled our blood, and on those rare occasions when we saw this martyr in her carriage we regarded her with the awe we might have felt for a victim of the Inquisition.

The oldest of the East Market Street houses are beyond the top of the hill, in what is now the East End, but on the verge of the hill are one or two that were new in a time no one can now remember: on the lower corner, a rambling soiled tumbledown place, built of vertical boards and battens, that in Mother's childhood was the neat, tight home of a German family of parents and nine children who had moved into it on their arrival in town, and had saved it from the dissolution that threatened what was even then an old house; and on the upper corner, a big brick house in a bigger yard that was all shrubbery and yellow roses, where my uncle and aunt lived, and my aunt's Aunt Cass, crippled and in a wheel chair, spending her days sewing most beautiful doll clothes, and silk quilts for the doll's cradle. And across the street was the house we called "old Matt Wilson's," though we had no idea who Matt Wilson might have been, and knew the name in no other connection. It had been built long before by a family named Inskip, since departed. It was Virginia transplanted, yet utterly lacked the glamor associated with tall fluted pillars, not because it was empty and the yard overgrown with briars, but because it had some time been painted an unwholesome yellow, and when we knew it that paint was peeling off in great flakes, leaving rust-colored patches to spread and widen.

Market Street is a succession of big houses built just before the Civil War or not long after, but in the block below are several that date back to earlier times. Next to the parking lot where the high school used to be, there stood until last summer the house that had been our first private school for boys and when we were children was the home of the very conservative, very distinguished-looking, erect, white-bearded old man who owned our daily paper. It deteriorated in the hands of later owners, but retained to the end its chief beauty: the wrought-iron work that framed the veranda: filagree bands, a light arabesque of leaves and fruit that supported the roof and underlined it, and a delicate row of lyres for the railing. Now that yard has been asphalted and added to the parking lot.

On East Main Street, too, are, or were, a few of these old nonconforming dwellings: across the side street from the post office, the square brick house with bay windows upstairs and down, where Miss Belle Paul lived with her lame nephew, which has made way now for the new bank; on the opposite corner, the Merrick house. Old General Merrick was a New Englander— one of the few in the town—and he built his house with its gable-end front door toward Main Street and its length along Collier Street; it has, somehow, a tight-lipped look. Next to it, set back a little, is a statelier square house, of smooth yellowish limestone with raised quoins, with tall windows: the dwelling place built a generation later by the General's son. Never, so far as I remember, have I been in the older house, but I feel that I know it well, for there Aunt Florence lived in her girlhood with her grandfather (Great-aunt Florence, the wife of one of my grandfather's brothers). She kept house for the old General after her father had married a second time and had set about bringing up a new family in his big house next door. When I was a child, all the Merricks had gone; even Aunt Florence lived in France with her daughter. The older house was made into offices and apartments, but in the stone house there lived for a generation one of the laughter-loving families of the town, whose children we grew up with and loved to visit for occasional turbulent hours. Now they, too, are married and scattered, but one of the sons lives in the house with his lot of children, and I doubt whether its atmosphere has much changed.

Beyond this original compact little town, bounded by Church Street and Third, by Columbus Street and West, lay the small farms cleared of the forest; a number of the farmhouses, since enveloped by the town, are as old as any in its original streets. John Hivling's first house was a farmhouse: my great-grandparents, the father and mother of the six boys of whom Grandpa was eldest, bought it and lived there after they moved to town. The house stood between orchard and meadows, a little east of Detroit Street, a little south of the creek. When Mother was small, grass and trees, the stone well with its sweep, and her grandmother's flower beds filled all that stretch between the farm lane and the creek. Now, across what used to be the lane, the house stares into factory windows, and it is barred from Detroit Street by dilapidated boarding houses and restaurants.

Farmhouses near the other, north fork of Shawnee were more fortunate in the neighborhoods that grew up around them: they have successfully acclimatized themselves to the tree-arched streets. The Robertses tore down their farmstead when they built the villa in what had been a field in the angle of Church and Detroit streets, but on the other side of Detroit one or two old farmhouses are left among newer homes north of the creek. On the next street to the west is Andrew Baughman's old house, where he lived before he built his villa next door. Once his farmyard went all the way to the creek on the north, and to Detroit Street on the east, and what was then his lane is now a narrow street; when you glance down its one-block length as you pass its Detroit Street end, you find yourself looking squarely at the front door of the one-time farmhouse. (Absurdly enough, this short passageway, joining King Street and Detroit, with not a house facing it, is "King Avenue.") When Andrew built the villa, the old house became his foster daughter's. Andrew had no children, and in time the villa was inherited by two spinster nieces: shy little women who never ventured from its gates except for church and missionary-society meetings. After they died the ornate mansion was empty for many years, while next door to it, in the farmhouse, the foster daughter's grandchildren were growing up. Finally the villa was knocked about and remade, its Victorian origin splendidly transformed, but the yellow-painted brick farmhouse next door, with its ivied shutters, its iron-railed steps, its high-pillared side porch, is still the more beautiful house of the two.

The houses that I have named are most of those that have survived from the town's first half-century: the latest of them was built by 1850, and the earliest of them long before that, when log cabins were being replaced by brick and clapboard. In the next score years, mansions were designed to a different pattern: they were huge, square, three stories tall, set well back in wide yards, with brick paths and iron fences. The biggest of these houses, although they number not more than a half-dozen, are conspicuous enough and sightly enough to date the town's coming of age. They are much alike except superficially, as in the design of their porches. They are centered in yards whose trees are taller than their chimneys, and so their solidity and bulk are not overpowering. Those chimneys are double, rising from the edge of the roof, two or three on each side. The roofs are flat; the widely overhanging eaves are supported on wooden brackets curved like question marks, and the length of the brackets is the width of the cornice. The brick walls may be painted or not, white or cream or gray, but the cornices, the brackets, and the window frames are white and the shutters green.

Interiors, too, follow a pattern: a wide central hall with a curving staircase separates two rooms on one side from two rooms on the other; sometimes, two parlors are on the right, thrown into one room, but having still two chandeliers, two fireplaces, and two doors to the hall; then, on the left, the rooms will be living room and dining room, with their fireplaces, their doors to the hall. Or sometimes the two front rooms are both parlors, or parlor and library, and in that case there will be solid partitions between them and the living room and dining room behind. But always there are four square rooms, high-ceilinged, with windows to the floor, shutters inside as well as out—and so thick are the walls that the inside shutters can be folded back into the window frames. Behind the square block of four rooms are those known only to the family, or to the friends of their children: a smaller dining room or living room, a butler's pantry, back hall and stairs, pantry, kitchen, and back porch.

These houses are safe only so long as they are handed down from one generation to another of the families that built them. On Market Street, cater-cornered from the Presbyterian church, is the one that we knew most intimately once upon a time, because the grandchildren who lived there were our close friends; and there we once had slumber parties and pillow fights, taffy-pulls in the kitchen, and marshmallow roasts around the marble fireplace of the back living room. That house is now a funeral home. . . . The one that stood at the west end of Main Street, on the crest of the hill, facing up the length of the street—the Kelso place, with its Scottish severity, its small porticoes, one on each of three sides of the house—was turned into apartments when there were no Kelsos in town to live in it; and in the general demolition that accompanied the construction of the new Dayton highway, it was torn down. On the hill just south of the railroad station, behind and above the houses built in what was once its yard, stands the Arnold house, red brick, with square porticoes and rows of long windows. When we were children it was derelict: we could look across at it from our attic windows, above the intervening creek bed and railroad station, and see its hanging shutters and weed-grown yard. It was rescued some forty-odd years ago, and restored—but I seldom climb to the attic windows now, and it is not visible from Detroit Street, and so it may have fallen to pieces again, without my knowing.

In the other direction on Detroit Street, next to the Reformed

Church, is another of these big square houses: this one has a porch that reaches across the front and down the side, ending in a porte-cochere. It has always been a doctor's house, and for many years was a private hospital as well. The doctor who built it put up later a smaller house in the side yard for his daughter, between his porte-cochere and the Florence Hotel: the big house might have rather a cramped look, if you were not too accustomed to notice it. The family who lived there when we were children carried their elbows close to their sides, anyway: the president emeritus of the Theological Seminary, his daughter, his doctor son-in-law. We were breathlessly in awe of him, because he was a saint and a scholar and very old; we were less in awe of his daughter only because she was less old: she too was reputed to be a saint and was certainly a scholar. She was plumpish and blonde and benign, but we knew better than to judge her mind from her comfortable ordinary appearance. Of her children, however, we were not in the least in awe. We were so presumptuous as to pity them. They were educated at home. This I feel sure was out of contempt for the public-school system and fear of corruption of the family saintliness, not out of snobbery; but as an inevitable consequence they had no friends their own age, and of course we pitied them. The son was occasionally allowed to play with us: he was so inexperienced in the art that he was likely as not to tag you playfully over the head with an iron bar found in a trash pile; games with him ended in his sullen withdrawal and a considerable mitigation of our pity. His sister was older, fair and gentle like her mother, but slender—rather, we thought, like Elaine in the towers of Astolat. The doctor's family who took their house when they moved away were different and easier to live with—at least for those of us unaccustomed to an exalted plane and a rarefied atmosphere. They were neither too bright nor too saintly for our daily food; their children grew up learning no more than the public schools and their own curiosity could teach them—and knew their contemporaries as friends and equals.

Three of these houses, on the corners where Monroe Street crosses Market, Main, and Second, have been until fairly lately or are still the homes of the families that built them; they stand now at the edge of the advancing East End. The oldest of the three is the Monroe house, at the top of Market Street hill. Built by the first Monroe to come from Scotland, it is a more austere house, outwardly, than the others; its recessed front door has not even a portico. Within, it was never austere: it was a hospitable house, full of life and the love of laughter, a treasure house of beautiful old furniture and of books—many books, lying open anywhere and everywhere. But now the Monroes that we grew up with are scattered and gone, their parents dead. The house was sold, and made into apartments, and is beginning to have a tenement-ish look. Better, perhaps, were it to be torn down, as the Matt Allison house was torn down a few years ago, when there was no one left to live in it—its mantels and staircase carted away to be saved, on the chance that some day someone might build a hall or parlor large enough to hold them; its cellar hole filled in, and sown with grass seed by the United Presbyterian Church next door, which bought the lot when rumors of a filling station began to be heard. Now the whole corner is velvety green lawn; only a few stubborn flowers persisted for a while in the corner of the hedge—daffodils, and columbine, and a white peony—to remind us of one of our proudest mansions.

The King house is on the Main Street corner; it is set far back from its iron fence, and except at the gate is concealed by shrubbery from the passer-by. "Old J. W." was not only a banker but a manufacturer of gunpowder as well; he built "The Kingdom" during the Civil War. The house is rather more elaborate than the ante bellum houses: its pillars are larger, and the roof line rises in a curve over the central windows above the porch; inside, the carved walnut woodwork is dark and massive. Old J. W. would have done better to have waited until the war ended to build his house. His too-great prosperity confirmed the suspicion (just or unjust, who knows now?) that he was selling gunpowder to the Rebels as well as to his own side. When the new mansion had been finished in every detail, and the family was ready to move in, some of his fellow townsmen hauled a cannon up Main Street, warned everyone in the neighborhood to open his windows, and let go with a blast that shattered every piece of glass in "The Kingdom." I never heard this story from anyone except my grandmother: she was never so in awe of the Kings as to think any shadow of scandal touching them should be forgotten, and in spite of her long and devoted friendship with J. W.'s daughter Ella, she told it with some relish. (I have an idea that Grandma was just enough envious of great wealth to be always ready to suspect the means of its acquisition). . . . And now the King family has long been gone. When Grandma was a girl, and visited them, before she married and came to town to live, the King daughters were young and pretty and gay. But only one of them had children. She died while they were still small, so son and daughter came home to live with their aunts. With that daughter Mother in her turn went to school and romped in the King house and climbed every tree in the yard. But her children did not in their turn grow up there; they had married and established themselves elsewhere before their parents came home to keep an eye on the aunt who had been left alone. After the mother died, they and the son's children gave "The Kingdom" to the American Legion.

The big house at the corner of Monroe and Second streets was built by John Hivling when the profits of bank, warehouse, and hotel had made it possible. Here there is an iron fence, and the path goes uphill to the wide porch across the front of the house. A granddaughter of John Hivling married John Allen, and John Allen built the brick Victorian house next door; in the fullness of time, the Hivling house came into the possession of the married Allen daughter; her daughters live there now, and it long ago became the Kinney house. When Mother was a child, it still belonged to one or another of the Hivlings: she played in it with a great-granddaughter of John, dressing up in the discarded ball gowns of the youngest aunt, or sliding down the laundry chute in games of hide-and-seek. Such days are relived now only when the youngest generation of nieces comes to visit; balls and ball gowns are part of a dead past, but the house's long tradition of hospitality has never lapsed, and all of us feel a vicarious pride in that tradition when we sit in solemn dignity in those beautiful stately drawing rooms at a Woman's Club meeting, or when we lift our eyes from the dining-room mahogany to the mid-nineteenth-century portrait of John Allen.

More numerous than these mid-century houses are the fantastic Victorian villas of the sixties, seventies, and eighties, with their balconies and pinnacles and towers, their mansard roofs patterned with particolored slates. Andrew Baughman's has been rebuilt, its perfect Victorianism completely concealed; but on the corner above it is Eli Millen's house, worsened by the heavy Teutonic porch of boulders arched like a Romanesque cloister that was added by a later owner. Across King Street with what was once the Baughman farm lane between them, are two of the big Victorian houses: one early and severe, unchanged except for a porch, with all its yard to the right; the other rebuilt and enlarged when its owners outgrew its first plan, with all its yard downhill to the left. Its Victorianism is largely a matter of porches and bay windows—added space. There were six children living there in my mother's day and generation, three boys and three girls; they were musicians, a cosmopolitan family, educated abroad, like a handful of others from the old houses—sons and daughters of the old families. They had what no other house in town possessed: a music room, on the second floor, where the grand piano stood in one corner, and an audience could sit in the sunny bay window among the ferns. But when we were growing up, friends of the grandchildren, it was not in the music room that we gathered, but on the third floor, where we played pool on the battered old billiard table their married uncles had left behind them.

Rather like this house is the one farther out on King Street whose yard runs for a block, from corner to corner. Here the children of the third generation were all bright-haired, red or golden: you remember them uptown in the sun, crowded squirming into the carriage. The house seemed less awful than others of its period because the yard was so wide, and because in a row behind the iron fence were the six most magnificent trees in town—elms, their trunks four feet through, their upper branches as high again as all neighboring chimneys, the noisy haunt of blackbirds on September evenings. But the elms were blighted and had to be cut down; the older generation died, the younger married and moved away; and the house, bigger and uglier without the elms, is a nursing home.

A more extremely Victorian villa, which was once surrounded by acres of ground, stands at what was in my younger days the very edge of town, where Detroit Street ended and the Springfield pike began. It has a tall square tower above the front door, square bay windows all around, a porte-cochere, a high-pitched roof of patterned slate crowned by an iron railing and broken by tall dormer windows. The history of the place—the full cycle—is that familiar to all who live in an old town: the children of the man who built it grew up there, married, and departed; it stood empty for a while, and then another father of a large family moved in—Dr. Webster, when he was professor of Greek at the Theological Seminary. His sons were our age, his daughters a little younger. They grew up, left home for college; the Seminary moved, and Dr. Webster with it. After another lapse of time, the house was bought by a lawyer with four children; they grew up in their turn; he died a number of years ago, his widow recently. The house was bought by an undertaker and made over into a funeral home. The change is not too evident: in the years since the Websters lived there, and the little girls made leaf houses in the big yard in the autumn, the town has spread well beyond it, building lots have been sold from around the edge of the villa grounds, and a dozen houses stand where used to be only trees and the shrubbery that banked the iron fences.

Another Victorian house is the white one on the southeast corner of Church and Detroit streets. Once, you were in and out of this house a dozen times a day, and played games with its six children over every inch of it, from the highest room in the round corner tower to the long-vanished stable and the high alley fence and the coops where chickens and rabbits and guinea pigs lived. Since that time it has been partially rebuilt: it is more impressive in its immaculate white paint than it used to be—it is emptier, with only one of our generation still at home with an aunt—but the spirit within its walls is so unchanged that however seldom, nowadays, you ring its doorbell, you still feel as much at home there as you ever did.

One of the things you remember is how one of the children of that house called one afternoon on the Robertses. The largest, most fantastic of the mansions built in the 1870's was the Roberts Villa, set far back from the northeast corner of the same streets. When we were children, there used to be picture post-card views of the Roberts Villa (always capitalized) for sale in all the drugstores, but by that time only three of the family were left: two Roberts sisters, very, very old recluses, and their elderly nephew, who minced out of the back gate occasionally, in his ladylike fashion, attired in dove gray or white, his side whiskers gleaming like silver. We children were consumed with curiosity about the place, but went no further to gratify it than to climb the fence and creep through the long grass to a vantage point under one of the tentlike maple trees, whence we would stare, seeing nothing but blind windows that flamed in the sunset. But the seven-year-old who tagged after us was not so easily satisfied. One summer day, when she had been "cleaned up for the afternoon," she went to call, most precisely like her elders. From the padlocked gate, which she had to climb, she marched steadily up the weed-grown drive without any visible hesitation; she plodded up the steps, rang the front doorbell, and was admitted. That was all we could see, but afterward she told us about it. The maid had asked her name and offered her a chair in the hall while she went to inform her mistresses. Soon one of the Misses Roberts had come downstairs to receive her caller, had shown her into the parlor, had made polite inquiries as to the health of her mother and grandmother, and had otherwise ex-changed such observations as ladies do exchange in the course of an afternoon call. We found it hard to accept this account until she added that Miss Roberts had come downstairs wearing white kid gloves. Such a detail, it seemed to us, could not have been invented—it was too odd and vivid: one could see the white-gloved hand sliding down the banister. That summer afternoon was many years ago; the Roberts sisters are forgotten; part of their land is now the park, given to the town by that seven-year-old's father; more of it is the spreading succession of subdivisions where shining new little houses are built every year. On the Robertses land have been built the "new" high school of thirty-five years ago, the newest high school of year before last, the field house, the county hospital. A street goes where the carriage drive used to be, and the mansion itself is the Masonic Temple.

All these houses are outstanding examples of what the Victorian builder could do when he really let himself go. More numerous—one in every block and in most blocks, two or three —are the less ostentatious houses of the mid-nineteenth century. These, too, are large houses, by modern standards: they are long and narrow, tall and thin-chested, with a porch down the side and sometimes across the front as well. The ceilings are very high; the rooms downstairs are dark, although the windows reach from floor almost to ceiling. The front door and the hall on which it opens are on the left side of the house; the stairs climb and circle and climb again to the third floor. On the right of the hall are the two parlors, and at its end the parlor bedroom or, nowadays, the library. Beyond the back parlor is the back hall, where the back stairs come down, and opening from it are sitting room, dining room, and kitchen. Once upon a time there were laundry, woodshed and coalshed and outhouse and stable beyond the kitchen. In the parlors and the front hall, the woodwork is walnut and the mantelpieces are veined black or green marble; the chandeliers have prisms; the tall doors all have transoms; and the banisters and newel post may be cherry instead of walnut. Of this pattern is the house we grew up in, where Mother had grown up before us; we have always known what it is like to live in one of them. We know how children can lie on their stomachs on a bedroom floor, over an open hot-air register, and listen to the scandal under discussion in the parlor below; we know how hot the attic gets in the summertime, and how far you can see from its windows; we know how perfect the banisters are for sliding down; and how impossible it is to catch a puppy who doesn't want to be caught where a way is open up the front stairs, down the back stairs, through the parlor and hall, and up the front stairs again, with an occasional diversion into the dining room and around the dining-room table. A number of other large houses, nondescript in architecture, sprawling and comfortable, were built in the nineties and early 1900's, filling the gaps in the old streets, until the last vacant lot, grass-grown and weedy, had been used. Between all these and among them are smaller houses, old and moderately old, shabby or immaculate in new paint; in odd corners, down crooked alleys are tucked away the very small houses: shanties, really, with crooked chimneys and trash-filled yards—all that we have in the way of slums. There are no new houses within the limits of the old town: the bright new houses are in the bright new (but treeless) subdivisions.

As in every town past its nonage, it is our big houses, old or new, and old houses, large or small, that have their names and pedigrees. It is not the same, in our tongue, to say, "That is where the Smiths live," as it is to say, "That is the Smith house." If it is the Smith house, there may be no one of that name living there now, but once and for a generation or more it was theirs, built or truly possessed by them. Only, with us, it is Scotch Presbyterian names like Moore and Monroe, McGervey, Torrence, and Frazer, or Pennsylvania Dutch names like Puterbaugh and Crumbaugh and Baughman that cling to the old places. Sometimes a house lapses into anonymity, when tenants are too impermanent to save its name: when that happens, it will before long be a rooming house, or apartments, or a hairdresser's establishment. But up to the present—the devastating present, when the merchants and the city commission are turning speculative eyes on every possible place where a house can be torn down and a parking space laid out—change has come to our older streets so slowly as to seem not to have come at all. The town has been conspicuously altered only around its edges, where the new little "modern" houses are going up, out of our sight and consciousness.

The young among us sometimes rebel in their inexperience,

saying "nothing ever happens here." They say it because they do not know the old houses. If they live long enough they will learn that everything has happened here, and may happen again. The town is Winesburg and Spoon River, it is Highbury and Cranford, it is even Illyria and Elsinore. Little that mankind knows and endures but has been here known and endured: even battles and sieges—Shiloh and Vicksburg, Chickamauga and Chattanooga, and all the others, before and since—have been fought here, in the minds of women who waited and the memories of soldiers who came home again.

But however many of the old houses stand today, to remind us of another time, no one can ever write a book based on the lives that have been spent under their roofs. To know about those lives you must be child, grandchild, great-grandchild of the town; and to tell about them you must betray kin or friends of your mother, your grandmother, your great-grandmother. Only a stranger could feel free to tell the old stories—and a stranger could not know them. A stranger would not dare imagine the preposterous kind of thing that has happened here. Nor would invention serve the native who is familiar with the pattern of events: your tale might be so unbelievable as to make you feel safe, yet someone would surely point to a door, a parlor window, a side porch, and say: "How did you know? I thought everyone was dead who might have remembered. . . ."

4. *The East End*

THE EAST END is the oldest part of town, taken over generations ago by the Negroes. There time and age seem almost palpable in the dim still air under the trees.

Our principal east and west streets climb the hill that rises beyond the post office and go on to the far edge of habitation. Beyond the top of the hill, they and the cross streets between them make up the East End. Once between the white town and the Negro town there was an indeterminate line, since no white family which considered itself respectable would live next door to a colored family. Now the two sides of the line, the neutral ground having disappeared, look exactly alike: prosperous white folk on one side of it, prosperous Negroes on the other. The line wavers between Monroe Street and Columbus Street a block farther east: here and there white families cling to their old homes above Monroe Street, not minding that they have Negro neighbors. Main Street just over the top of the hill is the East End's business center: this is a district of groceries, secondhand shops, beauty parlors, and neon-lighted "Nite Clubs," with several churches, notably Zion Baptist, scattered among them.

Beyond this section, as far as the end of the street where the Jamestown pike commences, lie long blocks of houses. Market Street is paved to the standpipe, and has churches and the East Junior High and Lincoln Elementary schools interspersed among residences. Most of the houses, from one-room cabins to verandaed and pinnacled mansions, are painted and in good repair, but even these two streets, in spite of their width and openness, have a quality, indescribable, of aboriginal age, of oneness with the earth.

And if this air of decay and fecundity commingled, one growing out of the other, is evident on Main and Market streets, it is still more pronounced where Church Street angles off into the country to become the Columbus pike; where Second and Third streets, unpaved, poke their way eastward in dust and ruts and weeds; where side streets and alleys cut crosswise and up and down. Everywhere east of Columbus Street the earth is encouraged to flower prodigally: every gutter is lined with trees, every fence buried under honeysuckle, trumpet vine, or hundred-leaf roses, every cabin half-hidden by lilac bushes, climbing roses, wisteria, hollyhocks. There is little space for grass anywhere between peonies, rose bushes, tiger lilies, sweet william, and phlox. Porch floors are edged with geraniums in tin cans; and morning-glories, cinnamon, and matrimony vines climb their neat white strings.

With the Main and Market Street exceptions, the houses are low, one or one-and-a-half storied. A few are of plaster-and-timber construction, built so long ago that cracks gape where the materials have drawn apart; some are of brick weathered from red to a dusty rose. But most are frame, in a few instances painted cream or white, more frequently saffron or lettuce-green or powder-blue, the brightness of the colors toned down by years of soot and smoke. Often they are not painted at all, and their wood has the silvery gray-black color of a long-dead tree in a sunny pasture, or the walnut-brown of a log lying fallen in moist grass or a stream. Shingle roofs, warped with age and forever shaded, are moss-grown like the floor of a deep forest. Here and there, a gesture has been made to indicate that

84

nature is being kept in its place: the trunks of trees are white-washed shoulder-high, and whitewashed stones line the path across a dooryard.

When we were children, no one of us ever walked alone in the East End. In spite of immeasurable affection for the individuals who entered our gates, and familiarity with those figures, not all known by name, that frequented the courthouse square, we were not so insensitive as not to realize that beyond Columbus Street, unless our errand was definite and legitimate, we were intruders and unwelcome. Once, indeed, a white newsboy had been tied to a telephone pole and left there until his family missed him, and sent the police on a search for him. The worst we ever met was the masking of mobile faces to blank secrecy, and the sudden hush of the river of over-the-fence, doorstep-to-doorstep talk—a hush that ran along before us, and closed in behind our heels. This resentfulness of intrusion was most open on the night when a half-dozen or so of us, high-school boys and girls, attended a revival meeting in one of the African Methodist churches. We went half with the impulse to mock, half with the romantic desire to see with our own eyes the singing, shouting, and capering we had read of in novels about the South. We found ourselves, instead, witnesses of a hysteria that seemed to us not in the least funny. The revivalist was a bitter, thin, ranting figure, cursing instead of cajoling, threatening hell rather than promising heaven; the response of his audience was groans of anguish, not hallelujah-shouts of triumph. We had heard of him as a miracle-worker; that night his only miracle, wrought by the lash of his tongue, his hypnotic gestures, and the whipped mass will of his audience, was to compel an old, old crippled woman to leave the wheel chair she had been in for a dozen years—to stand, to totter a few steps across the platform, where she collapsed in the hands of his "workers." Her thin panting voice screeched, "Praise the Lawd! I kin walk!" and she was echoed from the floor, "Praise the Lawd! She am raised from her bed!"—while we wondered whether the old woman would not die there before our eyes of shock or a heart attack. It was a terrifying spectacle. Perhaps we did laugh, reacting in that way to horror; at any rate the evangelist—already rumored in the town to be an instigator of racial dissension—turned upon us with unsparing denunciation. The center, even in our back pew, of glazed, inimical glances or of deprecatory, pleading, humble ones, we felt our faces grow hot; we were confused by shame. The preacher was right, and we were humiliated rather than angry. We should not have been there, and we knew it; curiosity had taken us to watch cold-bloodedly the manifestations of genuine and powerful religious emotions.

Nor were we angered—although, since we had done no wrong, we felt no shame—by the blank inscrutability we met in the East End. We were, instead, inordinately pleased by the greetings of those ancients who had been trained in slavery: the very old men who stepped to one side and stood bowing until you had passed, with straw hats held in two hands under their chins; the bandannaed crones who huddled on porch steps, smoking corncob pipes until they saw you, when they hid pipe in hand, and rose to bob a curtsey. Of course, by their obsequiousness we were puffed up with a deplorable consciousness of our superior status, but we did not resent the lack in other Negroes of what we realized was not at all our due. We, born white, had everything; they had nothing except what freedom had given them: private lives, and the right to keep them private.

However clearly we may have felt this true, without ever putting it into words, we did not therefore stay away from the East End. It was too picturesque, too vivid and full of color, not to be explored, but we walked there in threes and fours on Sunday afternoons, and talked as we went, pretending not to be looking, not to be seeing. (Negro children walked past our houses in the same seeing-unseeing fashion.) We went generally as far as the standpipe at the top of Market Street, and back again down another street. The standpipe had a dark fascination for us. It was—and is—the tallest thing in town, taller than the courthouse tower and the factory chimneys, or perhaps it merely seems taller, being set on a hill. To the traveler approaching along any road from the farm lands around about, it is the first sign to suggest that a town may lie beneath and behind the tree tops. It looks pencil-slender from a distance, but when you walk to its base you see that it is not slender, really: its circumference would encompass any of the cottages in the neighborhood. Up one side of it, all the way to the top, runs a narrow iron ladder. With our eyes we used to follow that ladder, up and up, knowing (as we thought) that into the open stand-pipe, thrown from the top step, went the bodies of all unwanted colored babies. I cannot understand now why we accepted such a calumny—against the evidence on every front step, gate, and porch that there was no such thing as an unwanted colored baby, or, if there were, why we could believe that such an un-necessarily hazardous method of disposal should be chosen. But even today, when I look at the standpipe, the old gruesome picture needs to be banished from my mind.

Separate and distinct as we thus recognized the East End to be, we never thought of it as not being an integral part of the town. It had been there almost from the beginning, and after a hundred years, for the white town to live without the Negroes, or the Negroes without the town, would have meant a reorgani-zation of the whole scheme of things.

The East End had begun soon after the first settlement of the frontier village. Virginians, Carolinians, and Kentuckians who disliked slavery came into the Northwest Territory to escape it, and a few brought their slaves with them, set them free, and sometimes bought them farms.

Some of those slaves freed by John Randolph's will were settled in the county; and there was at least one case of a concu-bine brought here with her children to a large tract of land presented to her by a plantation owner who did not himself leave Virginia. Most of these gregarious, homesick Negroes did not hold on to the lonely farms and log cabins, but drifted to town and made there a place for themselves as hewers of wood and drawers of water.

As early as the 1840's, escaping slaves came to add their num-bers to the East End. In that decade and afterwards, to aid and abet them, were abolitionists, few but fiery, among the Associate Presbyterians. One of these was their minister, leader of the small band of enthusiasts that called a state antislavery convention. The county refused them the use of the courthouse; the deacons, Associate and Associate Reformed, would not have the meeting in either of their churches; the opposition of the public made a street meeting impossible; and only the minister had the courage to open his house to the convention. A platform for the speakers was erected in his yard and the meeting held. A mob which collected on the other side of Market Street was held at bay by one John McClellan—"a stalwart old blacksmith," he is called in our undramatic records of that day. A village Voltaire, he stood at the gate, sledge in hand, declaring that he didn't believe in abolition, but did believe in free speech—and daring any of the mob to cross the street and try to molest his minister.

Among these same Associate and Associate Reformed Presbyterians were several who helped escaping slaves on their way to Canada. David Monroe was one; there was a price on his head in Kentucky, and so all slaves knew of at least one haven in Ohio, and the Monroe house became a particularly famous station on the Underground Railroad. We used to believe, when we were children and had heard much of this railway, that somewhere in the Monroe yard or barn or cellar was the end of a tunnel which ran all the way (sixty-odd miles) from Ripley on the Ohio. The Monroes of our generation were too much younger than we were for our games, and so we had no excuse for entering their gates and carrying on the explorations we so longed to make.

Certainly many of the Negroes, particularly in the years before the Fugitive Slave Act, did not go on to Canada, but stopped in the East End with kinfolk already there. Then, in the fifties, a Negro university, with the Cincinnatian Salmon P. Chase as one of its founders and trustees, was established not far from town, and thereafter more free Negroes came to live in the community, drawn by the hope and the chance of educating their children.

The university is several miles from the East End, on the Columbus pike. In the days of my childhood, when there were few automobiles and no buses, its campus lay outside our range, but we could not escape knowing when commencement week rolled around each year: it vied with September's Emancipation Day as a high tide of festivity for all the Negroes in town. In their gala clothes, whose bright hues put the sun to shame, they took possession of the courthouse square, gathering there to pile into hacks and cabs and carryalls, their gayety unrestrained, their voices, always raucous as crows' when they were excited, shattering the June quiet of our hot, slumbrous streets.

One old tale about the university used to overwhelm me, when I was young, with a smothering sensation of compassion and horror, and when I was grown could still move me to wish for an American Balzac to write it down. Balzac, because the story needs to be treated in the manner of *Eugenie Grandet*: daily life described in such minute detail in the beginning that the reader can feel it going on and on in the same fashion, year in, year out, while nothing happens except that time passes, and in the end you have a life wasted, nobility of purpose come to futility. But perhaps this life was neither wasted nor futile; I suppose that no one really knows: once upon a time, long ago, in Boston before the Civil War, when abolition was fought for passionately by those who believed in it, three young girls— innocent, hoop-skirted, naïve Victorians—solemnly pledged themselves to prove their belief in the equality of the races by marrying Negroes. One of them fulfilled her vow. All the remaining decades of the nineteenth century and into the twentieth she lived out at the university, while her husband, who was not without distinction among his people, rose from teacher to professor to dean to college president. In a community and at a time when the color line was rigidly drawn by both races, she saw only the guests he brought to the house. She survived him for a long, long while. All those years when I was growing up, she lived there in the same house, utterly alone, cut off from humanity. Year after year, when you went past it you could see how, by degrees, the place took on a haunted air behind its gloomy screen of hemlocks—how increasingly it came, even more than its neighbors, to have the look that Negro houses then had: shutters a little awry, steps a little broken, foundations yellow with rain-splattered clay.

After her death, not long ago, as generations are measured, a re-enacting of this drama began. "Men are lived over again; the world is now as it was in ages past." A member of the university staff, after a stay in the Soviet Union, brought back a Russian bride—she, in her turn, to be ostracized by two races. But I feel sure her story ended differently: we have not seen nor heard of her for many years, and indeed never did see her more than once or twice in town—a vivid picturesque young woman—and on one of those occasions she was haranguing the drug clerk on the other side of the counter: proclaiming her shock at the discovery of her situation; her surprise, because she hadn't understood; it was different in Russia, and how was she to have known? Her protests were made with such vigor, in her broken English, as to convince those of us who overheard that pity would be wasted on her: she was not one to submit to a lifetime of isolation; she could look out for herself.

The hardest years for the East End must have been those just after the close of the Civil War, when there was an influx of Negroes from the South. At least, one supposes that it was not until then that shacks, cabins, and "tenements" became hopelessly overcrowded. There passed through my hands not long ago, on its way to deposit in the public library, a book of records so interesting that I held on to it long enough to take notes: the records kept from 1866 to 1876 of "The Board of Health Examination of Premises"—local boards of health having been authorized by an act of the General Assembly "to abate and remove all and every nuisance in our cities." The document is invaluable, quite aside from its revelation of the appalling insalubrity of the town in that decade: on every street in every ward, each house was visited, its owner named, its condition noted: if anyone should ever want to know who lived in, who owned, any house in town in those years, he has only to consult this book. As for its scatological aspect—that in itself is material for pages of comment. It is a disillusioning subject, however, and best let along—except that one cannot resist noting that our oldest families (all of them are here: Hivling, Ewing, Allison, King, Puterbaugh, Millen, Allen) all kept pigs. They were sometimes ordered to clean their pigpens, and sometimes to build new privy vaults; they did not always obey the first order, perhaps resenting such an unwarranted interference in private and personal matters. The name of James Monroe (son of David, the abolitionist) occurs most frequently: he was a community servant: school trustee, church trustee, trustee of the "Hospital" (what in my childhood was known as the "Pesthouse"), and an East End trustee or property owner—and he must have been kept busy trying to fulfill the demands made on him by the Board of Health inspectors. He may not always have succeeded: the note on the Hospital, 1866, says, "J. B. Monroe notified to fill up privy vault and erect new one within 15 days"; the inspector of 1867 records that the Hospital is "a perfect disgrace to the city." The inspectors of the earlier years were primarily concerned with privy vaults; the later ones with pigpens. In 1876, there was a census of pigs. Practically every family had one or two, as noted, but the number of those who had more than two is counted at the end of each day's inspection: in the first ward, thirteen persons; in the second, eleven; in the third, nine; and in the fourth, which included the East End, only five. The Negroes were too poor, one supposes, to aspire to the ownership of pigs, and their part of town may have been less mephitic than the other three-quarters of it.

But the first and succeeding inspectors' horror at their living conditions gets down somehow on the pages, despite the brevity of the laconic and unpunctuated notes. In 1866, James Monroe was to be admonished as to conditions in an "Old Church": "25 negroes in this house very filthy." In 1867, in one Chas. Robison's house of four rooms there were ten occupants; in Matilda Brunnan's three rooms were nine. Jesse Thompson was notified of "privy vault full house filthy children dirty and alone"; he was to clean and disinfect the house. George Moxley was told to construct a new privy vault for three families (twelve persons) living in four rooms. That same year, in "the Old C.B. [Colored Baptist?] Church," twenty persons were living in four rooms, "filthy ventilation bad." If this is the same "Old Church" as that of 1866, five persons had moved out (or died), but living conditions could not have been much improved. Some of the landlords may themselves have been Negroes— Robison, Brunnan, Thompson, and Moxley are names without associations to link them to our time and knowledge—but most of them were white. The owner of one group of eight dwellings, in the Bottoms behind Third Street (shacks, not houses: I remember them well, although in my childhood there was one family to one shack), was a respectable white widow who no doubt looked out of her back windows and congratulated herself on the possession of good paying property. In 1867, in each of three shacks lived two families totaling eight persons to a dwelling; in another were two families adding up to nine persons; in another, two families, five persons; then came two with only one family in each, although one of the families numbered seven; and last: one shack of four rooms holding four families, twenty-two persons. Under eight roofs were seventy people—and for their health and well-being, the widow was ordered to build three new privy vaults.

It is an inescapable truth that in those days part at least of Negro living quarters must have been slums of the worst kind. But perhaps had the white citizens been accused then of "condoning a slum which shamed and disgraced the town," as we were to be accused by the eager reformers of the 1930's, they might have been as surprised as we were. The Board of Health reports of a century ago lead one to assume a callous indifference on the part of the white citizenry. Yet in anyone who knew the town as I knew it, growing up, that reaction would be somewhat modified by his own memories: it would not have been wholly indifference, but in part a kind of respect: an acceptance of the Negroes as adults to be trusted to solve their own problems. When the problems got out of hand and they needed advice or help, they would themselves go to some patron or employer, and ask for it. In the 1930's we considered the Negroes perfectly capable of looking out for themselves, and were indignant in support of our colored citizens against those outland critics who simply did not know what they were talking about. A slum is a rabbit warren of the underfed, the unwashed—it is made up of houses you enter warily, not touching wall or door frame, not sitting down. The East End was never like that when I knew it. The roofs might be sway-backed, but those who dwelt beneath them were well fed: they ate better than hillbillies, partly because Negroes know and love good food, but partly at least because in every household there was at least one woman who had been trained in a white family's kitchen. Nor did you stand away from the walls when you visited the East End to see whether you could hire Bob Johnson to mend the chimney, or Kate or Ida or Alice to help with the housecleaning. Instead, you went bearing rose slips or poppy seeds, and accepted in return a sweet-potato vine or a bunch of nasturtiums. You sat for a time in the parlor rocker, gossiping, while perhaps your eye rested enviously on the pride of the house: a luster pitcher or a piece of Bohemian glass that you wouldn't insult your hostess by offering to buy, knowing that probably it had been handed down from a grandmother who, as a slave, had been given it by a mistress when she exchanged old china or glass for new, or who, newly freed, had taken it from a devastated plantation.

The East End was not a slum, but like any community it had, and has, its slum districts. Notable among these was Frog Hollow, a triangle between the Columbus pike and Market Street and the railroad. Frog Hollow was flattened once by a tornado, and its shanties went down like card houses. My sister's hired girl, two-hundred-pound Alice, lived there. The family went at once to her rescue, and found her sitting placidly on a heap of salvaged furniture in the midst of broken walls and roofs strewn about like jackstraws. Her neighbors wailed and wrung their hands, but Alice said blandly, "Ah done tol' um, mah white folks look afteh me." But at the moment of calamity she must have been badly frightened, for she had climbed out of a two-foot-square window when the wind struck, and only terror could have made that miracle possible.

The days of Alice were few but unforgettable. I am not sure now whether it was the cost of feeding her—she could eat a loaf of bread for an afternoon "piece"—that brought about her dismissal, or the distasteful fact that she could get into my sister's clothes without actually bursting the seams. Alice possessed to an exaggerated degree the protean capacity of the old-time Negro for adapting his size to discarded wearing apparel; she could take one of my sister's old dresses, whack out sleeves, armholes, and a generous portion of the back, and pronounce it a perfect fit. For a long while my sister's daughters, growing up and desirous of borrowing this or that garment from their mother, were told, "You're exactly like Alice. Everything fits you."

A fortnight after the tornado, Frog Hollow had been put together again, all its boards collected and nailed back in place. Beyond offering succor at the time of the catastrophe, we did nothing about it. It was not our affair; and we should not have been thanked for interference. Community servants, such as the fire department and the public health officers, cover the East End, and there is a Negro patrolman on the police force to keep it in order. The rest of us go there only as one human being to another: to funerals, to inquire after the ailing, to hire work done, to carry Christmas gifts to the children of our friends; otherwise, we respect its preference for privacy.

Perhaps it was for this reason, as well as because we had known each other for so many generations, that relations between the races were always so easy and comfortable. The town was a whole: not two communities, but one.

That statement is not quite accurate, since Roman Catholic segregation-by-choice has always made us in practice two towns. Growing up, we knew far fewer Catholics than we knew Negroes: the clerks in uptown stores, those railroaders with whom we came in contact, and the scattering of Roman Catholic children who lived outside the West End, or whose fathers were Protestants, and who went to the public schools—and, in our teens, a handful who attended high school with us, since there was no parochial high school. As for the West End itself—those streets below West Street and south of Main—it might as well be a part of a town twenty or thirty miles away: it is as strange as that. I could not write about it. We never walked there, and never knew whose house this one was, or that one.

Fortunately when the Irish came they settled where they did, with the whole breadth of the town between them and the Negroes. And if for a while Irish Norahs and Katies threatened the livelihood of colored women by going out to service as hired girls, that did not last long, for the Irish were as quick as any other immigrant group to lift themselves to social equality, to scorn any labor that seemed to them, in a democracy, demeaning—and particularly demeaning when there must be competition with Negroes. Colored people did not then consider it beneath them to work as servants: indeed, prestige in the East End depended upon the prestige of the family you worked for, its wealth and standing in the community. Since long before I was born, domestic service was performed by Negroes. My generation grew up having known nothing else, and when I first went East to college, it made me uncomfortable at table to see a white hand beside my plate, putting down a cup of coffee: it was out of the order of things for white people to wait on other white people.

However, it may have been because the Irish Catholic immigrants of the mid-nineteenth century could find no work without competing for it with Negroes that animosity developed between them. In our town that animosity, for geographic reasons, was kept to a minimum except at election time, and election fights were rather a form of sport than a matter of bad blood. Those long-ago campaigns were spirited affairs, winding up with celebrations that rocked the town. Elderly Irishmen still speak of them with regret; and our mothers and fathers recalled torchlight processions, with dozens of flaming tarpots swinging on sticks, with transparencies spelling out slogans and insults, carried by Republicans shielded by oilcloth capes. The Democrats on their night would sally forth from the "Bloody Fifth" ward, with torches over their left shoulders and rocks in their "throwing hands," and would march east of Columbus Street on Main, where it could only be a question of time until they were attacked. On another night, in retaliation, the Republicans—the young gallants in spotless white top hats—would return the visit, marching with a fife-and-drum corps of Negro boys to a torchlight battle at the "Five Points" on West Second Street, where the procession would end in a melee of sticks and stones, with broken hats left behind to mark the high water of Republican invasion.

For weeks before an election small boys of both parties busied themselves collecting crates and boxes and lumber of all kinds, from cellars, woodsheds, and merchants' back premises, giving and receiving black eyes in fights for the empty tar barrels from the ropewalks. The morning after an election Irishmen went to meet the early train at the station, hoping that the edition of the *Cincinnati Enquirer* which it carried would display on the front page a triumphant crowing rooster. It almost never did, and the always-hopeful Democrats would in the reaction be too dispirited to put up more than a pretense of a fight against the Republican bonfire. That same night, boxes, barrels, and crates would be piled at the crossing of Main and Detroit streets, safely distant from inflammable buildings and as high as the second-story windows round about. Oil was thrown on the pile, and then it was set alight, to burn with a roar and a burst of flame that outtopped the courthouse elms, while small girls in office windows shivered with delicious terror, small boys danced about in the gutters as close to the fire as the heat would permit, and Negroes, none too sober, would prance in the street and sing "De yea' ob Jubilo." Twice, bonfires were Democratic—when Cleveland was elected; in one of those years there was a real fight: Republicans conceded to Democrats the right to the bonfire, but they had held the courthouse offices, and defiantly illuminated its windows. When all but a handful of them went home to supper, the Democrats broke in and tore down the illuminations. Republican forces immediately reassembled, rushed the courthouse, ejected the Democrats, and replaced their lights in the windows.

For sixty years or more there have been no campaign parades, no triumphs, no fights with fists or rocks; when I was a child, those days were remembered with relish by many, Democrats and Republicans, but I never knew them. Still, there was a sense of a bond between Protestant white and Protestant colored citizen. White children growing up knew many adult Negroes; some they did not like, as they did not like all white adults. Some they liked, and some they loved and remember still with enduring affection. Colored children we did not know, since we did not go to school with them. Our school situation was normal for a northern community of those days. Discrimination between races was prohibited by law, but a child was required to go to school in his own district, and the school board drew the district lines. Our board made Columbus Street the boundary; East Market elementary and East Main high schools were attended by Negro children and taught for the most part by Negro teachers. In my class there was just one little mulatto boy, whose family lived somewhere near the railroad station—a clean, quiet-mannered little boy who was ignored by us not because he was colored but because he was so meek, and would not whisper or throw paper wads or join us in any mischief. There were at least three boys in my class whom I disliked with a fervor that can warm me still, but Elmer was not one of them. But there was antagonism between us and those Negro children who were strangers, whom we encountered on such neutral ground as the library. They were noisy and self-assertive, with a provocative, truculent air; a meeting with them was like the meeting of strange cats on an alley fence. Nothing ever happened: we—and they, no doubt—were too well brought up to call names, and when they filled the sidewalk edge to edge, challengingly, then we got off the walk rather than collide with them, but sometimes we were hot with anger all the way home.

We did not feel at all like this about their elders, whose work made them familiar figures in the town, individual and idiosyncratic. Even the mill hands, streaming up at five-thirty from the West End, seemed like acquaintances, because Father had so much to say about them, particularly in the spring, when they all "laid off for a rest" because they could live on dandelions and poke greens, the fish they caught, and the chickens they raised. Up and down Main Street, up and down Detroit, dozens of

Negroes, all known by name, loafed at their work: livery-stable handy men, the hotel hack-drivers in long-tailed, brass-buttoned coats, the street sweepers cleaning up the gutters. On sunny summer mornings those who had pre-empted particular stands on the Greene Street side of the courthouse lined up there, with empty drays hitched to discouraged horses, or with pushcarts laden with brushes for housecleaning or sweeping chimneys. They waited all day long for chance customers, enjoying themselves in their own easy fashion, telling tall tales, their feet dangling over a dray's end as they rocked with laughter, their rich voices a familiar undertone to the noises of the town. And having them there was a convenience: a child could be sent in a few minutes to summon Mose Taylor or Sam to come and empty the ash pit, or chop and haul away the branch of a maple tree blown down in the yard. Occasionally Billy Rogers came sauntering down from the courthouse to join them for a moment before going on to his office. They greeted him respectfully. Fat, oily, little Billy Rogers, black as his own cigar, wore always a wide-brimmed black soft hat and a dark suit with a tight-buttoned vest on which his watch chain shone resplendent; he was the town's one colored lawyer, with an office on Market Street; he was sometimes a councilman, and always a power in Republican politics.

One owner of a decrepit dray and still more decrepit horse served us as garbage collector. He was one who never took his wagon near the courthouse square; he kept to the back streets, where the quiet air held for a long while the record of his passage. Between him and our half-breed spaniel flourished a mutual antipathy handed on through long lines of successors, so that for a generation the coming of the garbage man into our yard was anything but unobtrusive: it was instead a cyclone of snarls and growls, of Negro yelps and maledictions, and a stage-thunder rattling of galvanized iron can and lid. In those days when garbage was a gift, food for the pigs, to be had for the taking, we had to pay to have ours hauled away. One of our dogs, a big Airedale, disliked all Negroes, not only the garbage man, and lay in wait for them at the corner of the back porch; so the neighbors had perforce to grow accustomed to the spectacle of delivery boys leaving meat and groceries at the front door.

Some of our odd-job men were craftsmen, not to be casually engaged; negotiations with Bob Johnson had to be carried on at his gate, and on his part involved elaborate calculations of available free time. Bob spent no hours loafing in the courthouse square: if he was not laying bricks for white folks' pay, he was laying them at home. For several years before his death he devoted himself to building a new house. But he was a perfectionist, forever unsatisfied. Before he could get it done, he would be stirred by a new vision of beauty and comfort—he would hustle his family into the uncompleted house, and with the unused bricks begin another and more beautiful dwelling place on the other side of his lot. But before that was finished, he would have another idea; once more he would bundle his family into the half-built place, tear down the one they had left, and with the same bricks start all over again. Bob had the most beautiful iris and peonies in town, but behind them, forever changing yet never in essentials changed, stood two half-built houses, one with curtains in the windows, one without. And since his death, less exacting builders have finished both of them, two neat new brick houses squeezed on one lot.

In the smaller churches of the East End, ministers preached for the love of it, and earned their livings by such odd jobs as they could get. One of them cleaned our parlor wallpaper one spring—an arduous, even dangerous undertaking, since the parlor is one of those Victorian rooms some twenty feet square with a thirteen-foot ceiling. When he had finished he said to Mother gravely, "Now, Ma'am, Ah think yo'll find it's jes' as commojus as eveh." "Just as commodious" was one of our family phrases for years. (Grandma's encounter with another picker-up-of-words gave us our best family story. She had called in a handy man to whitewash the cellar; she took him down to show him how much wall space there was, and asked him how much it would cost her. He refused to calculate it. "Well," she said, "can't you approximate it?" "Ma'm," he replied firmly, "Ah kin white-wash it, Ah kin calcomine it, Ah kin 'proximate it, but Ah kain' tell yo' how much it gwun cost.")

Another of the preachers worked at the mill weekdays as a common laborer, and took care of our furnace besides. Every Monday morning he would tell Father how well the saving of souls progressed, but every fortnight, before payday rolled around, he would be on our front porch, calling Father from his six-o'clock dinner to beg for an advance in wages, so that he could bail his worthless son out of jail. The boy was finally sent to the penitentiary, and the Reverend John was freed of his importunities, but the failure to save the soul he most desired to save broke the old man's heart.

Every building around the courthouse square had its Negro janitor and handy man, every shop its delivery boy. There was bent, grizzled old "Jonevins" in the Building and Loan: you were half-grown before your mental eye corrected your ear, and you saw that his name was Jonah Evans. There was Roberts in the library, whose wife was a sister of Ellsworth at the City Building and Opera House, whose wife, in turn, was sister of Philip and Oliver, two distinguished chauffeur-housemen. Little could happen in town that was unknown to that group. Ellsworth had once been a waiter for the Elks, in the heyday of that lodge, when its dining room flourished; he was a snob of sorts: he claimed acquaintance with you if your father was an Elk, and inquired after him solicitously when you came to the Opera House to rehearse a play and he hung around, broom in hand, to watch, commend, and criticize. But if your father was not an Elk, he did not know you. Because of his experience and connections he was given the opportunity to don a white coat again whenever there was a big wedding or an evening party. Another Negro who was a familiar figure at formal dinners and dances was the colored barber; elderly, immaculate, stout and pompous, he gave a distinct air to any dining room in which he acted as butler; he had the most magnificent pair of Dundreary whiskers ever produced in town: silver in color and straight as he could make them, they swept out at angles from his jaw to his shoulders.

Janitor and barber took on these extra jobs less for the pay and the tips involved than for the standing it gave them among their own people. The most exalted in the hierarchy of those who helped with our parties was the cateress. No one could give an important luncheon, reception, or dinner without Maude's services. She was a superb cook; there was a certain sameness about her menus, but even that had its good point: your hostess was glad to have you whisper to your neighbor, after one glance at your plate, "Maude Guy in the kitchen." Our Luvenia always resented having Maude in command and being reduced herself to the rank of aide; she protested that she could do as well, given the materials to work with. Maude was provided lavishly at our house with the components of her art: Mother knew how certain ladies suffered a reputation for stinginess based on nothing but Maude's grumbling about them in other kitchens. Mother's efforts to please, her precautions, were endangered by Luvenia on one angry occasion. Every hired girl in town went home, when the evening dishes had been washed, with a basket on her arm; so long as the basket was not too large, no questions were asked. But that night, when Maude and her girls had been paid and were ready to go, Veenie stationed herself at the door and examined every basket. Veenie in a temper was more than a match for Maude: she removed from the baskets, and later displayed to Mother triumphantly, olives, celery, rolls, cake, and a whole fried chicken. . . . Maude worked for the town's hostesses for many years, and accumulated a good-sized fortune; then, like many another elderly woman, black or white, married a young n'er-do-well who wanted her money, and when she died, she died alone and in poverty.

All these Negroes were known to the town. Of course each family knew best and most intimately those who worked in its own kitchen and yard. Such close acquaintance with a series of individuals began for me, almost before I can remember, with the boy named Fred whom my grandmother had hired to do the yardwork. I pestered him so, and so hindered him from getting any work done, that Grandma gave him a white butcher's apron and promoted him to nursemaid. The neighbors wondered at Mother's permitting it: after all, Fred was just out of the penitentiary, where he had been sent after a cutting scrape: but Mother laughed at them—with me he was invariably gentle, amusing, and patient.

Grandma and Mother did their own cooking when I was little, but "Miz'" Simpson came to our house two or three days a week to do the family wash. Our laundry stretched from kitchen to woodshed between the driveway and the side yard; its walls were rough boards, unplastered, black with age; on one side a door opened beneath the peach tree in the middle of the lily-of-the-valley bed, and a step led down to the mossy bricks of the garden path; on the other side, small-paned cobwebby windows overlooked the driveway through a tangle of trumpet vines. When Miz' Simpson (the only colored woman I then knew who was honored with "Mrs.") was there on Monday mornings, the big copper boilers simmered on the laundry stove, and the steam intensified the damp rotten-wood smell the room always held. We kept Miz' Simpson company, my sister and I, on rainy summer Mondays, washing our dolls' clothes in miniature tubs just like hers. My first acquaintance with the sense of guilt, awful and profound, was connected with her: I had forgotten a pin stuck in a dress; she held up her hand to show me, its pale-pink sodden palm streaming with thick blood. . . . Miz' Simpson was a thin, tiny Negress, very black—and glum of disposition. I can understand her shortness of temper. The washing in those days was no light matter: besides the bed linen, towels, tablecloths, and napkins of a big family, there were lace-trimmed chemises and full embroidered petticoats by the half-dozen; in winter, woolen underwear, and in summer flounced and ruffled dresses, shirt waists, and white duck or piqué skirts, all to be boiled and scrubbed and starched and ironed. Looking back, I can forgive Miz' Simpson her grumpiness.

Later, we had colored girls to do the cooking and housework: Kitty, from the country; fat, wall-eyed Annie; and then at last,

Luvenia. Ours was the first family she worked for after she came north from Kentucky. She had been bred in the old tradition, and was pure delight to us for many years—a delight intensified in retrospect and only slightly marred at the time by her unreliable temper, which might explode when she was annoyed, or might simmer for days and become confused, finally, with "de mis'ry in mah back." She was neither lazy nor shiftless; she went through the house like a cyclone with broom and dustpan; she made beaten biscuits, and the walls rocked as her fists pounded the dough on the table and her voice soared to a high note. She scorned "light bread," and gave us biscuits, muffins, or corn bread every meal until she learned that other families were not so indulged. She despised "highfalutin niggers," but she learned from them the limits of what was to be expected of her. She came to us when my brother was a baby; she stayed until he started to school, and even after that came back whenever we had need of her. She left us to go to work in the tobacco factory, where she could earn more; she gave that up because the time-clock discipline was too rigorous; thereafter she cooked in at least two other kitchens before she turned to going out by the day, thus combining high pay with independence. Since Veenie never gave up any of her families, but continued to visit around among them, they are bound by a special tie: the things they know about each other—the never malicious or shameful but the sad or funny, and especially the funny, anecdotes that Veenie stored in her mind to tell. Of all the pleasures life held for her, the greatest was her pleasure in a good story.

In the years she was with us, she devoted herself principally to my brother: she carried him on her hip from kitchen stove to sink, while she spun him tales of possum and coon. She taught him to walk, and showed him off uptown to her friends and ours; he was at home in every kitchen where one of her friends was cook. But to the rest of us Luvenia talked, and we led her on, even to the detriment of the work in hand.

While she worked for us, she got into no serious scrapes, had no mishaps worth mentioning, unless you except that one time when we were all away and she was left to look after Father, when she staggered so violently bringing in his morning coffee that some explanation was necessary. She was not at all shamefaced: "Suh, you all's whiskey ain' lak what we git in Kaintuk'." He let her off with a caution against East End moonshine. It was a long time before he mentioned the incident to Mother; he didn't want Veenie dismissed, and he knew that hang-overs—if they were recognized as that, instead of being concealed under the generic term "mis'ry"—would not be tolerated in our kitchen.

Afterwards, working other places, for other people, Luvenia's life became one long series of misfortunes. First she had to have all her teeth pulled. The new ones looked big as dominoes, and Veenie was proud of them, rightly: they were unique. Then she fell out of the window she was washing on the second floor of the parochial school, and landed on the concrete steps of the areaway below. It would have killed a white woman, Dr. Will said: it broke her collarbone and some ribs. Veenie was not excessively superstitious but she was uncomfortable in her mind about that accident. She muttered to us about candles, incense, holy water (with gestures), and the sisters "lak big black bats a-swoopin by" (also with gestures), and it became clear enough that she thought some mumbo jumbo had been practiced against her. After that, or before, she cut a gash in her leg with a sickle swung too vigorously; then she ran a spike into her foot, and had a narrow escape from blood poisoning. She delayed going to the doctor until it was almost too late, and afterwards she didn't know which made her sicker: the hole in her foot, or the hole in her back, where she had been inoculated with antitetanus. I was at home alone when she came to tell us about it, afterward: I can see her now, sitting bolt upright in a sitting-room rocker, her basket on the floor against her knee, her white denture gleaming, her eyes rolling to emphasize the drama of her escape, as she told me "Ah could feel the raindrops tricklin' through mah grave clods."

For many years, Luvenia made no closer acquaintance than that with grave clods. Until she was an old, old woman she stayed on in the East End, comfortably well off, able to live on her savings and what her husband left her. When she was no longer able to care for herself, she returned to her daughter's in Kentucky, and died there. I had not seen her for a long time before she left town, but I am sure that she never changed in spirit from the days when she used to see me off to college, bringing to the train a farewell bouquet of "fall roses," their stems wrapped in damp newspaper. Life for her was to the end still full of drama, particularly melodrama and farce; from neighbors' irrepressible grins when I met them, on a bus or the street, and asked about her, I knew that even in her old age she not only retained her own delight in life, but continued to be a delight to others.

Several households in town had servants—cooks, housemen, chauffeurs—who stayed with them a lifetime, who identified themselves completely with the families they served, who sad "we" and "our" when they spoke of the cars they drove, the houses they cleaned; who knew perfectly well that they had brought up the children, and who triumphed accordingly at betrothals and weddings. We who were fed by these cooks and served at formal parties by these white-coated housemen, were driven by these chauffeurs and had their help with scene-shifting for the parlor dramatics of the Woman's Club—we knew them all. We were fond of them, and laughed at them, feeling that their rich comicality added to the color of life in the town. What we did not realize was that at their funniest they were trying hardest to be like us, carrying to the East End their version of what they had seen, so that they were in truth presenting us with a kind of picture of ourselves, and what we laughed at was a parody of our own activities. They liked parades and bands and speeches; so did we, although we did not march in such good time, with so easy a swagger. Luvenia was at the top of her form as a member of the Busy Bee Chapter of the Queen Lil Tabernacle, particularly on the occasion when the state convention was to be held in our town, and she lamented loud and long that she must wear a robe of purple sateen and a gold-paper tiara, when the Past Queen, a long-time rival, was to have purple velvet and jewels. It was funny, but white women too join lodges that are not without their humorous aspects.

Another thing we did not quite realize was how tight-knit a part of the community these colored servants were: how wholly they held us—upheld us, even—in their kind strong hands. If we knew them, so did they know us, and far, far better, since their fathers and grandfathers, mothers and grandmothers, had served our forebears. Theirs was the top place in the social and economic pyramid of the East End, and they were as closely related by blood and the ties of marriage as were the white folks whose lives they managed. Strangers among us, who were sometimes taken aback when they learned not only how well we knew each other, but how well we knew each other's grandparents and great-aunts and uncles, so well that everyone understood why everyone else was queer, or rich or poor or musical or stupid, and accepted second- and third-generation queerness, wealth, poverty, talent, stupidity, as natural and to be allowed for—such strangers would have been more amazed had they been told what we were hardly conscious of, but recognized as truth: that these servants in old families knew more about their white folks and their white folks' friends than any of us knew about each other. There were no secrets from them, and had not been for generations: they overheard family quarrels; they brought home the inebriated, and forwarded forbidden love; they were acquainted with stinginess, tyranny, capriciousness, and hysteria, as they were with kindness, generosity, and evenness of temper. They talked to each other, and if your own cook trusted you, she passed on, in hints and in mysterious whispers, a few glimpses of dark secrets behind decorous doors. For the most part, however, they were deeply loyal, and revealed to one of the white race only what was admirable, or at the worst, trivial and funny, about another white family—never what was shameful.

This older generation of Negroes is passing, although all of those, I think, whom I knew through being at home in one friend's house or another's, survived those years in the 1930's that brought about a change in the relationship between white and colored in our town. Since those years there has been no animosity between Irish and Negro, but there has been a drawing apart of the East End and the white Protestant town. The Negroes, who had always been Republican out of gratitude for emancipation, became, many of them, Democratic out of hope, fed on promises of equality by the grandsons of the men who used to throw rocks at them. There was no solidarity in their own ranks. Those of their race who said, "We don' want no trouble-makers roun' hyah" regarded with sullen anger those who, they thought, were looking for trouble—an anger which roused only contempt in the minds of the crusaders for equality. However, no trouble came, beyond a minor scuffle or two outside the moving-picture theater between Negro youths and white rowdies. There was resentment of this changed attitude in many Republicans, but it was resentment of the climate of government in those days, fundamentally, and was not transferred to any known, native, "misguided" Negro.

The separation begun in 1932 has deepened and widened. Convinced by the preachers of equality that domestic service is lowering, the younger Negroes were saved from the shame of it by the war: those who did not go into army or navy found work in Dayton factories or close to Dayton at the Air Force Base. That generation has made more money than their elders ever had. They have bought the East End houses that used to be rented, and have fixed them up, or have built new ones. They take pride in property and person. Those who do not want their children to go to Negro schools turn Catholic, and send them to the parochial school: early on every schoolday morning, spick-and-span colored children troop the interminable way to the West End. But this is no solution of the problem of making the town one whole: it is only a new form of segregation.

A generation has grown up that has never known the old close ties, and therefore cannot miss them. Those bonds of affection and trust are loosening and falling away as the older generation, white and colored, passes from the scene. Loss of love, whatever its degree and kind, is a grievous loss to the world. But that loss may be the price of equality, even as the price of liberty is sometimes life itself. And what white person would venture to say that the cost is too high? How can we know? The loss may be all ours; it may well be that our affection for our servants was never without a felt condescension, though we ourselves were unaware of it.

The feeling that younger generations of white and colored have for each other will never be that which we in our time knew. But there is a sure hope that the town will be one whole again, on a different basis—when all the schools are integrated, as the new high school has been from the day of its opening; when Negro and white children go to school together from the beginning and therefore see no reason for not going on together into the workaday world; when they know each other for a lifetime. Even now, the lists of graduates from the high school contain familiar names—names of children and grandchildren of those Negroes whom we used to know: handsome young people whose pictures are in the paper, along with those of their white classmates, when they win awards and scholarships. They are athletes and students, respected and liked, all with the beautiful manners learned long ago by their elders who served our First Families—in the days when there still were First Families and good manners. As for East End adults: here and there one encounters a Negro in some position on a level with any white person in town: a Negro librarian, whose departure was lamented when she went to Liberia with her husband on a government mission; a teacher on the high school staff; nurses and practical nurses at the hospital, and occasionally a nurse or a laboratory technician in a doctor's office. It seems very good—heart-warming, when it occurs to you to think about it—that in an encounter with one of these, both of you take it as a matter of course and, as any two people do who are bound to meet often, proceed to establish such relations that in time you may become friends.

In the meantime, the old ties between us and the East End have not been quite completely dissolved, and will not be while any of the older generation survive. Most of the old-time Negroes, whom we knew, and knew so affectionately, have disappeared from our streets. Years ago, Ellsworth retired from his job at the City Building, with the presentation of an inscribed gold watch to reward his faithful services. Jonevins is long gone, and Sam Taylor with his dray. The city collects the garbage, and is paid for doing so. But there are colored janitors still, and here and there an elevator operator with whom to pass the time of day, a few handy men who will do hauling, and a few yardmen. Above all, holding the town together still, after a fashion, is the straggling procession of a few aging colored women that drifts down from the East End, passes the town clock a little before four or a little after, and turns past the courthouse to the north end, or goes on down Church or Market, Second Street or Third: hired girls on their way to cook their white families' dinners. As they go, their eyes are on the sidewalk, their faces are masks, they do not seem to glance as they pass at the dark old houses behind the maple trees. Perhaps if you belonged to a town family that had skeletons in cupboards, you might feel as you met them, that the dark eyes lifted to yours were heavy with knowledge. But if you were a stranger you would not dream that here, rather than in libraries or in drawing rooms—here, in the memories of these shuffling women, is the best source (sealed, to be sure) of all you might want to know about the people of the town. They are not so unaware as they seem of you whom they meet, of the houses they pass; back in their own East End, they will have tales to tell, as Veenie used to tell them, with embellishment of simile and metaphor, with laughter and rolling eyes and clapping hands.

5. The Cemetery

IN THE FIRST DECADE of the twentieth century Calvinism in our town had somewhat abated its ancient rigors, but Sundays were still intolerably dull—desert intervals spaced regularly along a road through country otherwise rich in diversion. We went to Sunday school and church, returned to a heavy dinner, endured quietly a long afternoon to which ennui contributed heaviness and indigestion a headache, ate a bread-and-milk supper, went to Christian Endeavor, came home, and escaped into Monday by going to bed early.

Sometimes we were permitted to enliven the afternoon by a walk—on such occasions, I suppose, as the pressure seemed unduly high and some outlet necessary. These walks were never undertaken without the familiar admonition, "Remember what day it is. No running. No skipping. No loud talking or laughing." The commands were obeyed to the letter; no one of us, even if four or five managed to secure their liberty at the same time, would have dared to shatter the profound Sunday quiet by a lifted voice. We walked sedately, two by two, in our best clothes, preening our feathers. There were no challenges,

"Beat you to the next corner," or "Dare you to do this." We did not avoid the cracks in the sidewalk, nor balance on the curbstones, nor jump over every carriage step we passed. It was God's day, and the eyes of our townsmen might be upon us, to see that we kept it.

We never closed the front door behind us until we had fixed upon some definite objective. To have meandered indifferently in any direction, to any spot, and home again, would have been as dull as staying there in the first place. These Sunday afternoon objectives were limited not by necessity but by custom. If someone's impulse suggested the East End, we went to the standpipe and back. To the south, a good mile from town, lay the Orphans' Home; or there was the viaduct over the railroad yards, and the circle back down the hill and under the station bridge. North, there was the Fairground, and west, the cemetery. Nothing but a long-since-vanished love of decorum could have made the cemetery the orthodox end of a Sunday afternoon expedition in every country town in Amierca. We never went there, when we were children, at any other time.

At least, it was only on Sundays that we entered formally, by the gate. There was another way, well known, by which we could get in: we had only to follow the railroad track around its first curve beyond the edge of town to the foot of a hill crowned with tombstones; the wire fence between it and the railroad embankment was easy to climb. But in quest of one treasure only did we choose that comparatively furtive method of entry. It was not in search of chestnuts, although the trees in the cemetery were the only ones within walking distance from town. No adult, I think, ever suggested that we should not gather those nuts, yet we let the spiked burrs lie where they had fallen, in the grass where we found them. Not all our schoolmates were so squeamish. I remember the sick horror with which I learned, too late, that the nuts shared with me, one recesstime, had been picked up in the graveyard. But violets—the violets were different. For one thing, you didn't eat them. For another, they grew not in the old full deeply sodded acres of the cemetery, but on its fringe—on the slope just inside the wire fence. And although violets were everywhere in the spring—in the fields, in the roadside ditches, in the woods, along the banks of streams, until the ground was blue with them—still, those in the cemetery excelled all others in size and length of stem and depth of color. We picked them, therefore—but we could do it almost without admitting to ourselves that we had been in the cemetery: we climbed the fence and squatted down among them, and took care not to lift our eyes to the top of the hill, where the farthest-scattered tombstones were silhouetted black against the sky.

The high ground where the cemetery lies is properly approached from the other side of the hill, where a main road passes the entrance to the tree-arched avenue. Here stand, two on either side, the four Ionic pillars from the old courthouse, vine-wreathed and crumbling, like the last forlorn remnant of a ruined temple. This simile was first conceived, perhaps, in the mind of whoever was responsible for their being here; unfortunately for its truth, the workmen who set the columns in place knew so little of classic architecture that they crowned them with capitals turned sideways to the beholder. We are not pedantic; the error does not in our eyes detract from the impressiveness of the scene: the lonely pillars, and beyond them the straight line of the driveway, the gates, far, far away, and an occasional glimmer of white stone through the green that enshrouds the enclosure. Certainly we were impressed when we were children. The Greek-temple comparison pleased us, and we had found another for the driveway and its trees: we were in those days just experienced enough in literature to see the appropriateness of the forest-cathedral figure of speech, and not to know it hackneyed. None of us had ever been inside a cathedral, but we were ready enough to look upon the trunks as piers, the boughs as a vaulted roof, the footpath as an aisle outside the columned nave, and the osage-orange hedges, taller than a man's head, as walls that shut out the day. But this nave of ours is nearly a quarter of a mile long; our agile imaginations could not hold fast to one idea for the length of time it took to walk so far. Before we reached the end, it had become the road that led to some nobleman's terraces, and we followed it to incredible and fantastic adventures in a mansion either magnificent or mysterious, or both. Conversely, the actual scene became so much a part of our mental landscape that it would haunt us when we read "the rooks swinging in their lofty houses in the elm-tree avenue," or "we passed into the avenue, where the wheels were again hushed amid the leaves, and the old trees shot their branches in a sombre tunnel over our heads."

When we passed the superintendent's house, off to the left, where there might be observers behind the parlor lace curtains, we abandoned our games, and entered the iron gates of the cemetery with subdued dignity. The very stiffness of our ruffles proclaimed that we could be there for no other end than the contemplation of mortality suitable to the day and place. Inside the fence a labyrinth of drives winds in and out among the headstones and monuments. Here and there a weeping-willow tree or a flowering shrub ornaments some family lot; on and between the graves the grass grows thick and green; over all are the trees —once upon a time, chestnuts, and still today maples and that great trinity, oak and ash and elm. We used to follow haphazardly the twists in the road as they opened out before us. We might pause to note some new clayey mound, or cross the grass to see who had lain so long in the earth that the name on his gravestone had filled with lichens, or even, holding our breaths, to peek through the broken corner of a moss-grown sarcophagus. Sometimes we stopped to admire a particularly appealing angel, or to read with awe a summary of superlative virtues. If the thought of death touched us, it was death-impersonal, infinitely remote, death-the-end-of-all (did we not choose among the tombstones the ones beneath which we should be most content to lie?); it was never death-within-doors, death-the-despoiler—he had not yet touched our lives, nor left them less rich

As the sun declined and came into view beneath the branches of the trees, as the shadow of granite obelisks and marble angels lengthened athwart the graves and began to coalesce, we quickened our footsteps, quit our desultory wandering, and turned toward the gates. Sunset brought a touch of the macabre to the scene. We were not afraid of walking spirits, but shrank from the possible appearance of a pair of lovers among the trees. I wonder now how we knew what manner of woman might come creeping up the hill from the railroad tracks, a man at her heels. We did know. We must have seen such a couple, sometime, leaning against a tree trunk, part of the twilight, for that was the picture from which we fled; we were sickened by the morbid avidity with which they clutched each other, making of two persons one deep shadow. Why should they have come here, when there were woods and fields so close at hand? Was it a woman's device to remind a man that it was now or never, that hot blood would soon be cold and the bones unfleshed? "The grave's a fine and private place, but none, I think, do there embrace. . . ." But it is likely that they were brought there by no more profound a thought than that the cemetery grass was soft and thick and had no nettles in it.

We ran away at the approach of twilight, and yet we forgot— forgot deliberately—between one Sunday and another that we might not find the graveyard a perfect solitude, where trees were green and tall, where squirrels chattered from their boughs, where there were flowers on the newer graves, and every spot where a soldier lay was marked with last Memorial Day's rain-streaked flag. Life had no place within its fence. The goings-on of life became inside its boundaries horrible. . . . Buried bodies were buried bodies; if the dead were immortal, they dwelt not here but in some skyey region beyond our apprehension. Familiar headstones had no connection with the stories our elders told of well-beloved kin, or of the anciently notable. We knew that everyone in the town must end on this hill; it did not occur to us that the hill was the more populous part of the town—nor that today's story could be read in sunken and half-forgotten graves. And, indeed, it is not so. A graveyard is inspiration for the philosopher, not for the historian. What, after all, can be learned from a tombstone, or a thousand tombstones? "Their names, their years. . . ." Something perhaps of a family's taste as exhibited in the pomposity of carved granite or colored marble; something of its standing, social and financial, in the community. Nothing more.

Only a poet who can turn on his imagination as a tap is turned for water can make of such scanty material a *Spoon River Anthology*. He whose imagination must be primed, like an old pump, should go for what he needs not to the cemetery but—in lieu of the parish registers of an older country—to the cemetery records. The volumes that have been filled in recent years are no stimulus to the romantic mind: they are loose-leaf notebooks of printed forms supplied by the Bureau of Vital Statistics, and neatly filled in by a typist. The older books are a makeshift lot, as much more interesting to the casual inquirer into the past as they are less valuable to the statistician. They have accumulated for a hundred years, and have passed in the course of time from one hand to another. None of the courthouse records show any such variety of awkward and illegible scripts as do these musty ledgers. There is no snatching their matter at a glance. The pages are ruled in columns: date, name, next of kin, cause of death, undertaker and location of the grave. Physicians enjoyed a blessed anonymity; they are protected from the scorn of these more enlightened days when medicine is less empiric, and even laymen know the Greek and Latin names of diseases. As the pages are deciphered, line after line, a comprehension of the old life is built up in the mind: the daily vicissitudes of a time when there was for everyone as much likelihood of being struck by infectious disease as there is today of being hit by an automobile.

The first two or three pages contribute nothing to this enlightenment. The institution of the cemetery was followed by the abandonment of churchyard burial grounds in the town, and the first graves were dug for these disinterred bones. Only the names of those whose beds were thus changed are given, and the particular church in whose shadow they had at first lain, and where must have lingered the echoes of any emotions connected with them. It is with the end of this list that the book becomes something more than a catalogue. The column that records the ages of the dead makes the first impression. How young—how pitifully young they died in those days! But that is, after all, a matter of common knowledge: in what was hardly more than a frontier town, the proportion of elderly men and women was not large; moreover, in the first half of the nineteenth century, disease and not degeneration was the principal weapon of death. One's second thought is that an unfair number of girls' names are written here. Those were but girls, surely, who died at seventeen, eighteen, nineteen, inevitably—oh, so inevitably! —in childbirth. Young men died of consumption, but so did the young women. "Consumption, childbirth, childbirth, consumption": the alternation is proof of awful ignorance. When diphtheria and scarlet fever appear on the page, it is never once and no more: both repeat themselves, and usually in the same family. Infants were stillborn, or died in the summer months of "bowel complaint" or "cholera infantum"; children who escaped the infectious diseases had "cholera morbus." (As "cholrymorbus" familiar to our ears in childhood, warned as we were by our grandmothers when we would not leave green fruit hanging on the tree. But we consumed with immunity apples hard as pebbles and little larger, dipped bite by bite in the damp salt clutched in a grimy fist.)

Cholera infantum and cholera morbus, diphtheria and pneumonia: these terms exhausted our forefathers' knowledge of classic tongues. There was no appendicitis—there was only "inflammation of the bowels"; no variety of carditis, only "heart failure"; no meningitis, only "brain fever." A page or two of entries were made by a secretary who had no patience with the finicky distinctions of the doctors; in his time the men, women, and children who had to be allotted graves and buried in them died of "brain," "heart," "lungs," or—succinctly—"drink." No scandals were softened or slurred over in these books; no euphemisms substituted for plain speech. When the body of a newborn baby was dug out of a cesspool, the facts were coldly recorded.

Only a few pages need to be read before a picture of the town takes form in the mind: unkempt, muddy streets, plain houses edging the footpaths, picket fences guarding the yards between them, each with a barn larger than itself—large enough for a horse and a cow, a carriage and a buggy; each with a chicken yard, a rain-water cistern, a well, a shed, an outhouse; and each with a scarlet fever or diphtheria or smallpox placard on the door. The simple life of a hundred years ago may have had its charms and its virtues, but they are not suggested here. The whole story, of course, is not contained in these columns: it is impossible to know how large a proportion of those who caught them died of the infectious diseases, or how large a part of the population was immune. One's heart shrivels at the sight of names repeated—brothers and sisters—three, even four of them. Were families wiped out—or were there other children who escaped? The town, after all, did survive and grow by a few score, from year to year, but there are surnames in these columns, familiar subjects of old stories, which are owned by no one known in our streets today. Were they families whose every member has a line in the cemetery records, or did they move away, farther west, and leave their dead behind them? On the other hand, there are names here that are only too notorious still, which take precedence, in burial dates, of our Best People, although they belong to families that one could not suppose had an ancestry, nor to have survived more than a couple of generations, so feckless are they. Our most ubiquitous clan of poor whites, hangers-on of every church in town, successively, was as numerous then as now; they died as respectable deaths as anyone, employed the most popular undertakers, and were not buried in paupers' graves. Were they even then objects of charity —or have they degenerated, and why? Here are many half-told tales, which tantalize the imagination. Sarah Gray, aged eighteen, died in childbirth, but there is no "Infant Gray, stillborn," on the next line. What became of the baby, boy or girl?—who nursed it?—who became its stepmother? . . . The body of an unidentified man was "found drowned in Shawnee Creek"; no one could drown in Shawnee unless he lay flat on his face, drunk or unconscious. How did the unknown come to be there, and who was he? Did anyone ever know? Perhaps the coroner of 1857 investigated, and found it an accident to a drunken tramp —or perhaps the murder of a well-dressed mysterious stranger. At any rate the body was buried by the town, without a name.

The Civil War steals into the ledgers unobtrusively; there are no capital letters, no italics to announce its beginning. In the winter of '61–'62, between the names of two children, brothers, who died within a week of each other of scarlet fever, is the first recorded burial of a soldier: "John Scarlett, aged 20, —th O.V.I. Fell off a gun-boat and drowned in the Ohio River." . . . What an unheroic death! One can visualize the scene: tiny gunboats pushing up the river slowly through the fog of a wintry morning, their icy decks crowded with skylarking boys, careless out of the enemy's country—the not-unfriendly scuffle, the splash, the horrified outcry, the attempt at a rescue . . . there must have been such an attempt, since the boy's body was recovered and sent home for burial, out there on the hill, beneath the chestnut trees whose burrs he may have robbed, once, of their nuts.

The gunboats were no doubt on their way to Fort Henry. But the attack on the fort was months after Bull Run and the West Virginia campaign, neither of which has any mention in these pages. There was at least one regiment of Ohio troops at Bull Run; my grandfather, when he was very old and tolerant of his own youthful weakness, told us how he had run from that battle, and how he had hidden, when the long day had ended, beneath the arch of a stone bridge, how he had spent the night there, lost and too frightened to move. It was funny, when he told it, but the field was not a bloodless one. Why, then—? But of course, soldiers slain in conflict were buried where they fell. Only those could be brought home who died by accident, in some brief cessation of the storm; only their names would be written in this book. One turns the leaf, after so reasoning, only to be startled by the significant uniformity of the next half-page. The same words are repeated beneath each other until they fall into columns: "—th O.V.I. Died of wounds received at Shiloh." Only the names are different, and the ages. Even beyond that first solid half-page, interspersed with the familiar diseases, are the words "Died of wounds received at Shiloh."

Here is actuality, in these lines; this is not fiction; one catches one's breath. If all these men died of their wounds, how many were left dead on the field? What was it like, the grief of the scattered country villages of the young Middle West, in those first weeks after Shiloh? Who has imagined it, who has described it, more heartbreakingly than it is here described, in that damnable iteration, "Died of wounds received at Shiloh"? In the hand that held it, the pen that wrote the words was none too steady; the script is the uncertain script of an old man. An old man, left at home, keeping the records straight, writing down his neighbors' names, knowing each time how a sick hope had been cherished by a family, from the first report through news of infection, amputation, and gangrene, with death the only possible end—knowing how the only consolation was the return of the mutilated body to be buried here in peace . . . an old man, spreading his ledger on the counter between himself and some boy's father, come to buy a grave. His pen shook in his hand; beyond that he left no hint of emotion, his own or another's; he confined himself to the necessary data—and all the battle-pages of the historians are less moving.

For our town there was not again anything so devastating as the battle of Shiloh, but the war has its place in the succeeding pages. Men died of fever and dysentery in the swamps around Vicksburg, and their bodies were sent home; men were wounded in every battle in the West, and died of their wounds. There is one odd entry. By its date one can place the occurrence as early in Sherman's campaign about Atlanta: "Walter Taylor, —th O.V.I. Shot by a Rebel at Maxwell, Alabama." The words tease the mind, the distinction implied is so obscure. Was not every one of these boys, after all, "shot by a Rebel"? Where was Walter Taylor, and what was he doing? Knocking on someone's door? Looting, perhaps? Or, lost and alone, was he walking warily down the middle of a dusty street in a dusty southern hamlet, questioning whether its desertion was fact or seeming? Was he shot there, to collapse in the street? Wherever he died, his comrades must have been near at hand, since they rescued his body and sent it home.

It is strange to think, staring at the yellow pages, how, long ago, one had seen all these graves scattered through the cemetery, marked by flowers and the flag, and had taken it for granted that the bones beneath the sod were old men's bones. The annual Memorial Day parade had—perhaps inevitably—

linked together in our minds veterans and the graves of veterans: if those who carried flowers were old men, those for whom they carried them had been old, too, before they died . . . but it seems a strange and regrettable failure of the childish imagination. If we had thought of those graves as the resting places of boys brought home from their battles, we should have been even more powerfully moved by the flags and the flowers and the stories we knew of old unhappy far-off things. It is too late now to feel any perverse pleasure in the melancholy truth.

In the records, the end of the war, as its beginning, is unnoted. Casualties dwindle. One reads half a page and finds no soldier's name. At the top of the date column the year is written—1866. It is all over. The cripples, the invalids, the unscathed—all are returned, and will live or die in their beds. One is almost ashamed of a sudden lapse of interest. The next pages are an anticlimax. An imagination stimulated by the thunder and lightning of battle and siege does not respond to childbed groans. . . . But it is not wholly that. The sixties were long, long ago; the seventies were day-before-yesterday. That decade, in the tales of men who remembered it, was dull, unpicturesque, unheroic, and the deaths men died no matter for epics. The ledgers are robbed of their last antiquarian interest by the improvement of at least the nomenclature of medicine. They may well be closed on the page dated 1870, and returned to the safe where they are kept.

It is enough to have learned how handily accessible is all that material. Historians and novelists may turn to it when they please, and re-create with its help the town of a hundred, or eighty-five, or seventy years ago. Anyone whose interest is in the portrayal of men and women will do better to confine his researches to it, and not take the long walk west of town, past the Ionic pillars and down the avenue to the cemetery. There he might be persuaded from his intention "to trace . . . Who are the dead, how died they . . ." and "to snatch some portion of their acts from fate." The angels in marble make it impossible to imagine back to life the bones that are buried at their feet. Inflexibly benign, they point to heaven. The cemetery is a pleasure ground for children only, and for philosophers, who can look upon these monuments and not be discomforted; being hopeful of another world, they are fortified by these admonitions. The historian should stay away, lest he be convinced against his will of the futility of any attempt to bring back to memory the forgotten men whose mortality on earth is here proclaimed in letters of stone.

6. *Church*

THE BIG Presbyterian church down on Market Street is the church in which I was brought up. My great-grandparents had belonged to it in their lifetime; my grandmother and mother, my aunt and all her family, attended it Sunday after Sunday. Searching back in my memory, I find no beginning of my knowledge of that vast auditorium, bare and clean in a cool clarity of light, its amplitude of air shaken by the music of the organ when all the stops were pulled for the doxology.

The pale-green ceiling is so high overhead that no one can have seen it since he was young enough to squirm unrebuked into a half-lying position, or was just so tall as to be able to put his head back against the round top of the pew. When you were still of an age to comprehend the height and width and depth of that space, the congregation on the floor below seemed dwarfed and doll-like: not only the bent old ladies in pansied bonnets, but the deacons taking up the collection. The space had not the utter emptiness of air, however, for in its center hung the chandelier, glittering and bright as icicles, made all of mirrors and prisms: hundreds of prisms in concentric circles, each diminishing circle lower by the prisms' length than the one above it. Perhaps no one saw the chandelier, either, after he grew so tall that trying to count the prisms gave him a crick in the neck, for one time when the walls were painted, the decorator from the city was allowed to take it in part payment for his work. I grew up before that desecration; so long as I could look at them the prisms hung there, motionless themselves, but breaking the light that fell on them, shifting and changing it.

The bare side walls have two tiers of windows. The lower tier of waist-high sash windows with crude red, blue, and purple panes stands open on a summer morning, and gives upon depths of green—leaf, bush, and branch all lighted by the sun or dripping with rain. Above are pointed windows of grisaille in tiny diamonds; sunbeams are strained through them as through a honeycomb, and on the most garish day fall softly within.

The walls were painted a cool green, like the ceiling. Only one thing relieved our Presbyterian austerity: the pews were made long ago, when the wild cherry was still a plentiful tree in the forest; on the sloping floor they curve from one front corner to the other, from one side passage to the other, in sweeping arcs twice broken by green-carpeted aisles, and the deep color of their wood is rich and warm. At the time of the loss of the chandelier, the congregation could still see the pews, and refused to let the decorator have them; they have the patina of age, and of wear given them by four or five generations of broadcloth-cloaked spines and children's warm hands.

On the floor of the church between the center front pew and the edge of the pulpit platform, stood the communion table, its polished surface bare except on the four communion Sundays of the year. The platform, green-carpeted like the aisles, with steps at either end, had on it only the carved pulpit, and two massive Gothic chairs set back against the green curtain that hid the knees of the choir. Behind the banked rows of the choir, the golden pipes of the organ climbed to the tallest and stepped down again, the width of the platform. The organist sat between choir and organ, in the center, with her back turned to singers, preacher, and congregation. A little square mirror hung over the music rack. When I was a child, I thought the mirror was there so that the organist might keep watch over the congregation, restraining any restless child by a reflected glittering eye. She was indisputably the best organist in town, but such was her character that you flinched if you caught her eye in the mirror: she never spoke or thought kindly of anyone, and you preferred to escape her notice.

Halfway along the outer aisles are side doors that used to be propped open a little way on summer mornings. The end of my grandmother's pew was close beside one of them, but the narrow street visible beyond offered no distraction; nothing—no horse, no dog, no child—ever went past that door on Sunday. Across the rear of the auditorium a curved balcony repeats the curve of the last row of pews on the floor below. The two inner aisles end under the edge of the balcony, and in a line with them, beyond the space behind the pews, are the pairs of swinging doors that open on the Sunday-school room; across that room two opposite doors give on wide landings above and on either side of a wide vestibule. From each landing a flight of stairs in the front corner leads up to other Sunday-school rooms and to the balcony. Three or four steps down to the vestibule reach from front wall to inner wall, the full length of each landing. The vestibule is an empty square space, steps and a blank wall on three sides, on the other, the two pairs of double doors, Gothic-arched, with a stone shaft between them, and stone steps down to the sidewalk. High above, in the center of the wall, is the rose window with its intricate stone tracery and its dark rich-colored glass.

That was the church of my younger days; it stands so now, unchanged except for a different chandelier, an organ screen, and additional coats of paint, of varying colors applied at intervals over the years. But the church of my childhood was also more that is now lost and forgotten, except as it may be revived in the mind by the smoothness of cherry wood under the fingers, or the smell of rain and wet leaves across a spattered window sill. Then for a moment you know again, without trying to remember, all the little things that were a part of Sunday-morning church. The scratchiness of green-rep pew cushions under that inch of thigh that was bare when you had squirmed your petticoats up. The scent and flavor of peppermint balls from a crumpled thin-striped paper bag in your grandmother's purse; the irrepressible rattle of the Sunday-school paper, read surreptitiously when the sermon was overlong; the final resort to counting: organ pipes, lights, and—an attempt forever baffled—the prisms in the chandelier. The slick stickiness of your grandmother's white mohair suits, and the softness of your mother's flowered lawn; your own scrawny hands folded in your lap, and one or two of the dresses they lay on: a cream-colored challis with little green leaves and flowers in it, and a made-over Nile-green silk that had belonged to one of your fair-skinned aunts, in which you must have looked the color of a dried peasecod, but which you loved because it was the first silk dress you ever owned.

With these memories there come to mind all those, dead and gone, who were then members of the congregation. Grandmother's and Mother's acquaintances, whom we knew and accepted and were indifferent to, and those of our elders for whom on our own account we felt affection: Miss Carrie and Miss Fannie Allison, the old maids who lived across the street from us, and whose pew was in the middle of the church in the midst of other Allisons. The two black-browed, long-lipped Irishwomen who sat well back on our side of the church: one, the elder, a widow, grandmother of children younger than we, shaped like a broad-based isosceles triangle, her Quaker-gray skirts long and full, her bodice tight, her shawl spread decorously on her shoulders, her bonnet minute on the crown of her smooth head; the other, the younger, more conventionally dressed, the bookkeeper at the shoe factory, and famous as the baker of the best cakes anyone ever sat next to at a church picnic—and both of them as Presbyterian as Belfast, as gay and witty as Dublin. They were always in their pew, and were generally accompanied by the widow's son and his family, even though he might have been end man in an Elks' minstrel show the night before. He was a necessary part of any home-talent play, and would surely have been a professional actor had his mother not been so adamant a

Presbyterian. . . . The Wests, just a few pews behind us: he desiccated, thin, unsmiling—white-haired, white-mustached; she equally little, but plump, drawing her chin in as she smiled at you, until it swelled over her collar. Like Grandma, Mrs. West never wore bonnets, always wore hats. You admired them for holding old age at bay, not realizing that the bonnets were worn by ladies fifteen to twenty years older than they were, and in their minds at least—however it might seem to children—not even of the same generation.

Mostly our eyes were on those of our elders whom we knew less well, but who were more picturesque: eccentric and intellectual, like Miss McCracken and Professor Ormsby—or eccentric and rich like Miss Paul, or just old-fashioned like the Kingsburys, whose pew was a few rows in front of ours. They were a sturdy little couple, she straight and upright in her decent black taffeta and jet bonnet; he, Irish as a St. Patrick's day cartoon, round-shouldered in a long-tailed broadcloth coat, his bald head with its fringe of white hair refulgent in a Sabbatical glow. He was a shoemaker all his life: in a little cubbyhole next to the blacksmith's shop on the side street behind the church, he worked at his bench, leather-aproned, with tobacco juice staining the corners of his mouth, never really focusing his vague blue eyes on you when you carried him shoes to be half-soled; in a little ancient red-brick house down on Church Street he lived with his wife, stubbornly independent of a son who had made much money and lived in one of the town's big Victorian houses.

Between us and the Kingsburys was the Bakers' pew. There was nothing picturesque about the Bakers, nothing odd about them except in that summer when zealous, philanthropic Mrs. Baker tried to make Presbyterians of one of those families that our more earnest reformers were always trying to uplift. (More tolerant citizens regarded them indulgently, because by their completely successful and always legal efforts to live without toil, they kept the town supplied with a series of stories, each more preposterous than the last.) She accomplished something: she got two of the daughters to church—for a while. They sat with the Bakers, which no doubt was more than she had bargained for—and the whole congregation smiled. The girls were then, I suppose, fifteen or sixteen, but in school, which they attended sporadically, they had never got beyond the fifth grade, and I had caught up with them. The handsome Baker boys were about their age: they would bow Hester and Ruth into their pew and would then sit through the service in a rigidity of discomfort not to be missed by anyone who was behind them and could see their necks and shoulders as they dodged the saw-tooth brims of the gaudy white lace-straw hats.

Directly in front of us sat another bonneted old lady and her two middle-aged daughters, one a widow, one a spinster. The widow was a square, solid woman, with a firm jaw and unemotional eye; the spinster was bony and lachrymose: she had once upon a time been engaged to a carpenter, but had lost him through some fatal combination of roofs and ladders. Every sermon wrought her to tears at some point in its delivery; there was a fascination in listening, in thinking "this will do it," in swinging the eye to her corner in time to see her bring out her white handkerchief and push her glasses up.

The other end of the pew belonged to a more worldly couple. He was portly and pompous and bald, with a heavy watch chain calling attention to his portliness—but at least he got to church on time. She was a bosomy, fashionable woman with elaborately coiffed hair and the last word in hats; she was always late and came down the aisle like a full-rigged ship as we sang, "Praise God from whom all blessings flow." She moved with a jangling of bracelets, a swinging and clashing of the necklaces which she caught up, just too late, as she squeezed into her seat. Once she swept majestically forward while the minister was reading the Scripture lesson; as she went banging into her pew he came to the verse, "Behold the noise is come . . . and a great commotion. . . ." I haven't an idea where in the Bible that passage occurs, but I know it is there; I couldn't forget it.

The Ormsbys sat on the other side of the church, behind us but not so far behind that we could not watch them. The tedium of the sermon was relieved for everyone by Professor Ormsby's restless progress from one pew to another. The most amusing move, which the whole congregation watched for, was the first one he made. He would come down the aisle alone from the Sunday-school room, his white hair as untidy as Carlyle's, his expression as grim. Presently, when he was nicely settled, Mrs. Ormsby would come to join him. He would rise to permit her to enter the pew, and would then go elsewhere to sit.

There were several memorable old ladies in the church, like Mrs. Harper, who at eighty-odd still treated grave and dignified Judge Harper like the stepson he was. Oldest of all the congregation, next to Grandma Bigger, who was housebound, was Aunt Maggie Allison. Of that once great and flourishing family only women were left: sisters, widows, daughters, nieces—and Aunt Maggie was head of the family. Among her tall kinswomen, she was short—either humpbacked or stooped with age; she wore a bonnet, and from beneath it her strong-boned face, slightly bearded, jutted out like that of a grenadier. She lived alone, quite self-sufficient; she ruled her family, the Ladies' Aid, the Missionary Society; she was good and kind and unsentimentally humorous, and was loved in spite of the vagaries of old age.

Farthest back in my mind lies the memory of Miss Paul. The others lived through the years of my growing up; Miss Paul is a figure of my early childhood vividly but so preposterously remembered that I might question the truth of the picture could I not hear also echoes of Mother's and Grandma's defensive, "But there's no better woman in town than Miss Belle Paul." We used to go to the church vestibule after Sunday school, to watch for her arrival. Her gleaming black victoria was driven to the curb by the Negro coachman. With difficulty, because of his clubfoot, her nephew alighted, his massive gray head bare, his silk hat in one hand, his cutaway coat and striped trousers elegant beyond our standards. He helped her out of the victoria. We always held our breath: we could hardly believe from one week to another that anyone could look so queer. She was tiny, with bones like a sparrow's; under her bonnet she wore a frizzled red wig; her fine-featured, withered face was painted red on the cheekbones, and all the wrinkles were filled with caked powder. On her nephew's arm, her white-gloved hand looked like a claw. They both walked with sticks; limping together they came up the outer steps; in the vestibule we fell back before them, and they climbed to the landing, limped across the Sunday-school room and down the aisle.

As a child I watched and noted all these people. Now, looking back, I realize they were not the members who made the church what it was. Those who did were the great majority of ordinary folk who failed to interest a child: substantial farmers, three judges and their families, three or four doctors and their families, and particularly, the half-dozen or so merchants and manufacturers who considered themselves leaders of the town. The women proclaimed by the assured unself-consciousness of their bearing what they assumed to be true, and had half-persuaded the town to accept: that to be important in Society, you must be a Presbyterian. That dictum was sometimes uttered by Presbyterian mothers-in-law (advice to brides "from away"), and sometimes it was resented, not secretly. Then the town scoffed, and Grandma would sniff: "Society! In a town this size! What do they think they mean by Society?" If they meant by it, giving and being invited to receptions, calling and being called on, in white gloves, with engraved calling cards, then she and Mother were a part of it—but if they meant elaborate card parties, and dances at the Masons' or the Elks', then Mother and Grandma were in outer darkness. Grandma may have thought that a few of her co-religionists were a little smug—but there was a certain amount of truth in the position maintained by the Presbyterian ladies. Our membership did not include more of the well-to-do descendants of old families than did the other churches, nor was discipline strong enough in any denomination, except the United Presbyterian, to prevent all participation in the amusements of Society. But Presbyterians could dance, play cards, and go to the theater, and send their children to dancing class, with quite untroubled consciences, because the members of the church who wanted it so were in the majority; they could set the congregational tone, and choose the minister. No bigot, no fanatic even on the subject of total abstinence, was long tolerated. Since the church was what they made it, those well-to-do families were its

mainstay: they filled the pews on Sunday mornings. Now, looking back, you realize how much that color of material success, of
ease and well-being and graciousness, contributed to the sense of
untroubled, even somnolent peace that went with Sunday-
morning church.

And their responsibility did not end with their attendance, nor
with dropping their envelopes into the collection plate. Those
same women who played cards on some afternoons, on others
entertained the Missionary Society; they offered their bedrooms
for delegates to District Meetings; they belonged to the Ladies'
Aid, and at church suppers worked alongside schoolteachers and
clerks and bookkeepers without condescension. They sang in the
choir and they taught in the Sunday school—a handful of them.
And for those few at least, I can speak: however worldly they
may have been, they were still good Calvinists. They knew
Presbyterian doctrine, and passed the knowledge on to us. We
worked hard in Sunday school; and although we may have
grumbled, to Sunday school we went as unfailingly as to public
school, excused only by illness.

As in most conventional American homes, Sundays began for
us with the maternal inspection: in turn we stood beside Mother
where she sat behind the coffee pot, while hair ribbons and
sashes were retied or at least pulled into shape, while the hang of
petticoats was corrected and, sometimes, stockings were taken
down and readjusted over long winter underwear. After breakfast, Mother went with us to the front hall to see that hats were
on straight and jackets were respectable. Seldom did our family
finances run to Sunday coats for the children; dresses, shoes, and
hats, yes—but the same wraps were worn seven days in the
week. Once, feeling to see whether I had a clean handkerchief,
Mother dipped into the pocket of my jacket as it hung on the
rack, and her finger tips encountered the snails that had come
out of their shells since I had put them there on Saturday. She
was somewhat hardened—there were always cocoons about,
tucked behind pictures, and minnows and tadpoles in their season, in glass jars; she had learned to look carefully at any cardboard box before she opened it: if holes had been punched in the

lid, it held some living creature, probably a caterpillar. But snails were too much: I started for Sunday school that morning with burning ears, jacketless.

When the front door had closed behind us, we pranced down the steps and through the gate with starched petticoats swinging, Bible and Quarterly under one arm. But the rapt expression on our faces was rather concentrated than devout: the short walk to the church was given over to a rehearsal of the catechism. The first question and answer, "What is man's chief end?" "Man's chief end is to glorify God and enjoy Him forever," took us no further than our own tulip tree in the fence corner; how many questions beyond that could be asked and answered in three blocks depended on how often we forgot, stumbled, and had to start again from the beginning.

We went "through the alley" to the church. To the local tongue the side streets that crossed the town above and below Detroit Street were "alleys" because of their narrowness. (A slight distinction in phraseology made clear what we meant. To go "down the back alley" was to take a short cut past stable doors, back-fence gates, and garbage cans.) On weekdays the alleys were crowded, but on a Sunday morning there was no traffic of ice or delivery wagons, or of Negro garbage collectors or old-rag-and-bone dealers. There was nothing in the three blocks before you to distract your mind from the catechism; there was nothing of interest, even, in the houses you passed. First, the Cooper house, on the corner, with its round shell-bordered flower bed in the center of the front lawn; then the white cottage tucked behind it, whose small yard blazed with an untidy mass of flowers—ragged robins and coreopsis even poking their heads through the picket fence. Beyond the back alley stood the red-brick stable of the Allisons, bigger than the cottage you had passed, and their back yard and porch, their side yard, then high over your head their dining-room windows and the living-room bay. You knew all these were there, but you hardly saw them; you were muttering, "What is God? God is a spirit, infinite, eternal and unchangeable. . . ." You crossed Second Street, deserted except for the buggies at the Methodist hitching rack, a little way down from the corner. Then came the Darlington house, red brick again; the Darlington backyard, shielded by a solid board fence so high it was like a blank wall towering over you; the Darlington stable, its door sometimes open, its carriage room empty. The end of another back alley, and then another stable, this one frame, ramshackle, empty; another tall board fence; another house—a very old house, set flush with the sidewalks on the Main Street corner, so that not a blade of grass was to be seen. You passed it, asking yourself to define the decrees of God, replying, "The decrees of God are His eternal purpose according to the counsel of His will, whereby, for His own glory, He hath foreordained whatsoever comes to pass." How those words sang themselves in the mind: "He hath foreordained whatsoever comes to pass"!

Main Street seemed infinitely wide on Sunday morning: unless the interurban car was starting for Dayton, nothing stirred as far as you could see. When you had crossed it, you came to the little brown-brick house where the Wests lived, built at the edge of the walk, with a side door on the alley and steps to be gone over or around; and beyond the kitchen window, another high, solid board fence stretching to another back alley. At that point you cut catty-cornered across to the side door of the church and were presently, in a circle before Miss McCracken, demonstrating what progress you had made with the one hundred and seven questions of the Shorter Catechism of the Westminster Assembly of Divines. No one ever expressed any curiosity as to what the Longer Catechism might be like; it was enough that we must write upon the tablets of our memory this presumably simplified version of Calvinist doctrine. That we accomplished it is perhaps not marvelous: it is easy for children to memorize, and we had long ago, in the beginning of time, learned the Ten Commandments which made its middle section. What does seem remarkable to me now, holding the catechism in my hand, is that we supposed ourselves, when Miss McCracken had expounded it, to understand what we had learned—the doctrine of Original Sin: "The sinfulness of that estate whereunto man fell consists in the guilt of Adam's first sin, the want of Original righteousness, and the corruption of his whole nature (which is commonly called 'Original Sin') together with all actual transgressions which proceed from it"; then, the doctrine of the Elect: "God having out of his good pleasure, from all eternity, elected some to everlasting life, did enter into a covenant of grace to deliver them out of the estate of sin and misery, and to bring them into an estate of salvation by a redeemer." We did not feel baffled by Effectual Calling: "Effectual Calling is the work of God's spirit, whereby, convincing us of our sin and misery, enlightening our minds in the knowledge of Christ and renewing our wills, he doth persuade and enable us to embrace Jesus Christ, freely offered to us in the gospel"; nor by the benefits of Effectual Calling: Justification, Adoption, and Sanctification. But we must have relaxed strained mental sinews when we arrived at the only comfortable creed set forth in the catechism: "Is any man able perfectly to keep the Commandments of God?" "No mere man since the fall is able in this life perfectly to keep the Commandments of God, but daily breaks them in thought, word and deed."

We were proud to have learned all this; we were proud of a church that gave it to us to be learned; the catechism of our Episcopal friends seemed absurdly childish. And I know that we thought we understood it, because we sometimes argued in its defense through angry school recesses, whenever the Methodists were excited by one of their revivals. The arguments were always between Presbyterians and Methodists; applause or reprobation came from our German Reformed and Baptist and Episcopal schoolmates, who had apparently no very distinct ideas about the dogmas of their churches. What we Calvinists would have called "Our Religion" was purely doctrinal, and could be argued as loudly and fiercely as could, for example, the tenets of the Republican party. And however dispassionately logical the dogma was in itself, its defense not only taxed our intellects, but roused our emotions: fierce loyalty, indignation, and even a scandalized horror.

No one has ever denied that the Westminster Catechism, once its premises are accepted, is rigidly logical: Methodist children retreated step by step before us until they reached the premises, which they had then perforce to reject. That might have overthrown us, had not such denial seemed blasphemous even to Baptists and Episcopalians. First, the Methodists expressed disbelief in the doctrine of Election. In vain we reminded them of those Methodist saints in town—old men and particularly old women—who were so sure of their State of Grace as to believe themselves relieved of any necessity to attend church or to worry about their souls' salvation. That was different, we were told: they had achieved Grace, not been foreordained to it. Methodists did not believe in Foreordination. Then, we demanded, how could God know what would happen next, if it might happen some other way? Did they deny foreknowledge too? They tried not to, for to deny Omniscience to God was certainly blasphemy, but their position was a hard one to maintain. And with our triumph was mingled something like awe of those who had courage to face life believing that not even God knew what was about to happen to them or to the world.

Long afterward I realized that ours was the continuation of persistent argument between Methodists and Presbyterians—Arminians and Calvinists. Such disputes had been acrimoniously pursued, even in print, since there had been a Methodist church. After my grandmother died, when we cleared out the attic for the first time in fifty years, I rescued and preserved the books on religion that been my great-grandfather's. Among them was *The Difficulties of Arminian Methodism*, written by a Presbyterian D.D. and published in Pittsburgh in 1838; it is a point-by-point rebuttal of Methodist attacks on Original Sin, Foreordination, the Doctrine of the Elect—and, by way of riposte, a thrust at the Methodist doctrine of Sinless Perfection, and at the government of the church, in which section the old Presbyterian abhorrence of bishops is emphatically restated.

How much longer, after we were grown, the teaching of the Westminster Catechism was carried on in Sunday school I do not know. I do know that a generation has grown up in most denominations that knows little of dogma and cares less. If that were not true, there would not be talk of uniting and making of

Arminian and Calvinist one church. Why I should have the slightest regret at the idea of such union I do not know—I who cannot now believe in the Westminster Catechism, except—perhaps, sometimes—in that beginning definition of God: "God is a spirit, infinite, eternal. . . ." But regret it I do: I unreasonably want some Presbyterians still to stand fast, remembering what their forefathers died for: *Pro corona et foedere Christi.* Even if dogma no longer matters to Wesleyan or Calvinist—even if young newcomers to town choose their church for social or business reasons—surely they must go where they feel at home, and church still differs from church in organization and in tone and attitude: staid or revivalist, liturgical or plain—and that tone must derive if not from dogma then from some philosophy, Pelagian or Augustinian in its basic assumptions. It is hard for me to believe that Methodist and Presbyterian could ever be one.

Even when all Presbyterians became one church—United Presbyterian—having to take the name made one wince a little, made acceptance hard to "plain" Presbyterians who grew up knowing the unbending, inflexible United Presbyterians as well as we knew them.

For we were by no means the only Calvinists in town: there were two big United Presbyterian churches. Their young people gave us little vocal support in our childish arguments with the Methodists: their religion was too grave and solemn to be aired on a graveled public-school playground—but they ringed us round, and the silent weight of their agreement helped us to bear the Methodists down. "Of course," they would say, when we appealed to them. Our doctrine they shared, but in other matters having to do with church we were apart as the poles. We said "Sunday," they said "Sabbath." We celebrated Christmas and Easter; they considered recognition of those sacred days "popish." Saturday night was for us the festive time of the week; their Sabbath began at sundown, and they could not come out to play after Saturday supper. We put pennies, given us for the purpose, into the collection plate at Sunday school; they solemnly "tithed." After Sunday dinner we read what we pleased, or took sedate walks, or visited relations; they were immured behind drawn blinds with Bible, catechism, and sabbath-school paper. They believed so firmly in the divine inspiration of the Bible, and in the immediate cessation of divine inspiration after the recording of the last word of Revelations, that they would sing only psalms in church. We never discussed these things with them; they were superior in the assurance that they were right, and we pitied them because they were so burdened by prohibitions.

Although we might have guessed it from their numbers, we did not then realize that the United Presbyterians had founded the town, had made and kept it different from all the other towns round about. The county seat nearest us to the southeast is a Quaker community, supporting a Quaker college, while we had in those days no more than a handful of Quakers. North of us is a city still Lutheran, with a big Lutheran college, while with us that church survives with difficulty. A religious atmosphere of this sort persists in a country settled as ours was, in biblical fashion; two or three men would come on horseback to spy out the land, and when they had found a likely stretch of forest wilderness, they would return for a wagon train of relations, friends, and neighbors, who would cross the mountains together, or the Ohio river from Kentucky. The new community would set up first a few log cabins, and then a log church.

To our section of the land of Canaan came a few single exploring Scotch-Americans, and then, close on their heels, their various congregations. The first to arrive were those sternest of Covenanters, the Reformed Presbyterians, who had left Scotland because the state church was to their minds too lax, and who, after the Treaty of Greenville, departed from the Carolinas for the Northwest Territory, where slavery had from the beginning been excluded by the Ordinance of 1787.

The first congregation settled in the northeastern corner of the county. Other, later groups came from Kentucky, from Virginia and Pennsylvania—from all that mountain-frontier fringe of the Scotch and Scotch-Irish. In 1810, the first Calvinist church was built in the town, ancestor of the two United Presbyterian churches of my time, which had gone through all the permutations and combinations possible to hair-splitting logicians: Associate, Reformed and Associate Reformed Presbyterian, "Old Light" and "New Light" Covenanter, and were sometimes two churches but sometimes three, if there had been a serious split in their ranks. Our church, plain "Presbyterian," was founded a few years later by settlers with a different background. Their ancestors had come to America early in the eighteenth century, not from Scotland for religious reasons, but from Ulster for economic and political ones. There were Scottish names in the congregation, and still are: Adair, Anderson, Stevenson, Watt, Gowdy— but somewhere along the way, in Ireland, or Maryland, or on the Pennsylvania frontier, the old Scotch Covenanter sternness had been mitigated somewhat. Also along the way they had been joined by Dutch Calvinist families like my grandmother's, who had found themselves too few to support a Dutch Reformed church. Almost from the first they differed as widely from the United Presbyterians as they could, while still holding stubbornly to the Catechism. They went to church in the mornings, but did not stay all day; they had hot and bounteous Sunday dinners; on weekdays they played cards and danced, some of them. And I doubt if they were fanatical on the subject of slavery: it is mostly United Presbyterian families—descendants of Covenanters who had hidden their ministers from Claverhouse—that have inherited the handsome old brick houses with secret rooms or cellars where fugitive slaves were concealed from a pursuing sheriff.

It was the United Presbyterians who set up educational institutions in the county and brought us professors as well as ministers. In the 1850's, the seminary of the Associate Presbyterians was moved here from Pennsylvania, and until it was moved again in the 1920's, it helped to give the town its Calvinist color. For its "theologues" the church provided its best scholars; the professors who lived their adult lives in our town and brought up their children in our schools were learned and distinguished men. They were bigoted, some of them; they had their idiosyncrasies: we laughed at them, but we respected them. President-Emeritus Harper, for instance: an aloof, white-haired old man who took solitary walks along the swamp paths and through the woods; he went with head bowed and hands clasped behind his back; he never saw us, even when we stood out of his way to let him pass, but we watched him go, head and shoulders rising above the cattails, and thought him queer indeed—grownups never intruded into our world of wood and swamp except in the fall, with guns. And that other white-haired saint, who was president of the seminary when we were growing up: tall, bent, fragile, frightened into confusion when he met us skating on the street, yet rigorous and unyielding as John Knox himself in matters of theology; he was unfit to cope with the world as it was wagging in those years.

The younger professors were more like ordinary men, or we knew them better because they had children our age—children who were not particularly angelic—and we were in and out of their houses familiarly. They were scholars—archeologists, classicists, divines—but Dr. Webster was the single one we knew not as parent only but as teacher. The others were red-haired, Scottish in bone and color as if they had come themselves from the old country; Dr. Webster was a black Celt: his hair, his eyes, his heavy brows, his long mustache, were all quite black; his hair was shaggy, his eye flashed. When we were in high school, he held a beginner's class in Greek, open to any who wanted to join; love of Greek or love of teaching moved him, since he charged no fee. Public schoolteachers and their pupils attended the class together. I am sure that no female had ever sat in the seminary classroom before, but that particular innovation offended no United Presbyterian. It was of course New Testament Greek that we learned; to this day I cannot hear "In the beginning was the word"—Εν ἀρχῇ ἦν ὁ λόγος—without seeing again that bleak room, and Dr. Webster, pointer in hand, his dark hair tumbled in his eyes, standing at the blackboard.

For retired United Presbyterian divines, the town was a paradise on earth—a paradise furnished with books of theology, scholars and theologians to argue with; when they grew too old to teach or to preach they stayed on in their dark tree-shaded brick houses. Dr. Carson lived on the corner of the alley a block beyond our church. He had been minister of the Second Church in the days when theology was a life-and-death matter to its members, and so long as he ministered to the congregation no relaxation of discipline was permitted: rebels held their peace or went elsewhere. Some while after the close of his ministry an organ was installed in the church. On the first Sunday morning it was played, he rose from his seat at the first note and stalked out. This was a gesture—an ocular demonstration of his disapproval: by that time there was no church without an organ to which he could turn.

But Dr. Carson had two weaknesses which involved him in the world's affairs. One was a passion for politics. He was a Republican who cherished a conviction—unspoken but to be inferred from his conduct—that skulduggery was not skulduggery if committed in the interests of the party, and he engaged with effect in the machinations of practical politics. His second weakness was for chess. There were not many expert chess players in town, and what few there were, like my grandfather, were not notable churchmen. Dr. Carson must play with them or not play. He played.

When I was a child and knew him by sight, he was an old man, long a widower, living alone except for a housekeeper; he was a burly old man, like Dr. Samuel Johnson, who rolled when he walked. His high, stiff collars empurpled his jowl and double chin. He wore a long tight-buttoned black vest, a long frock coat, and a yellowed straw hat, hard as a board. He had the Doctor's growling, ungracious ways, and like the Doctor was oblivious of any possible beholder. He did his own marketing; and in those days when the grocers spread their wares under awnings as far as the curb, he poked at the vegetables with his cane to indicate his preferences, and then rumbled home, his market basket over his arm, carrot or onion or celery tops dangling over its edges. Marketing done, he spent the rest of his day in his study; when you passed the house you saw him through its undraped window awake at his desk, with a knotted handkerchief on his bald head, or asleep in his leather chair, the handkerchief over his face.

The town was full of active clergymen, in addition to the retired United Presbyterians. At the two Methodist churches, pastors came and went, seldom there long enough to become figures in the community. Rectors came and went at the Episcopal church, too, because it was small, chiefly supported by a few wealthy families, and had little to hold ambitious young men. The Baptist minister, on the other hand, was a figure out of all proportion to the size of his church: he was a little dark-bearded Englishman with a beautiful rich voice and a twinkling eye, who dressed in summer in immaculate white linen and walked in our streets behind his wife's wheel chair; he stayed until his sons were grown and he was ready to retire. The German Reformed church, like ours, changed ministers when the incumbent was called to another charge, or when the congregation grew tired of him. We grew tired of ours oftener; we had as many while I was growing up as the Reformed church had had in all its history.

But however many churches there were—however important their pastors, or large their congregations—still Calvinism dominated the atmosphere of the town. Consequently, although for many years we have had the reputation in our part of the country of being very strictly pious, ours is piety along Calvinist lines, and confusing to a stranger. It consists mainly of adherence to the first four Commandments and most particularly the fourth. Certain sins it frowns upon—sins against man—but is prone to commit: theft, for example—theft in strictly legal ways from the widow and orphan, or in less law-abiding fashion from the county or the state. The thief in such cases is seldom punished or even ostracized, but must be aware of the contempt felt for him. Sins of the flesh which Moses and the prophets forbade—adultery, fornication, looking on the wine when it is red—are regarded more leniently, and if the sinner contrives in their commission to make such a fool of himself that we rock with laughter, the affection which we feel for him may even be increased. This is contrary to all conventional ideas of the Calvinist, the Covenanter; it may have come about because so many of our families followed the long way round, through Ulster, and by the time they reached our shores were as much Irish as Scotch. Perhaps it is cold climate and thin blood that make the Presbyterian in Scotland intolerant of the sins of the flesh (if he is) rather than his doctrine: "No mere man since the fall is able in this life perfectly to keep the commandments of God, but daily breaks them in thought, word and deed." Or perhaps that even more comfortable section of the United Presbyterian Confession of Faith has been added since they left the old country: "We declare that although the moral law is of perpetual obligation and consequently does and ever will bind the believer as a rule of life, yet as a covenant he is by his justification through Christ completely and forever set free from it, both as to its commanding and condemning power, and consequently not required to yield obedience to it as a condition of life and salvation."

At any rate, however it came about, love of laughter and delight in the ridiculous errors of mankind are inbred in us and only noticed by the alien observer. Strangers are baffled and confused by this contradiction between our piety—so obvious and so famous—and the tenor of our favorite anecdotes, old and new, whose central figures, living and dead, are named in tones of fondness and in gratitude for their provocation of mirth. This indulgent attitude toward the comical sinner has been characteristic of us since a church was first established in the county: otherwise, old stories would not have been remembered and passed on, to be quotable today against those who are righteous overmuch. That oldest church was the Massie's Creek Covenanter church, northeast of town, whose congregation lived scattered in the forest and rode for miles on the Sabbath to sit through two long services in an unheated church—to eat their cold dinner in the churchyard between the sermons of a minister who had to cross the unbridged creek on stilts from his cabin on the other bank. When, in 1812, they set about building a new church of hewn logs to replace the first one of peeled logs, the work was divided among the congregation, and the minister was to supply the whiskey—a gallon of it. Squire Galloway agreed to haul the logs, but in his hands the oxen, which he had hired from a "wicked Gentile," were unmanageable. The Gentile, to prove that success with oxen demanded the use of profanity, cursed them heartily by way of illustration. Swearing was against the law; the Squire then and there fined him fifty cents. He had a dollar, the Squire had no change; the Gentile ripped out another oath. "There," said the Squire, pocketing the dollar, "that makes the change.". . . Of course this anecdote has been preserved in the annals of the Massie's Creek church because its humor lies in the discomfiture of the wicked Gentile—but what rejoices the heart of one who stumbles upon the tale in the pages of old chronicle is the matter-of-fact announcement that the minister was to supply the whiskey for the occasion.

Only the old stories, the half-forgotten and the mildest ones, can be put down in print. But we watch the progress of those now being acted out and await their conclusions, storing them in our minds to embellish for our grandchildren. Meetings at night, in the deep shadows of curbside trees, do not go unseen, nor does the simultaneousness of errands to bank and drugstore escape our notice. On summer evenings there are interested observers on front porches, and by day post-office and bank clerks are not too busy to see an inebriated leading citizen practicing new and fantastic dance steps on his way up the courthouse path. But we cannot laugh freely until the comedies have been worked out to their ends, nor put any tales down in print until the last of a family has died or moved away. For illustrations of that queer reverse side of Calvinism one must therefore go back to the days when Mother was a girl, or even to the time when Grandma was young; then, foundlings were left on United Presbyterian doorsteps, and stern and strait-laced elders were confounded. Other divagations were revealed when mulatto children grew up with conspicuous resemblance to certain white girls and boys. Here and there on Main Street, above the groceries and saloons, unregenerate bachelor sons of leading families kept their mistresses behind lace curtains; everyone knew it, and no one approved, exactly, but since it was better to pretend not to know it, the bachelors were only looked at a little askance, and went their way unpunished.

When the Robertses built their villa in the 1870's, the town was not so much awed by its magnificence as it was delighted by

"Caje" (Micajah) Roberts's stable arrangements, made for his peculiar needs. The hayloft floor, by his desire, was built low, and its window was directly over the stable door. That window was left open nights so that anyone who came home late, incapable of walking, could stop his horse in the door, and from the saddle could pull himself into the loft, roll into the hay, and sleep it off. History does not record what provision was made for the horse.

Certain of the men who were young in the 1880's had names famous in story long before they died: those men who left the town and scattered over the country, and became wealthy, some of them, and some of them millionaires. They used to come back occasionally, when I was a child—a richly chuckling, red-faced, cigar-smoking group of men, telling stories on themselves and others. One story the town remembers is of the night long, long ago, when they went to play their usual game of poker with the hotel proprietor, and allowed their curiosity to be so aroused by his winks and nods toward the room at the head of the stairs that their public downfall resulted. They went from the proprietor's room by an inner door, picked up a stepladder in the service quarters, and with it crept up the back stairs. To see through the transom of the interesting room, they were forced to put the ladder dangerously close to the top of the stairs from the lobby. They were not so quiet as they should have been, and the gentleman within, resentful of their intrusion, fired a shot from his derringer through the door. It sounded like a cannon to their startled ears, and their reaction was enough to upset the ladder over the edge of the stairs, and ladder and youths went tumbling and crashing down all the way to the newel post —to the noisy delight of all who had the luck to be in the lobby.

Of course we never heard the best tales until we had grown up; nevertheless, as children we somehow shared, without any real knowledge of it, the town's attitude. Even some of us who on occasion argued about the catechism, on other days listened with shocked delight to whatever guttersnipe stories the boys were willing to tell us. And when we grew up to high school and were for a few weeks so excessively pious that we joined the

Methodists and United Presbyterians in refusing to dance—still we continued to play post office (Methodists and United Presbyterians, too), and to sit in close embrace under the robe on a bobsleigh.

For that little while only did most of us who were Baptist or Episcopal or German Reformed or Presbyterian pretend to ourselves to be deeply religious—religious enough, for instance, to consider even remotely the possibility of becoming foreign missionaries or of marrying ministers. The town had indulged in the most frantic revival in its history, held in a tabernacle built for the purpose. Our participation in this revival was frowned on at home: by Mother, who was a Presbyterian and had no faith in a sudden conversion springing from overwrought emotions; by Father, who was an outspoken skeptic, and saw to it that we considered the possibility that all we were taught just might not be true. We were no doubt the only ones of our contemporaries who had to plead to be allowed to attend. But, conformists like all the young, we could not bear to be too peculiar in the eyes of our friends, and so were allowed to go occasionally, on a Friday night. (And now what I remember best about that revival is that it gave the science classes a piece of information about their teacher which had been long and vainly sought. His initials were P.A. That was all we knew. No other teacher made a mystery of his given names. When he was converted, he joined the Baptist church, which meant that whether or not he had been baptized before, he had to be baptized then. Not many of his students were Baptists, but it took the news no time to spread: *Pearl Alfonso.* Our unholy delight must have been clear to him: I hope that saving his soul was worth what that shy man must have suffered.)

The emotional fever roused by those weeks soon subsided, for the most part. For me it was a brief attack indeed, lasting only until the history teacher assigned "The Higher Criticism" to me for a report. The necessary research, on top of my father's caustic remarks, resulted in a paper that shocked the teacher and startled the class. But to the revival, where we learned that all denominations are equal in the sight of the Lord, I owe what little familiarity I have with other churches than my own. After it was over, there continued to be union services on Sunday evenings, in one church after another. Remembering those nights, when young people of a denomination sat together, having proceeded to the church from their own six o'clock meetings, I realize just how odd were the impressions left on my mind. For one thing, if you were used to the Presbyterian church, in other auditoriums you felt smothered and breathlessly impelled to push the ceiling up. For another, the eye accustomed to cherry pews found varnished yellow pine raw and cheap. Only the Episcopal church did not offend in either particular: its roof was peaked and timbered, its straight pews of dark oak. The Baptist church, too, had dark pews, so high that you could see little of your neighbors except their hats. The tight little Baptist church was altogether dim and dark, small-windowed, its most spectacular feature the baptismal font, of the shape and size of a sarcophagus.

I was even more bigoted in my reaction to the various services, concluding that since Episcopalians read their prayers out of a book, and rattled them off in an unintelligible singsong, they could not be putting much real heart into them; that all their bobbing up and down, on and off their knees, was tiresome, and left no time for revery, which is the proper business of church. That Methodist hymns were loud and noisy, and, if you were a Presbyterian, made you shrink up inside instead of rousing you to the emotional pitch proper for a Methodist sermon. That the United Presbyterians were stiff-necked and ungracious, since although you went to their church and sang willingly "Oh how love I Thy law" and "Keep me as the apple of Thine eye," they came to yours and stood through hymn-singing—a whole line of your friends and contemporaries—not only mute, but with mouths clamped shut in hard stubborn lines. Only the service of the Reformed church was not objectionable: the congregation stood to pray and sat to sing, instead of the other way round, but that was unimportant. You could imagine yourself becoming one of them, if only you knew how they stood on the vital matters of Foreordination, Election, Sanctification, and Grace.

That was fifty years ago. I have not been to a service in any of those churches since that time, but I doubt whether those I once visited are very different inside, either in their decoration or their services. (But United Presbyterians did finally give way over the singing of hymns—else how could we ever have become one with them?) I know that externally wall and window, roof and spire, are exactly as they were, brick of the nineteenth century, stone of the twentieth. Passing them now and then, I might be seeing with the eyes of my childhood, except that my architectural judgments have altered, and I see the oldest churches as the best, however shabby they may have grown.

The church in town that is most worth preserving is the original Reformed Presbyterian: a one-room church without spire or tower, its square windows alternating with brick pilasters, its only ornament the classical motif carved in the center of its lintel. It stands at the top of Market Street hill—has stood there for somewhere near one hundred and fifty years, surrounded by its ancient tall trees. Negroes live around and below it, and it was sold long ago to one of their smaller congregations. Poverty has put its mark on it: it has been painted a dingy gray, and the paint has here and there peeled from the crumbling bricks. The windows are lurid even from the outside and the foundations are stained with splashed mud. However, the trees so conceal these defects that it is easy, particularly at twilight, to imagine the Covenanters eating their Sabbath lunch in the yard in the shade.

Our poorer congregations have done most for the town. Their first small brick churches, built in the last years of the Greek revival, have never been replaced, and have long been subdued to the pattern of our streets, mellow and ancient almost as the trees themselves, crumbling mortar and worn bricks even adding to their air: the Lutheran church down the hill on lower Main Street, and the Baptist church on Market, with its Corinthian pilasters around the square tower above the door and across the front, and the arches recessed between them. Later than these, and larger, built in the middle of the nineteenth century, are the Roman Catholic church, its brick veneer fortunately disguised by creamy yellow paint, Trinity Methodist Church on upper Main Street, and the Presbyterian church—their architecture imitation

Gothic, with spires bursting into crocket and finial above the roof line. But large as they are, they belong to the scene. The two Protestant churches particularly are in harmony with the brick houses near them; they are warm and dark in color, and unobtrusive. Other denominations have newer churches: squat, smothering stone churches—Methodist, United Presbyterian, Reformed —or—the Episcopal—a stone church which is neither squat nor smothering, but a copy of an Early English parish church. Like the others, it was built when we were children, but the years since have covered its walls with ivy, and it has an air of having been there always.

I check my surprise at recognition of that look of age: after all, we were young enough in the years of its building to have paced the circuit of its rising walls every summer evening when the stone masons had gone, and to have crawled between the joists under the floor when it was being laid—to have spent hours breaking up scattered chips of granite for the pyrites in them. We knew the pyrites were fools' gold, but they looked real enough to us, and were therefore hoarded in small cloth bags with drawstrings, like those that forty-niners carried in the stories about them; the bags had no doubt once held jackstones or marbles, but for a while were put to a more romantic use. The Methodist, and one of the United Presbyterian churches, were built a few years earlier, when we were too little to scramble over unfinished walls, and the Reformed and the other United Presbyterian church just a short while later, when it would have been beneath our dignity to make them a playground. . . . And so I think of them still as new churches. The truly new ones are those of the various fundamentalist sects that have come with the influx of new inhabitants; the only old congregation to have built a "modern" church is the Friends'—on their hill in the south end, beyond the railroad station, where for some reason the Quakers have always lived and had their meetings.

Because I have not for so many years been inside those churches that I was once familiar with, I cannot be sure they have not altered within their four walls, unchanged as they outwardly seem. That the Presbyterian church is different I do know. The bonneted old ladies were gone long ago; the next generation of merchants, doctors, lawyers, and farmers who once made the church I remember has followed to the grave, and their sons, daughters, and grandchildren may or may not be in their pews on Sunday mornings. The honeyed light that slants down through the grisaille falls on few familiar faces among the strange ones. The church is fuller than it ever was in my day; the size of the congregation has doubled, along with the population of the town. The newcomers are as prosperous as were their predecessors; the born United Presbyterians refer to our congregation, with something of their old superior feeling, as the "country-club church." And so in the minority are those members who have for a lifetime loved the old church building, that at a congregational meeting a year or so ago it was voted to build a new one, a modern one, somewhere in the expanding north end of town. All too soon there will be a gas station or a parking lot on that corner of Market Street. The high brick walls and the spires will be gone; the vast auditorium, the cherry pews, the grisaille, the rose window will be only a nostalgic memory in the minds of a few of us.

I have long since forfeited any right to protest. Mine has not been, by and large, a churchgoing generation; it is the younger people who are crowding the pews. Perhaps not much was ever asked of them in the way of belief; perhaps they were never given dogma to learn and accept. (Churches seem, indeed, to have become either social or social-welfare institutions.) Perhaps, on the other hand, too much was asked of us in the way of acceptance, so that when we reached the age of reason and rejected a part of what we had learned, the whole structure fell away. I think that even in my childhood what I thought of as "religion" was purely doctrinal, and not real religion at all. It is true that you tried with more or less constancy to be "good," you said your prayers before you went to bed, you thought of God occasionally at other times than in church. For the most part you read the Scriptures no more emotionally than you read any poetry or history: your attitude toward the Good Book was reverent because of what it was as much as for anything you found in it. In Sunday school there was something in the way the Bible stories were taught that gave them a tone of Aesop: a tale, and a moral. The moral was always true; therefore the tale was true essentially, in the same way that a chapter out of stories of ancient Greece or Rome was true, and you never asked while you were absorbed in it whether things could have happened in just that way. Noah and Abraham, Isaac and Jacob, Joseph and his Pharaoh, Moses, Joshua, Gideon, Saul, David and Jonathan, Absalom and Solomon: you knew them all, as you knew Jason, Cadmus, and Theseus, and Romulus and Remus, Horatius-at-the-bridge, and Cornelia and her jewels. If you believed in Gideon and the trumpets, so did you believe in Ulysses and the Trojan horse. There was the same dark fascination in the story of Medea as in the bloodstained history of the Jewish kingdoms that reached its climax in those chapters which told of Jehu who drove furiously, and of Jezebel who was thrown down to him from her balcony and trampled under his horses' hooves, and whose flesh the dogs did eat.

But your reason was persuaded by the logic of the catechism: the articles of faith you stumbled over even in those days were not set forth there. You assumed they were in the Bible, although you did not know where. They were rather, I suppose, misinterpretations unshakably established by generations of simple, practical, literal minds. Particularly, I was reluctant to contemplate that heaven we were all striving to attain. The teacher asked one Sunday morning what we should be leaving behind when we got there; pleased at the chance to have my doubts cleared away, I shot my hand into the air. I was going to say "books." Fortunately she called on someone else; the correct answer was "sorrow." I blushed at my narrow escape, and withdrew my hand quickly, accepting the necessity to join the conspiracy and pretend that heaven with golden streets and nothing to do but sing would be a happy place.

Instants of truly religious emotion, which I suppose I was not alone in experiencing, would not have been called by that name at all. Few of those sudden and brief apprehensions of the Infinite and the Eternal had anything to do with church. Certain passages read from the pulpit Bible had sometimes this power to sweep the mind out of itself: "The heavens declare the glory of God," "Let not your heart be troubled," "For I am persuaded that neither death nor life. . . ." "Remember now thy Creator. . . ." But most of your breath-taking revelations of that unnameable experience that now, looking back, you might call knowledge of the immanence of God, came out of doors, and were a compound of awe, ecstasy, and terror, when the depths of the summer sky, with a swallow circling almost out of sight in the late dusk, or the brilliance of a winter night, with the stars hanging low and Orion climbing aslant from the east, proved to you, once and forever, infinity and eternity and your own oneness with them—and made you feel, when you jolted back to earth, the burden of separation, and rebellion at having to be a person bound and limited by a name for however many years.

Now, when you are growing old, you go to church—if you go —not out of loyalty to the creed of your forebears, since you have rejected Calvinism (insofar as you can reject it: there still lies deeply buried in your mind, a foundation for all your thinking about dubious battle and certain death, an ineradicable persuasion that all ends are inevitable, and that the future can no more be altered than the past). Nor, certainly, do you go hoping that you may be lifted to exaltation in the old way when you hear from the pulpit, "The heavens declare the glory of God"— for you know that the "vision splendid" has vanished forever, and you are grateful, like the poet, to be able merely to remember what was so fugitive. You go, rather, seeking what would once have seemed not worth the recapture: that peace so profound that it came close to being boredom—that utter and abiding security that you knew when, sitting between your grandmother and mother, you dreamed your dreams undisturbed through Sunday morning after drowsy Sunday morning. The substance of those dreams you have forgotten—"What the mind at home in the spacious circuits of her musing had liberty to propose to herself of highest hope and hardest attempting"—but you do remember how good and how tranquil they left you feeling. Although meditation is still the proper business of church, it is not so easy as it once was to withdraw your attention; it is harder not to hear the sermon. Nevertheless, you find—sometimes—what you have sought: remembering, your mind becomes again innocent and quiet, loving God, the earth and the fullness thereof, while the service goes on from "Praise God from whom all blessings flow" to "Now may grace, mercy and peace . . . be and abide with you, now and forever."

The Depot, built in 1850 by the Little Miami Railroad, was both a station and a hotel. For many years it was the only first-class hotel in Xenia.

The Opera House at the corner of Detroit and Market Streets. The Opera House was originally built in the 1860s to house the town officials: the police station, jail, and offices were on the first floor; a hall with a stage, on the second. In this photograph, the Xenia fire brigade is posing out front.

Circus parade on Detroit Street, 1880s. Detroit and Main Streets marked the center of activity from the town's earliest days.

Funeral procession on Detroit Street, 1886. Eight members of the same family died in the May 12 flood of that year and were honored with a single funeral procession through town. The Opera House stands at the corner opposite the courthouse square.

Xenia's police force in the 1880s.

Citizens National Bank employees posing for a picture. The man seated on the curb is holding a (presumably pet) raccoon.

A. R. Grandall & Co., a dry goods store at the corner of Main and Whiteman. The building is still standing today.

Fickering's, another West Main Street grocery.

Sadler's Grocery on West Main Street. Like other groceries of the day, Sadler's displayed its wares outside in baskets and burlap bags.

A grocery store. Grocers and butchers, many of them children of German immigrants, kept shops south on Detroit and east and west on Main. At the "finest store in town," the grocers "were neat and spruce in navy blue serge or black alpaca jackets and they never never wore aprons."

The Xenia Candy Kitchen on Main Street. This popular confectionery store was owned by a Greek family.

A typical clothing store of the day. The Santmyer family liked to shop at Hutchison and Gibney's, where they would patiently wait to be served by their favorite salesclerk.

The "dinky." This small interurban trolley carried passengers between the courthouse downtown and the Soldiers and Sailors Orphans' Home.

Helen Hooven Santmyer, December 25, 1911. Photo courtesy of
John Williamson.

The Xenia Camp Fire Girls in 1913, the first such group in Greene County. Helen Hooven Santmyer is the fifth girl from the left, and her sister Jane is the fourth from the right.

Detroit Street looking north, 1930s. The Allen Building at the corner of Main Street is at the far left.

An algebra class at Xenia's YMCA summer school program.

A nineteenth-century house on North King Street. Such Victorian houses are noted for their towers, curved verandas, fan windows, and graceful ornamentation.

The Walter Harner Home, built in the 1800s. The house was in the possession of The Greene County Historical Society when it was destroyed in the tornado of 1974.

Eli Millen's "baronial villa" on North King Street at Church. Santmyer is critical of "the heavy Teutonic porch of boulders arched like a Romanesque cloister . . . added by a later owner."

7. *School*

SEPTEMBER was passing, but it seemed like summer still, and we spent the time of twilight on the front porch. I sat on the edge, with my feet planted squarely together on the step below, dreamily watching the street and the neighbors who passed by. I was aware—without turning around to see, without hearing them, for they had little to say at the day's end, only a word now and then—of the presence of Mother and Grandma in their rocking chairs behind me. Before it grew dark, Miss Baker would pass by on the other side of the street, on her way from boarding place to rooming house. I would stiffen, scuff my feet— and perhaps mutter a word or two, for Mother would always re- monstrate gently, saying, "Now you know you like your teacher."

I was never persuaded. Perhaps I "took after" Grandma; she seemed to have disliked all her teachers. I had started to school that fall; years and years that must be spent in the schoolroom lay ahead of me, and I suppose that Mother was touched with misgivings at sight of my sullen brow. She need not have been; I loved school, and Miss Baker was the only teacher I ever hated;

the worst I ever felt for any of the others was a kind of amiable contempt. But only a week or so after I entered the first grade, Miss Baker shook me until I bit my tongue because, mutely but stubbornly, I refused to stand up straight at the word of command. After all these years, I can see her striding up the aisle, brushing meeker children out of her way. The feeling roused in me by the sight of her—even on the other side of the street—made a bond between Grandma and me, and so on those September evenings, while the katydids shrilled, there began the telling of all those stories of her long-ago but unforgotten school days, stories that went on until I was grown—and even Mother was sometimes carried away, and remembered, humorously but fiercely, her year with "Old Anna Galloway."

Grandma had not lived in our town as a child, and so she could not point out to me the scenes of her earliest anecdotes. But she had been sent there to the Female College when she was sixteen, and although the college buildings at the top of Church Street hill were well outside my orbit when I was only six, I grew up to be familiar with them—with what you could see of them, fenced in as they were, and buried in trees. There were still two buildings then, the dormitory and the schoolhouse. The schoolhouse has long since been torn down, and the dormitory turned into an apartment house. Driving past, you are aware only of unbroken shade, a screen of trees before a dark façade, and the sprawling bushes of pink and red roses on the bank that rises from the pavement. It is easy to forget that the one building is still there, not only because it is so withdrawn, so hidden behind low-hanging boughs, but also because now it lies within the verge of the westward-crawling East End, and has been taken over by the colored people. Black children, soft-voiced, in bright clean garments, tumble around each other in the long grass where once upon a time our grandmothers played croquet.

The one-time dormitory looks today exactly like the engraving which survives from the 1860's: austere, rectangular, three tall stories high, with its gable end toward the street, its brick walls broken only by the evenly spaced windows. The wide overhang of the eaves is supported on curved brackets, and above the eaves stand the broad chimneys, five on each side. The first floor windows are some feet from the ground, and the front door in its dark recess is approached by stone steps with iron handrailings. The picture restores the schoolhouse to its place beside the dormitory. The buildings were alike except that the long side of the schoolhouse paralleled the street, and but two chimneys rose above the eaves at either end.

In the engraving there is no sidewalk; a close-picketed white fence guards the lawns within from the horse and buggy in the street; the trees outside this fence are trim saplings, each in its white-picket box. Inside, the trees are larger and more numerous, but only a few—four or five—are taller than the chimneys; they do not shadow and darken the scene in the way it is shadowed today by the same trees grown older. More sun lighted the grass in those days; in this sunshine, in the picture, a few bell-skirted young ladies play croquet, others stroll arm-in-arm on the paths. When I was a child, I regarded those tiny figures with a lively interest, since one of them might have been Grandma.

Grandma's tales of her schooldays were lively enough; it is only now, looking back, that I realize how singularly incapable she was of seeing her youthful self in a humorous light. Her judgments of people and of her own conduct had not changed in fifty years: other girls had played funny pranks—had even done what they shouldn't—but she had had good reasons, which she remembered, for all her own actions. Her teachers were still, in the eyes of a woman of sixty-odd, what they had seemed to a girl of sixteen. Professor Smith, who under the jurisdiction of the Methodist church served the college as president, was a stern taskmaster whom one respected but could not possibly like. Mrs. Smith, who managed the housekeeping and taught history, was regarded with detestation. When Grandma mentioned Mrs. Smith, she made you think of Lowood and Jane Eyre; every story she ever told included the recollection that boarders could have either butter or molasses on their breakfast bread, but not both. This restriction was typical, I suppose, of a niggardliness which sat ill on daughters of middle western pioneers whose tables were abundantly, even lavishly, supplied.

Only one of Grandma's stories, from frequent repetition, sticks in my mind. Measles broke out in the school; she knew that she would catch it, knew also that that was the last place in the world to be sick in. On the fatal evening when she discovered bumps behind her ears and a rash on her chest, she dressed herself in inconspicuous clothes, tied a heavy black veil over her bonnet, and slipped out and away to the depot. She was going home. She was frightened: she had never been on the steamcars alone before, and it was night, and the train was full of rough soldiers on furlough—but she found a corner seat and cowered there, her flushed face hidden behind her veil, and no one so much as spoke to her. She had her measles at home, in comparative comfort, and afterwards returned to school, unrepentant. "Indeed and indeed," Grandma used to say defiantly, as if the memory of ancient scoldings still rankled, "I was not going to be mewed up at school, quarantined for three weeks."

Grandma's friends were Ella and 'Lissa, Phoebe and Jenny—now all long dead and gone, as she has been for forty years. But until fairly recently there were old ladies still living in our town who were not many years behind Grandma at the college; among their mementoes survived old catalogues of the school. In those pages, along with the Claras and Emmas and Sallys are the moss-rose, lace-valentine names which deepen in one's mind that sense of the faraway and long ago, the faintly sentimental, the faintly absurd, that is wakened by the memory of Grandma's tales. Selina, Parmelia, Alida, Alphareta, Vandalia, Calista: hoop-skirts, dimity ruffles, parasols; surely they led their lives on grassy lawns, playing croquet—or, perhaps, bending gracefully over a tombstone beneath a weeping-willow tree, black-bordered handkerchief in hand. There is more than a suggestion of that aspect of Victorianism in the catalogue: in, for example, the address delivered by the secretary of the Alumnae Association at the meeting in June, 1867. In delicious melancholy she dwelt on the thought of the year just passed:

Gleamed with joy and dashed with tears, another year has glided over us. Twelve months more have departed. Where are

they? With the years beyond the flood it has gone—the year—
and with it

> "Many a glorious throng
> Of happy dreams. A mark is on each brow,
> A shadow in each heart."

It came, and ere it passed in its swift course, millions of graves
by the lonely forests, by the shore of river and of ocean, in lonely
country graveyards and in beautiful cemeteries near thronging
cities have been hollowed out, filled and closed. But not one has
been snatched away from our loved band by the icy fingers of
Death. "Over the river the boatman pale" has borne no member
of our sisterhood. We are all, all here, in full life and bliss,
vigorous in youthful energy, with brave hearts ready to meet the
shadowy future, particularly for the right, and knowing that the
great drama of life demands earnest action. We aspire to be
contenders, not dreamers.

> "The Father mild inclined His ear
> And spared us all another year."

For this kind Providence we offer devout and solemn
thanks. . . .

Today our darling Alma Mater, our girlhood's home, wel-
comes back its scattered band, and warm caresses and clasped
hands bring back days of yore. Old associations gather the tints
of distance and on uplifted canvas short memories paint vivid
pictures of bygone days. They are bright, beautiful and very
lovely. These we enjoy and cherish for only one short hour. But
we will not remember that they cannot always endure, nor with
what rapid wings the golden hours fly. We will only think how
far more sweet will be our greeting when we meet, an unbroken
band with the innumerable host gathered in peerless beauty
above, and are permitted to join in the high response of cheru-
bim and seraphim, and that there will be crowns and palms and
robes and mansions for all; "enough for each, enough for all,
enough for every man."

—Sophia E. Wright
Class of 1866

No one could read this high-flown effusion without amusement. Sophia E. Wright was just a year out of school when she

made her address, and you laugh at her a little for being solemn about the "days of youth," and for congratulating her fellows on their survival. But in the Alumnae Roster a shock awaits the forgetful modern mind: in that catalogue, published in the spring of 1868, less than a year later, there stands beside her name one of the not uncommon stars, explained at the foot of the page by the one word: "Dead."

When I first saw that star, my mind stopped at it, as one's mind stops at sight of a familiar name in the newspaper's obituary column. I was curious about this schoolgirl, dead so young; when I went uptown and consulted the cemetery books, I found her record at once: "Sophia Elizabeth Wright; Aged 18. Died of consumption, Jan. 3, 1868." When I saw that, it ceased to seem to me funny that her mind had been full of "millions of graves," that she should have been aware of the clutching "Icy fingers of Death." It was perhaps not remarkable that she should have congratulated an association, no one of whose members could have been over thirty, on its escape from "the boatman pale."

There are too many stars in those margins. Perhaps it is wrong to smile in unbelief at the thought of Parmelia and Calista shut in for long hours over their books. It may have been that they studied too hard—that croquet on the lawn and a diet of bread and butter-or-molasses could not save them. . . . If one could believe that they learned all they were supposed to learn as set forth in the catalogue, then perhaps they were too rigorously confined.

The purpose of the college was to give Young Ladies a thorough English or Classic Education; the course covered one year of preparatory study and three or four years of college: three years if you were content to be an M.E.L., or Mistress of English Literature; four if you aspired to be an M.L.L., or Mistress of Liberal Learning, with Greek and German included in your curriculum. The faculty included three men who were Masters of Arts, three ladies who were Mistresses of Liberal Learning, and three who were Mistresses of English Literature only; the students numbered one hundred and seventy-five.

The college was supported by the Methodist church; therefore the spiritual welfare of the girls was amply provided for. Each student was expected to attend the services of her parents' church on the Sabbath; religious exercises were held at the school morning and evening, and there were besides two meetings a week for prayer and religious conversation. The books of Matthew, Acts, and Hebrews were part of the college course of study, one each year. Above all (judging by the capitals) there was NO VISITING EXPECTED ON THE SABBATH.

The curriculum is outlined specifically and in detail, with the names given of every text used in each of the three terms of each year. The course in mathematics included arithmetic, algebra, plane and solid geometry, and trigonometry. The sciences, although taught without benefit of laboratory, are all there: geography, physiology, botany, chemistry, astronomy, household science, zoology, and geology—only physics is omitted from the list. Philosophy and logic began to be studied in the first year; among the texts are listed Paley's *Evidences of Christianity* and *Natural Theology* and Butler's *Analogy:* familiar titles of books you are astonished to discover were once not only read, but studied. In the languages the orthodox classics were translated: Xenophon's *Anabasis* and *Memorabilia;* Caesar, Cicero, Vergil, Horace and Livy; Fénelon, Racine; Schiller's *Joan of Arc* and *William Tell.* Weakest in representation were history and English: perhaps it was taken for granted in America in the mid-nineteenth century, as it was for so much longer in England, that an educated person would acquire without direction a knowledge of history and a familiarity with the literature written in his own tongue. Students might add to their course of study, if they so desired and could pay extra for them, lessons in Music and the Use of Instruments, or in Drawing, Crayoning, Water Colors, and Oil Painting.

Except for the extras, there was no election among these subjects; the course was prescribed for those who aspired to degrees. It seems like a heavy load to be carried by the Victorian miss as we have imagined her, but I have done enough teaching to know that a college catalogue's description of courses offered is the expression of an ideal to be aimed at, but seldom attained in practice. I wish that my grandmother's textbooks had survived; they might give one a clue—but apparently her distaste for school prevented her adding them, in spite of a saving habit and an enormous attic, to the other relics of her girlhood which were stored away.

In the end, one can only judge a system of education by its results. Grandma and the two girls who followed her at school and into my grandfather's family—they married two of his brothers and thereby became in time my great-aunts—may have been exceptionally frivolous for their day and age; certainly when I was a child they never impressed me as being learned, or intellectual. More representative of the Female College, perhaps, was that group of elderly ladies who were distinctly, in an elegant, white-gloved way, Blue Stockings, and who, through the Woman's Club, the D.A.R., and the library board, spoke as the town's authorities in all matters literary, artistic, and historical. When on the Thursday afternoons of your childhood, the Woman's Club assembled at a house in your neighborhood, you suspended your rowdy games while carriages stopped at the curb; you watched with something like awe until they were all indoors; and then you withdrew to a remote back yard, lest the rude breath of another world disturb the delicate air they breathed. Years later, when you were admitted to the Woman's Club, you remembered that awe with derision, and, fortified by your own B.A., were prepared to be amused by the group of those once Olympian figures that had survived. But you never could be, quite. They accepted all Victorian writers, up to and including William Dean Howells, without question; although they read widely and tried to be open-minded, they could not wholeheartedly approve of very much of what had been written since. In their essays and book reviews they used the critical adjectives which rang sentimentally false in our ears—yet they knew Shakespeare, Racine and Molière, Schiller and Lessing, Wordsworth and Browning better than the later generations knew them, and, whether because of their schooling, or their birth and background, or the number of their years, they had keener wits, more ironic, more detached, and more fastidious, than the women who were their daughters and granddaughters.

The Female College persisted, although progressively less flourishing, until 1887, when it was merged by the Methodist church in a larger and sounder institution. By that time the public high school had so developed that the college lost all local support, but in the transition period, in the late 1870's when Mother was a child, the failing institution shared its classrooms with an elementary private day school. The tone of Mother's memories suggests that only a lingering genteel tradition, making a last stubborn stand in the face of Irish and German immigration, could have enabled this day school to survive as long as it did.

Mother was not like Grandma in justifying as an adult her early misdemeanors—no doubt, too, she was naughtier. It rather shocked her, as a grown woman, to look back, and she never told us anything of her school days until we had passed the age when we might excuse our behavior by reference to them. The photographs which she preserved show little boys with fair curls, plaid kilts, roundabouts with wide white collars; little girls with high buttoned boots, pantalettes, full skirts and pinafores, and flowing hair held back by round combs. Boys and girls alike are solemn, wide-eyed, innocent—but Mother's tales belied the ingenuous appearance that she, her brother and sister, and her playmates affected before the camera.

The school was conducted by a widow who no doubt appealed to the town's compassion; she was kin to leading citizens, and as learned as a lady could be, but either her griefs had broken her spirit or she was a cynic, indifferent to her duty to her patrons. The children decided for themselves at who knows what precocious age, or deduced from the whispers of their elders, that she took drugs. She sat at her desk nodding, until her hair slipped out of its net and down her shoulders; she taught—after a fashion—between nods. One by one, boy and girl would slip into the aisle, and on hands and knees would scuttle to the door and out; by mid-morning there would be no more than half a dozen pupils in their seats; the others would be out playing beneath the trees.

How this could have gone on as long as it did, or what final revelation or catastrophe put an end to it, I never learned, but Mother must have been eleven or twelve at the time. The private school was the closest she ever came to the Female College, except that, as she fondly remembered to the end of her days, she was a great pet of the grown-up boarding pupils. She had an uncle, Grandpa's still unmarried youngest brother, who was one of the town beaux, and on his account the girls enticed her to their rooms, fed her with candy, entrusted her with missives and with oral messages, and gave themselves away completely.

The history of education in our town, before Mother's day and after, is like that of other towns of comparable age and location. The first schools were "subscription schools" that "kept" for a term of three months. The schoolmasters were any men who happened along through the winter. The first schoolhouse was built of logs, in 1805; it had a dirt floor; the next one, also of logs, had a puncheon floor and was therefore comparatively luxurious. These log schoolhouses were furnished with seats of hewn planks, and desks made by driving pegs in the wall and laying slabs across them. Windows were covered with greased paper; the fireplace filled a third of the length of the wall—fuel in those days could be had for the cutting.

Until 1838, these subscription schools and the various "academies," physically like them but better taught and more expensive, were all that the town could offer its children. In that year the first board of education was organized, and the free school system initiated. But no history of the town, however eulogistic, pretends that the schools were good before the days of Professor Ormsby. In the sixties and seventies that fierce, cranky little man set up rigorous standards for teacher and pupil, and saw to it that they were met. The academies declined and died because a classical education could be acquired free under his supervision. The day school in the college building attended by Mother's generation was the last to surrender; when it did, the young barbarians who had gone there were tested, sorted, graded, and popped into the proper class of the grammar school.

Anyone with pedagogic sympathies must shudder away from the thought of that invasion of orderly schoolrooms. From Mother's vigorous recollections of "Old Anna Galloway," however, one must conclude that her teacher was equal to the assignment. Whether Mother's respect for the public school was genuine, inspired by the violent and doubtless salutary change, or whether it was assumed, from a parental desire to set an example, at any rate we used always to be assured emphatically that in *her* day, you had to *work*.

That year when she entered Miss Anna Galloway's sixth grade was the year when the original "Central" grammar and high school was building, and so she attended the old West Street schoolhouse. West Street, in the beginning the boundary of the town, had later become the line beyond which the West End grew and spread. The parochial school was not a block from the little brick two-room public school. West Street in that neighborhood was not pleasant for little girls who disliked sticks and stones flying through the air: I know because I too began my education in that same old building, and the same old hostilities were being carried on between Catholic and Protestant small fry. When I was six, the McKinley school was under construction, replacing an older building, and the board had again opened up for use what must have been one of the first brick schoolhouses in the town.

For two years I went there, learned to read and write and add, and began a twelve years' association with some forty boys and girls: came and went with them, played with them at recesstime on the triangle of pebbles behind the school. We played singing games: "London Bridge," "Farmer in the Dell," "Round the Mulberry Bush," "Go in and out the Window," and another lost game that was mysteriously forbidden to us of which I recall only a fragment of the chorus, "Water, water, wine cup. . . ."

Often, listening to Grandma's stories, while my own days were passing so slowly and were so unexciting, I wondered how she could remember all that had happened to her in school—why it had not been blotted out by the important years of her life, especially since those important years were themselves so far in the past, when after the Civil War she had married a soldier, and had borne her children. But now I know that remembering is easy: your school days are never longer ago than yesterday, and the dullest adult could fill a book with anecdotes. Not that there is anything out of the ordinary about your most vivid recollections: any of your contemporaries could remember the same or similar experiences.

There was the third grade, when you first went to the new McKinley school and to a young teacher of whose inexperience you took advantage. Whether the picture you still see is of one day or of day-after-day you can't be sure now, but it is ineradicable: a noisy roomful of children in motion, where chalk, erasers, spitballs, and wet sponges filled the air, and where there was running in the aisles with splashing inkwells held like baseballs. Because they were so appropriate-sounding, you remember the names borne by the two most irrepressibly mischievous: a plump little girl and a plumper little boy. Dickens might have chosen just such suitably plump-sounding names as theirs: Nina Puckett and Mahlon Womble. (Mahlon disappeared early from the scene, but Nina was still with us through the first year of high school: I remember trading with her: Latin exercises for algebra problems.) From that room you went on to the fourth grade and a mad-tempered woman who, at the least hint of disturbance, without a pause for investigation, chose always the same victims for punishment: strode down the aisle and beat them where they sat—thrashed her long switches about their heads and across their shoulders until the wood broke, and bits and pieces flew in every direction. She subdued us properly, and we passed to the fifth grade docile but acquainted with injustice.

In the fifth grade you learned geography, *learned* it, so that all these years later you can singsong the states and their capitals in exactly the rhythm you adopted for "now you will repeat in concert. . . ." (Post-Dewey teachers may hold up their hands in horror, if they like: that firmly lodged bit of knowledge has many a time proved useful.) In the fifth grade you had your first bobsled ride and your first kiss. The boy, I suppose, acted rather out of respect for the conventions than from any real emotion; he had not even waited until he got properly sat down, so that when you smacked him he lost his balance and went tumbling aft, over the tailboard of the sleigh bed into a drift. And the Valentine's Day of that year is the only one you remember for a particular incident, though Valentine's Day was always a high spot of the year. On every February fourteenth there was a crepe-paper-covered box in the schoolroom, from which the big envelopes were distributed twice, at noon and in the afternoon. To have your name called many times—to have your desk heaped high—was necessary to your happiness, yet you were sensitive, too, to the hurt of those who were left out. Except as the heart responded to some extraordinary proof of devotion in elaborate and expensive lace paper and embossed cupids, Valentine's Day was not, for children, a season of romantic love; it was rather a time when you were moved by affection for all your schoolmates. And that is why you remember the fifth grade, and Lena. She had been in our room only a short time: her Russian parents had started her in the parochial school, but because she was Orthodox, not Roman, Catholic, the sisters had been unfriendly or had been considered so, and she had been transferred to our school. When the box was opened on that particular Valentine's Day, she sat with frozen face, not looking at anyone, her hands clasped tight at the edge of the desk. I was thankful to the bottom of my heart that I had thought of Lena in time: mine was the only valentine she received, but one was enough to save her from shame. I had not been so noble as to make the gesture anonymously, and I was a little surprised that Lena hadn't waited in the cloak hall to thank me. Instead she had run off ahead of us all. But that afternoon there was a penny heart in the box for me from "your friend Lena"—and when school was out she stopped me. When I had said "thank you," she explained in tears and broken English: she was ashamed because she hadn't had a valentine in the box for me in the morning—but her father hadn't understood about valentines, and wouldn't let her spend any pennies. When she went home with the heart I had given her, so beautiful—then her father had been so pleased, so thankful, that right away he had given her a penny and told her to run uptown on her way back to school and buy one. I thanked her again, and told her I would keep it always, and I was near to tears myself, it seemed so sad that anyone should be pleased to the point of weeping by just one paper valentine.

We began the sixth grade with Miss Harper. Even now I find myself baffled, trying to explain her, and our feeling for her. In appearance she was the cartoonist's schoolteacher: bony, ungraceful, gray in tone—clothes, skin, tight-knotted hair, the eyes behind her glasses. Her eyes were very large, purely gray, serene, untroubled: the only redeeming feature of a homely, weak-chinned face. And she was prim, too, and narrow: when we came to France in the big geography, she asked what Paris was most famous for—someone ventured, "It's the most beautiful city in the world"; her eyes widened, and she said sternly, "It's the wickedest city in the world." She set such rigorous standards for us that we were almost afraid to take our report cards home. Yet we loved her with passion, with an adoration which withheld nothing. We would have died for her. We did tiptoe for her, and refrained from whispering, and from turning to look over our shoulders. Once we whispered when she left the room, and then suffered an agony of shame when she returned and looked at us reproachfully, and we had to watch the slow blood climb into her face until even her ears were red, while she told us quietly how disappointed in us she was. After the holidays she was transferred to another building; we walked in one morning to find her place at the desk taken by a stranger: a young woman, slim, almost pretty, with a great crown of honey-colored hair. We were stunned, outraged, heartbroken. I tried to put my emotions into writing, to make up a story that would express my loss: "On that sad morning the beloved gray head was gone from behind the desk, and a golden head was bent above it instead." I went no further than that, for I saw that it would never do; no one reading it would be convinced of a grief arising from the substitution of a coroneted golden head for a tight-bunned gray one. But for some reason, the attempt made me feel better. And presently we had all melted toward the new teacher. We forgot about being our better selves, and a more natural atmosphere prevailed in the room, with the normal amount of hair-pulling, whispering, and note-passing. . . . As I grew older and knew Miss Harper better, I wondered a little, even while I liked her warmly, and recognized her goodness. If she had been a Catholic instead of a Presbyterian, she would have been a nun certainly, and perhaps a saint—and there may always be something a little morbid, a little unwholesome, in the influence of saintliness.

There were at any rate no more saints in store for us. We plagued the seventh-grade teacher by ways known to twelve-year-olds, until she sent us to the superintendent's office. In the eighth grade while Miss Clark was absent for a long while, nursing a dying father, we were bad as could be, driving out one substitute after another in tears and despair. The girls were split by a most terrific feud. All but one or two pacifists took sides, and we spent the recess periods hurling invective and insult. "Our side" organized a club whose only activity was wearing on our bosoms blue ribbons initialed in white: J.F.S.C.—the Just for Spite Club. One of the neutrals pleaded to be allowed to join; we took her in, but we did not wholly trust her, and made up an innocuous title to fit the letters. When Miss Clark returned to school, she listened from the window through just one recess, and then called us in, and attempted to get to the bottom of the trouble. One of the grievances the other side held against us was our "secret society," with its mysterious initials. Miss Clark looked sternly from one beribboned bosom to another—and settled on the neutral. "Margaret, what do the letters stand for?" And Margaret answered blandly, self-righteously—and in all innocence— "Jolly Friends' Sewing Club." Our escape was so narrow that all other feelings were swallowed up in relief, and we were quite willing to obey Miss Clark's command, and be reconciled.

All these incidents, whatever the calendar says, happened not a great while ago. They are clear in the mind, with no blurred edges. It is only when you begin to think what school was like day in and day out, when you get the feel of it in your bones again, and smell chalk dust and unwashed winter woollens, that you know the weight of the years that have passed. When we were children, in the West Street building and in the new McKinley school down on Market Street, there had not been much essential change since Mother's day. We learned to write on slates; we were supplied with sponges and water and rags that we put to various uses, the most innocent of which was filling the pencil groove with water, in the spring, and laying it full of white violets. Later we progressed to inkwells set in the desk tops, where flies drowned in warm weather, and you angled for them with your pen. We learned the same things Mother had learned: arithmetic, geography, grammar, and history, and we studied them in textbooks. We read aloud, in turn, from McGuffey's readers, and we had spelling matches, using the word lists in McGuffey's eclectic spellers. We sat beside and behind children from the notorious "Flats" on Main Street, as Mother had done, and ran the same risk of catching ringworm or impetigo or worse.

We went to school by the same streets, from the same house, and saw high above our heads the same board fences that shut from view possibly glamorous backyards. When you were tall enough to see over those fences, you were grown-up. In the winter you walked with your face lifted to the falling snow, and learned that although the flakes might be white, against the sky they looked like soot coming down; in the spring your eyes searched the ground, and you discovered that the poplar catkins dropped first, and then the maple flowers.

Every year ended with an Exhibit, on the last day of school. All winter long the teacher preserved the best paintings, maps, and copybooks; during the last weeks especial efforts were put forth: poems were carefully written into booklets; relief maps were molded of salt paste; arithmetic problems of extraordinary difficulty were copied neatly in ink. Finally all these evidences of skill, knowledge, and talent were pasted on great sheets of green cardboard that were fastened up around the walls, covering the blackboards.

On Exhibit afternoon you wore your best summer dress to school, and so did everyone else, including the teacher. On her desk were bowls of pink roses, and the boys all had yellow ones in their buttonholes. The windows were open, the warm, sweet-scented wind scurried down the aisles, and the full-blown roses at its touch dropped their petals on the desk, on the floor. At two o'clock guests began to arrive, come to see the Exhibit. You were all supposed to act as hosts or hostesses in your own room, but the boys mostly escaped, and each girl hovered over whatever of her own handiwork was the apple of her eye, waiting for her parents, hoping meanwhile to overhear words of praise. Sometimes my father got away from the mill early for School Exhibit; Mother always came. As I stood beside her, looking over my works, the stubbornly retained ideal images faded from my mind, and I could see how the paints were smeared, how the writing ran downhill, how the erasures showed on my arithmetic papers. "It isn't my best," I always insisted to her, to the end believing imagined perfection within my power of accomplishment—the next time. At any rate, my pleasure in the day was never spoiled. I led Mother around the walls to see my friends' work, and went with her to the other rooms. Every parent said nice things to every other parent, to every other parent's children, and particularly to every teacher. Through every west window the sun shone; it was June and the beginning of vacation, and next year you would be a good step further along toward being grown-up at last.

While Professor Cox lived, the schools could not change very much: "Daddy" Cox, high school principal in Mother's day, school superintendent in ours, driving his meek little brown mare from building to building, the light ramshackle buggy tip-tilted to one side by his weight, the tilt exaggerated by the foot swinging down, outside, over the buggy's step. He was a great, burly, bearded old man: I remember him best in spring, in the end-of-school, yellow-rose days, with his Panama hat and his black alpaca jacket. He was a noisy old man, too, who made crude sounds, hawking and snorting, and bellowing from deep inside his chest the moment he stepped inside the building. No matter how deep you were in fractions, no matter how many halls and closed doors lay between, you could hear him, on the instant. You should have been afraid of him, but if your mother had been his pupil you weren't, because he always began what should have been a painful interview with: "See here, now, Susy—what's your name?—I knew your mother when she had long curls"—and his eyes would twinkle and your knees cease trembling.

I can hardly believe that Mother wore long curls when she was in high school, but perhaps she did; it was there she first knew Professor Cox. It was in high school, particularly, that in her day students "really worked": Latin and mathematics; Professors MacMillan and Cox; astronomy, chemistry; history and Miss McCracken. But since certain textbooks survived on our attic shelves whose blank spaces were full of doggerel, and whose pictured Apollos and Venuses were bearded, mustached, and supplied with pipes smoking like volcanoes, I have always been a little skeptical of that earnestness we used to hear about.

The years when those dog-eared books were new, and a strapped burden on youthful shoulders, were the years when commencement programs included a valedictory, and a Latin as well as an English salutatory—when commencement exercises were held on sunny June mornings in the Opera House, and stately young ladies in white ruffled frocks and white ruffled hats, with long-stemmed roses lying across white-gloved arms, stepped from their carriages at the Opera House curb. Programs of those commencements turn up, now and then, in odd boxes of mementoes, or tucked away in old photograph albums. In their pages, Parmelia and Alphareta have given way to Estella and Grace and Maude—and these are not just names, usually, but people you knew, Mother's friends. Appalling to a modern mind is the length of those exercises, with all their duets and solos, and all their essays: "Effort the Price of Success," "Cobwebs," "The Mind of a Portrait Painter," "Unheard Melodies," "Gathered Fragments," "Whispers from History."

When we were children, commencements were still like that: slim, wide-hatted girls with roses coming down tree-shaded streets, while we watched with awe and wondered if our turn would ever come. (It did. It really did, eventually. And except that the exercises were by that time held in the evening, so that the girls went hatless, they were much the same as they had always been: the long white dresses, the elbow-length white gloves, the roses; the Orations: "The Scotch Bard," "Climb Though the Path Be Rugged," "Power of Initiative," "Woman's Right to Suffrage," interspersed with music—Boys' Quartet, Piano Solo, Girls' Quartet, Violin Solo. And finally the Awarding of Diplomas. The president of the school board in those days was a wispy insignificant-looking little man, who was actually far from insignificant: he was a hidebound Methodist who never yielded an inch; so long as he ruled, there was no dancing at any school function. The long-anticipated top social event of the school year was the reception given by the juniors for the seniors, just before commencement; for junior girls it meant the first real evening dress, first long white kid gloves, first corsage. It was perforce a banquet, held at whichever local restaurant gave the juniors the best terms—a long-drawn-out banquet, with toastmaster, toasts (drunk in water) and music. Why those of us who had been dancing all year at private parties should have found the Junior Reception an exhilarating experience I do not know, unless it was that so many of us had an unwonted chance to exhibit in our toasts a scintillating wit and a profound wisdom.)

By the time we entered its doors as freshmen, the high school had a timeless, been-there-forever air. It stood deep behind an iron fence in a yard that ran from Market Street through to Church and almost the length of the block. Two gates were open on a kind of W of brick path, with oblique lines meeting at the school steps and straight lines cutting back across the grass, beneath the trees, to the playground. (The playground for the children still in the grades; in spite of its name, only the third floor of the building and part of the second were occupied by the high school.) In each of the two front corners of the schoolyard, outside the walks, stood square, tapering sandstone columns each stone marked with the year of a graduating class. These columns were weather-stained and green with lichens, and a tangle of grass and vines was thick about their bases. The year of Mother's graduation was a date on one of the lowest stones, but in spite of a child's exaggeration of parental age, the high school seemed more venerable as a building than did Mother as a person.

It was venerable, and not unimpressive. The years of its building must have been years when brick was cheap indeed. Its first story was high above the ground; its walls rose past three floors to an attic with dormer windows and a high-pitched roof. The Market Street façade was broken by a square central tower that contained the entrance door and vestibule at the top of white stone steps, and above the door, on the second floor, the superintendent's office, and on the third, the school library. The tower soared high above the roof with an empty room at the attic level, and a bell in the steeple.

The years of my life spent in that building are but a very small proportion of the whole, yet I think that I could build it up again brick by brick, and that I should know the sound of the bell that has been silent now for forty years and more. When we were in high school that bell rang for five whole minutes before the tardy gong sounded; if we clanged our gate shut behind us on its first note, we could reach school in those five minutes—hurrying. My feet could follow that path if I were blindfolded: slantwise across our street to midway of the next block, half a block to Detroit Street and across it (the "wrong side" of the street was quicker), two blocks of dodging and twisting around people, past shop and saloon and livery-stable doors to the bank corner, catty-cornered across Main Street to the courthouse fountain, and around the courthouse square. However desperate the necessity, no one ever cut across the grass in the square; besides, in going round it, you dropped to a walk, both because of the pain in your side and because of the reassuring closeness of the sound of the bell. Then, when you reached Market Street, you were able to run again—in one last long diagonal to the gate. There were still the brick path, two steep staircases, and a wide hall ahead of you, but you could slide into your seat before the bell stopped ringing—especially since the janitor of those years never sounded the tardy gong until the last echo of feet pounding up those stairs had died away into silence.

Inside the building there was as much space wasted as there was in use: ceilings were high, and interminable flights of stairs led one panting past the grammar grades to the high school. On each floor there was a barnlike hall, vast, dark, echoing, empty, and perfectly useless. Classrooms surrounded the halls. On the third floor, the study hall stretched two-thirds of the way across the front of the building, behind the little cubbyhole of a library in the tower. The long room ended at a platform surrounded by blackboards, with a tall clock hanging on the front wall. On the platform were crowded a desk, revolving bookcases, and a grand piano. The principal "supervised" the study hall at the same time that he heard his algebra classes on the front benches. Algebra problems were worked on the blackboard (more or less honestly) behind the screen of grand piano and bookcase. The principal was a dapper little man with a fringe of gray hair, watery blue eyes, and a crisp, grizzled mustache, who moved about the building in an agile, high-stepping sprint. If, being scolded, you looked him in the eye, he assumed you were unrepentant, but if you looked at his vest buttons and wiggled a little, he thought you were ashamed, and let you off easily. He paid very little attention to the study hall behind his algebra benches. It was usually quiet, because chronic disturbers of the peace counted on his not missing them if they were not there. On one historic occasion his eye was caught by whole rows of empty seats; he called the roll of those who should have been present, and discovered that some forty of his students had wandered off downtown for ice-cream sodas.

You could play tricks in the laboratory, too, where the desks were in double rows, to make room for the tables along the sides; if you were alert, you could find a seat whose mate was empty, and slide back and forth out of whichever row was at that moment being harassed by questions. By the time my class was working in the laboratory, the walls of that north wing were none too stable, and if the boys began jigging their knees and feet up and down, in concerted time, beneath their desks, the windows would rattle and all the bottles knock against each other. A new teacher would look startled, even frightened, while the quake grew in intensity, until the boys themselves would be scared into stopping.

There were not many new teachers: with the same school board year after year, and the same superintendent as long as he lived, we also sat, for the most part, under the same men and women who had taught our uncles and aunts and cousins—or had at least gone to school with them—and had been teaching ever since. Few indeed were the liberties we took under their eyes: they held us close to "the sum of the squares" and "the quality of mercy is not strained." We were held close to the English poets: to

> Look how the floor of heaven
> Is thick inlaid with patines of bright gold

and

> When I consider how my light is spent

and

> Virtue can see to do what Virtue would
> By her own radiant light, though sun and moon
> Were in the flat sea sunk.

Every line of poetry learned has not only its own intrinsic meaning, but is also ringed about by the light, by the voices, of the hour of its learning. No one could count for how many in our town certain beautiful fragments of Milton and Shakespeare rebuild on an immortal foundation the southwest corner of the old high school, and restore to it the gallant, gay, and witty romanticist who was its presiding genius for more than forty years. Of all the classrooms, that was the only one furnished with separate, movable, cane-seated chairs—it was the only one that could have been so furnished—and there, at least, the boys behaved like gentlemen, simply because gentlemanliness was taken for granted. The desk was lined with books, and had generally flowers on it; there were revolving bookcases, full to overflowing, and pictures on the walls: Stratford and Kenilworth and Windermere. On Friday afternoons we stood in turn beside that desk, under those pictures, and entertained the class with monologue or recitation, or in groups presented scenes from Shakespeare: the boys in stewpans for helmets and sheets for togas murdered Caesar and fought at Philippi. I question whether many of those boys would confess today to a love of literature—that is a difficult admission for the masculine midwesterner—but I feel sure that not one of them would deny that he enjoyed while he was reading it whatever he read in that classroom.

Although I think that I learned a lot in those four years, and although I know that I filled dozens of notebooks, yet fixed in my memory are all the views from those third-floor windows, as though I had done little but look out of them. East and south from the study hall you looked into treetops: in the spring and fall you saw foliage in the sunshine; in the winter, bare wet gleaming branches and an intricate filagree of twigs against a leaden sky. Household chimneys and a few soot-streaked roofs were above the level of the window sills. In the library you could sit close to the windows, or even on the sill, and then the whole scene came within reach of your eyes: the steps below, the brick paths, the flagpole, which swung a little, its chain brushing against it with a lazy metallic clink . . . clank . . . , the gates, Market Street and its houses; and beyond the roofs, the courthouse tower, where the clock, if there were clouds behind it, seemed to be swooping across the sky.

Perched on that window sill again in your memory, you see with something of surprise what you had for many years forgotten: the row of horses and buggies fastened to the hitching bars along the Market Street curb. High-school students who came from the farms beyond the city limits either roomed in town with aunt, cousin, or family friend for five days a week, or drove a horse and buggy all the way to school every morning, leaving a patient animal tied for the day to that hitching rack. By that time there were many automobiles in the county—we had got past the need to justify such a possession on the grounds of necessity, as once the doctors had done, and the real estate dealers and insurance agents. But few families got rid of their horses and buggies, surreys and carriages, just because they had acquired other but still unreliable means of transportation. Young people did not drive the automobiles—they would not have dreamed of such a privilege—but the horses were there for the use of those who were willing to hitch and unhitch them. So our rides were taken two by two in a buggy, or a cutter in the winter, tucked under a buffalo robe; or four by four in a surrey or a sleigh; or by the dozen in a bobsled drawn by a team of farm horses in late winter when the maple sap was running and a farmer's son or daughter entertained the class at a sugar camp deep in the snowy woods on a moonlit winter night.

Even more tantalizing than the view of Market Street from the school library was the outlook toward the north, from the windows of the Latin room. All of your class studied Latin, beginning in the September when you were fourteen with *amo, amas, amat,* and concluding, in the June when you were eighteen and you had read Aeneas' journey to the end, with "Ancora de prora iacitur; stant litore puppes"—"The anchor is cast from the prow; the ships stand by the shore." To the north of that room in those days there was little but open country. The sleepy whistle of a quail on a warm afternoon became inseparably associated with "Forsan et haec olim meminisse iuvabit." Passing from the class, your book under your arm, you stopped at the window to search the horizon. You were higher than the tops of the playground trees, and over them and beyond Church Street you could see fields and pastures stretching away to the distance, one gentle slope beyond another, whence came in June the scent of clover—acre after acre of wheat or rye or barley, which were green as emerald in April and then grew tall, so that the wind blowing over them sent light and shade in waves to break against a fence. You looked, and longed to be out and away, whether just to cross those fields to the nearest woods, where violets and wild phlox grew—or whether to cross the horizon, and never came back, forever and ever.

Time is so long-enduring whose hours are mostly dreaming of

the future that those years of looking at the horizon seem as many as all the others since—but they passed, and were over, and we scattered. Before I was home from college the school bell was silenced: the vibration of its ringing might bring the tower crashing down through the roof. The air above our treetops was quieter at eight-thirty than at any other time of day, or seemed so, and it was a miracle that anyone could get to school on time. Then the whole third floor of the building was condemned, and the lower grades were moved into a barnlike temporary structure on the playground to make room for the high school on the second floor.

Then, finally, the new high school was built. For a while afterwards the old one was left standing, a hollow shell with no glass in its lower windows, its tower an invitation to disaster. It has been gone now for a long time, and we are used to the town parking lot where it used to be. The "new" high school, across Church Street in what was once the Robertses' front yard, between villa and fence, is so like all the other high schools of that decade in a thousand American towns that there was no necessity for the words cut into its lintel: it is long and low, yellow pressed brick where it isn't window, with a flat roof and stone battlements. That thirty-odd-year-old building is the junior high school now, and filled so near to the bursting point that a second one is to be built next year. The newest high school is a vast complex of modernistic buildings behind the library, where once upon a time the town's cows were pastured. And it, too, is overflowing; there are many, many times the number of students there used to be, and more every year, along with new teachers and new methods.

But just as in our day, at any hour there seem to be as many high-school pupils downtown as could be left for any of the study halls. Perhaps they are busy about their various "projects" —or perhaps they are on the way to the drugstore. They are as merry as we ever were; they are taller and stronger and handsomer, but I cherish an elderly conviction that manners, discipline, and intellectual standards have deteriorated. Students are more cosmopolitan and sophisticated: country fields have been pushed back from their windows. And if by chance they do hear the quail calling, spring or autumn, they are not at the time studying Latin. But perhaps, since learning has been made a painless process, there would be no point to their getting by heart, as we had to do, "Forsan et haec olim . . ."—"Perhaps even these things will one day be pleasing to remember."

8. The Library

COURTHOUSE, HIGH SCHOOL, AND CARNEGIE LIBRARY: in any middle western country town these are buildings impossible not to recognize; particularly, all Carnegie libraries are so alike that one's memories hardly seem associated with an individual set of yellow-brick walls, white stone trim, and granite steps. One might have sat on any one of a hundred parapets to strap on a pair of roller skates: whatever town one drives through, past whatever library, at the sight of an unknown anonymous child bent over a skate buckle, one remembers rough stone through a summer dress, the sun on one's back, the pull of skates on shoe soles, and accepts as identical one's own and all others' experiences. The soul of one architect, although guilty of aesthetic sins, has achieved a certain measure of immortality.

Yet, however ineradicable and long-enduring the memories associated with it, the Carnegie library in our town is still, to me, the new library. Innumerable were the times when I left a pair of skates behind the pillar by the door and slipped through the screen with no inch to spare, so that the dog couldn't get in (Miss McElwain didn't like dogs)—so innumerable that my fingers can imagine the handle of the summertime screen and the big brass knob of winter's oak door. When I am away from home for a while, I see the library as it was in those days, when I was eleven or twelve: raw, with naked foundations, coarse grass scarcely covering yellow clay, a few thin saplings set out along the path, a thin line of new privet hedge against the sidewalk. And all the while I know that the foundations have long been buried in shrubbery, that the hedges, shoulder high, have become impenetrably thick, and that the trees are full grown. One of these trees was a tall maple so covered in the spring with clusters of seeds as to look like a pale green waterfall; it was a beautiful tree and one that helped to make the spring. Home again, I see with blank surprise and shock that the tree has been cut down: no matter how little you feel your age, you cannot deny it when a tall tree has died that you saw planted as a sapling. And sometime in the fifty years that passed after they were planted, the hedges grew so wide in the sunny corner and so thin and scraggly in the shade that they too had to be chopped down and rooted out. . . . And Miss McElwain has been gone for a score or more of years. Now, like the buildings housing other institutions, the library is sadly inadequate; it is so cramped and overcrowded that there is scarcely room for patrons between the overflowing shelves of books; it is time and past time for it to be replaced by something larger and—one hopes—more beautiful.

It would be easier to accept as fact the passage of all these years if it were not so easy to remember what the north side of Church Street was like before the library was built. In all its length there was only the Roberts Villa, buried in trees behind its iron fence, hardly to be discerned between tall grass and low-hanging maples, and—far up, on the top of the hill—the empty buildings of the Female College and two or three houses built in the corner of what had been the college grounds. Between the end of the villa's iron fence and the slope of the hill, there was a lane with a barred wooden gate, then a wire fence, and behind the fence, grass in the spring and weeds in August. The lane led to the pastures rented by townspeople who kept cows; where it was not overgrown with grass it was marked deep, in dust or mud, with the prints of hooves and bare feet. The boys who drove the cows home for milking and back again swung open the wide gate to the lane, but going that way for a walk you went over the gate: it was easier. The lane took you to rolling pasture land, which you crossed keeping a wary eye on the crest of the hill lest a cow appear too suddenly; you waded through a wheat field and came eventually to a creek, with a two-board bridge across it; beyond the bridge you followed the creek bank for a mile or so to the woods. That was a favorite walk in the spring, for there were spring beauties in the pasture, marsh marigolds along the creek, wild phlox in the woods, and violets everywhere. You seldom went that way in summer: there wasn't a tree in the length of it, except a few clumps of thorn and locust, and willow scrub along the creek: in the summer there was nothing at all to take you up Church Street and down the lane, past and through Queen Anne's lace and bergamot, dog fennel and tansy. You let it bake, deserted, in the merciless sun—and yet, not having gone there in dog-fennel days, still you can remember how it smelled, harsh and acrid. And because you can remember the lane, the footprints in the dust, and the pastures beyond the fence, the library seems new. Let a cellar be dug and foundations laid where your feet have been free to wander, and the walls that go up there may stand for a lifetime without ever seeming really old.

And then, the years of one's early childhood are so long that they cannot be measured on any calendar: if I was eleven or twelve when the Carnegie library was built, then I had already, for a lifetime, been using the old library, up on Greene Street.

I can still remember the moment of discovering that I could read. The realization came with all the suddenness of a thunderclap when there has been no lightning. It had nothing to do with school. I was in the first grade; no doubt I had been struggling for weeks, with other six-year-olds, through primer and first reader, but I think that I could not have looked at any other printed words with the hope of recognizing them. The hour of revelation came at home, in the kitchen at suppertime, and the book was a "liberry book."

I always asked Mother, when she went to the library, to bring me *The Snow Baby* that I might hear it read once more. I cannot, now, account for its fascination: since the hour when I returned it to the library for the last time, I have not felt the slightest interest in Eskimos or the Arctic. But *The Snow Baby* I loved; that evening in the kitchen my tall aunt leaned against the table and read it to me, while I sat cross-legged at her feet. When she put the book down and turned to help with the dinner, I picked it up and opened it. I could find the place where she had left off. I could even go on. I could read for myself.

Never again, after that, did I have *The Snow Baby* read to me, or any other book. The pleasure of seeing words on a page was incomparably greater than the pleasure of hearing them read. When the page was before you, then came the capacity for losing yourself utterly, for becoming one with the story's person, and with that person being baffled, then enlightened, suffering, rejoicing, weeping. When you outgrew that phase and could read half-objectively, even then, with the page before you, you would see the heroine moving through your own familiar house: you would imagine rooms larger or smaller, richer or poorer, but still the stairs went up in the same place, doors opened in the same walls, beds stood in the same corners.

Mother let me use her library card: a sacrifice, since in those days the rule was one book to one card, one card to one adult and none to children. Mother let me go to the library whenever I asked. Because it seemed safe, I made the library my first test of independence, and instead of saying "May I?" said at noon, "Mother, I'm going to the library after school." Perhaps she didn't even notice, but I held my breath. The sky held its place; she said "All right."

The library in those days was in the short street that cut off the courthouse square from the block to the east; it was on the second floor of the building just beyond the alley. The stairs that led to it were like those in all our half-dozen uptown blocks:

narrow, rickety, dusty wooden steps, squeezed between two buildings, or boxed in and hanging over an alley. They led to dentists' offices, and lawyers', to photographers' studios and job-printers' shops. The building which had the library upstairs was a big one, with the post office on the ground floor, and a milliner's shop, and the Woman's Exchange; the library was in a rear corner room just inside the stair door; the corridor went on past it to the offices of a lawyer, and a printer's shop. I don't remember that I ever went past the library door, but the lawyer and the printer had their names in large letters on the front windows, so that you could read them if you walked on the courthouse side of the street.

So long as the library was there, in that room, it hardly changed from what it had been in its beginnings, in the 1870's, when a library card cost a dollar, and the ladies who had organized the Association took the desk in turns, two afternoons a week and Saturday evening. Miss Bontecue, one of the ladies, was the niece of old Eli Millen and the housekeeper of his baronial mansion down on the corner of Church Street and King. She had procured for the library the use of the room in the Millen Building, there across from the courthouse square, where it stayed long after Eli Millen was dead and his estate divided, and Miss Bontecue too was gone and forgotten except as a name.

One of the old catalogues of books in the library archives includes on its title page the names of the ladies who, in 1882, made up the Board of Managers: Miss Clara Allen, Miss Elouisa King, Miss Elizabeth Ewing, Miss Anna McCracken, Miss Sallie McDowell, Miss Isadora King, Miss Belle Gatch, Miss Emma King. I read that list of names with a mixture of emotions: respect and admiration, compassion, amusement and amazement. The amazement is first, and is due to the fact that I knew them —most of them—so well. In 1882, they were all old maids, in their late thirties or early forties; they were some of them school-mates of my grandmother, her age or a little younger—yet thirty, forty, fifty years after that catalogue was printed, all but three of them were still leading the intellectual activities of the town, and of the three, two had moved away, and only one had died. In other ways than in longevity that was an unusual group of women: had they grown up a few decades later, they would have gone out into the world in pursuit of careers; born when they were, they perforce devoted their energies to what they could put their hands to in the town—the library, the Woman's Club, the D.A.R., and the causes of Temperance and the Foreign Mission Field.

Of them all, Miss Sallie McDowell alone is a name to me and nothing more. But she was so outstanding a figure in the childhood of my mother's generation that the name came alive for me. "Damascus" McDowell she was called, because—daughter of a missionary family—she was born in the Middle East; I connect her in my mind, perhaps for no reason, with bonnet and shawl and a straw basket full of tracts. Miss McDowell was the only one of the ladies to whom the library was second in importance to the mission field.

I cannot remember that I ever saw Miss Elouisa King in the flesh, but she was a person in my mind from my earliest childhood, never just a name. After having been accepted for years as one of the town's old maids, she married and went to a neighboring county seat to live, but she was still, and to the end of her days, a friend whom Grandma's memory kept lively. As "Ella King" she appears in Grandma's diary: they were classmates at the Female College, and summer visitors in each other's towns. One particular visit of Grandma at Ella's house, after their graduation, is recorded in minute-by-minute detail. Grandpa had been honorably discharged from the army in the spring of 1864, physically unfit; his family lived in our town, where Grandma had gone to school and where Ella lived. Grandpa doesn't sound so awfully sick, in the diary: there were picnics, fairs, band concerts, Sunday-evening calls. In the February following, Ella returned the visit and was bridesmaid at Grandma's wedding. We have a daguerreotype of Ella King among our old photographs: tiny and dark, with sleek hair and black eyes like saucers—composed and grave—there is nothing in the picture to suggest the fire of life that was in her.

Perhaps I should hardly claim to have known Miss Lizzie

Ewing: she too had been gone from town a good many years before she died. She made her escape in the one way open to spinsters with money: she traveled and lived abroad, coming and going as she pleased. But she did at least return for visits, and I remember her from my childhood. She was the niece of the old ladies who lived hidden and secret lives in the villa— old ladies whom I never saw but pictured as trembling crones, because Miss Lizzie, after all, was Grandma's age or near it, and her aunts must therefore have been old beyond belief. In her sixties, Miss Lizzie's hair was still red, she was still slender and graceful. I can almost—not quite—see her again on the villa driveway: red hair, a parasol, ruffled skirts caught up in gloved hand. The last time she was in town—thirty years ago, perhaps —her hair was still rather sandy than gray, and although her white skin was waxen and crumpled, and her hands shook, her green eyes were still alive and quizzical.

The rest of the ladies were living here up to within the last thirty years. Miss Emma and Miss Issie King, Ella's younger sisters, stayed on in their father's big house in its big yard up on Main Street. Richer than anyone else in town, in their old age interested in the D.A.R. to the exclusion of all else, the Misses King grew so retiring and aloof that few outside that organization could claim to know them well. They appeared together— and, after Miss Issie died, Miss Emma appeared alone—at important functions; but toward the end they had few if any intimate friends. The town was for a long while chiefly interested in their cars, for only in their cars were they seen in our streets. First, long ago, they had a little electric which they themselves drove until the day it took them over the curb, up the bank steps and down again, with Miss Emma helpless at the steering bar but unflustered and stately as so small a woman could be. After that they got a larger car, and a chauffeur—and year after year still larger cars, none of them ever with so much as a scratch to mar its polish. Miss Emma was almost blind toward the end of her life, and her last automobile was a spectacular limousine, painted one-half sky-blue, one-half cobalt, so that she could find it at the curb when she came out of a shop. Poor Miss Emma!

She lived on alone for years in her big square pillared mansion, at the far end of a lawn whose every blade of grass was in place, behind an iron fence which barred from the street all consciousness of what was beyond it. She lived there blind and dependent on a retired schoolteacher hired by the day to read her books aloud to her, and on her niece and her niece's husband, who came back to town and bought a house across the street from The Kingdom to be close at hand when needed.

Miss Clara Allen, born at another time or into another kind of family, would have been an actress; the only outlet afforded her by circumstance for her lively sense of fun, her wit, and her gift of mimicry was the parlor dramatics of the Woman's Club. Her other energies were devoted to her family, to looking after the property that belonged to her, her sister, her sister's children, grandchild, great-grandchildren. An indomitable little figure until she died, well past ninety, Miss Allen went about her affairs in the town, and her plain, comical, friendly face gave pleasure to everyone who saw it. She was almost stone-deaf, but if that deprived her of any of the pleasure of living, no one knew it; it was hard to remember how old she was, so that when she died—quickly, without a struggle, as the very old do—it was a shock that colored the whole winter for those who had known her.

Miss McCracken was another who toward the end of her life found only in the Woman's Club any chance to live what she really was; daughter, sister and aunt of scholars, she was born to be a scholar herself. She was one of the earliest graduates of Oberlin, but the field open to her for use of her knowledge was limited, in Mother's day, to the town high school; in my childhood, to the Presbyterian Sunday School; and for all the days of her life, to the library and the club. Her interest was rather in ideas than in people—particularly young people—and she never made a competent teacher; she was scrupulously honest and not in the least conciliatory; she thought of what she was saying, not of whom she was saying it to. She was at her best and most characteristic at Woman's Club meetings, where she sat in the circle of ladies in some prim twilit parlor; she might nod, with closed eyes; she might even snore, gently—but she never missed a word of whatever essay was being read, and never failed to startle its author by enlightening, ironic, or contemptuous criticism spoken sometimes with her eyes still closed, as if nothing she had heard made it worthwhile to open them. Miss McCracken cared nothing, when she was old and poor and lived alone, for what people might think: she wore, year in and year out, grotesque hats above straggling white hair, and rusty black silk dresses, or mohair skirts short enough to reveal high laced shoes and thick stockings that slumped in wrinkles above them. Everyone in town knew Miss McCracken; no one was bothered by the stockings.

Miss Gatch, as alone in her old age as Miss McCracken, and poorer—desperately poor—had yet grown up in the genteel tradition in a well-to-do family, not in an atmosphere of scholarly contempt for appearances, and to the end of her days, however wild her eye or unkempt her mass of white hair, she contrived to look well dressed, even elegant, in an old-fashioned way. For twenty-five years or more, I suppose, she hadn't quite all to eat that she needed; it is small wonder that long before she died she crossed the line between "queer" and "cracked." For Miss Gatch I feel now, looking back, not only compassion, but remorse; I knew her well, once upon a time, as children know their neighbors. It is fatal for a lone spinster or widow to antagonize the children who live round about her, for they will bedevil such an enemy almost out of her wits. Miss Gatch would not let us play in her barn, or cut our initials in her quince tree; worst of all, she made afternoon calls at suppertime. We used to suspend our games when she came out of her gate until we could see where she was going; then someone would groan "There she goes, and Mom'll be sure to ask her to supper." In our innocence it never occurred to us that poor Miss Gatch might be just plain hungry: we supposed that her dropping in at mealtime was a device for getting us placed before her helpless, with clean hands and party manners, while by pretended playful remarks to us, she contrived to let our parents know what we had been up to. But we retaliated. Miss Gatch had once been a

Methodist, but she had taken up spiritualism: she had acquired a reputation for "hearing things," which meant that everyone thought she heard nothing, except in her mind. Everyone was wrong: we saw to it that she had real voices to hear. In her barn loft once we overdid it, groaning so lustily, with such watery gurgles, that not even she could believe that it was spirits. Fortunately we decamped when we saw her scuttling up her brick path, petticoats snatched up to her knees, for she sent for the police to come get the drunken or dying tramp in her barn. The barn was empty when they arrived, and they went away shaking their heads.

Miss Gatch communed with the dead, and was as impractical a soul as ever lived, vague and inattentive. A friend gave her some seeds one time which she planted; later she called the neighbors in to tell her what she had grown in the flower bed along the side fence: the foliage was so feathery and pretty—it looked so familiar—but wasn't it strange there were no blooms on such healthy plants? What she had was a fine flourishing row of carrots. But in spite of her helplessness somehow she contrived to live to extreme old age without starving to death. Her relations with those of us who had been her sworn enemies were more cordial after we grew up, but I suppose that none of us was ever really able to like her. It is for that not liking her that now I am remorseful, because I know that it was Miss Gatch who did most, who worked the hardest, to get the library established. It was she who, in the seventies and eighties, stood most frequently behind the library desk and took care of its patrons; Mother said, and so did others who remembered: "Yes, they took turns, but usually it was Miss Belle Gatch."

In those days, books were kept in locked cases. One either looked them over through the glass doors, or ran a gloved finger down the pages of the catalogue kept at the desk. It was only when a choice had been made that the case was unlocked and the book taken down.

Several of the old catalogues survive. It would be easier to study them objectively if one had never known the ladies responsible: collectively, their amateur standing as librarians; individually, their characters, predilections, and backgrounds. One suspects that the book lists, particularly the first of them, reflect the taste and intellectual standards of the ladies rather than of the reading public. The oldest, a little pamphlet not more than three inches by five, is dated 1875; in it the books are divided into categories: History, Biography, Travel, Fiction, Religion and Theology, Law and the Congressional Record, Literature and Miscellany. But in each classification there is sequence without reason; one can only assume that the easiest method was followed, and that the books were listed and numbered in the order of their acquisition. Numbers 1 and 2 are Blake's *Pictorial History of the Great Rebellion;* 3 is Robertson's *History of the Middle Ages;* 4 and 5, Whitelaw Reid's *Ohio in the War.* That many of the books were discards from paternal libraries, or contributions from interested citizens, is indicated by the possession of volumes three to seven of Hume's *History of England,* twelve to fifteen of Bissett's, and two and ten only, of Smollett's.

Comment, principally humorous, might be made on the hodgepodge of titles under Religion, and the even stranger collection under Literature and Miscellany, which includes in its four-hundred-odd titles Parton's *Smoking and Chewing, The Boys' Book of Battles, Green on Gambling,* Combe's *Phrenology,* a *Treatise on Cattle, Fifteen Years Among the Mormons* by Mary V. Smith, and others of like heterogeneous nature, scattered through the Irving, Thoreau, and Emerson, the De Quincey and Carlyle, that represent Literature. But most conducive to speculation is the catalogue of fiction. At first glance all the standard authors seem to be there ("all" once the admission has been made that of course fiction began for spinsters of the 1870's with the proprieties of Jane Austen and Sir Walter Scott). Dickens, Thackeray, George Eliot, Charlotte Brontë, Mrs. Gaskell, Mrs. Mulock, Kingsley, Reade, Irving, Hawthorne: these were all titles to be included in any self-respecting library, whether the ladies bought them with their first subscription money, or were given them. Perhaps it was because our grandfathers could not yet spare them from their own shelves, perhaps because the ladies' own taste did not run to the lurid, that there was not in the library any Cooper, any Bulwer-Lytton, Wilkie Collins, or Disraeli. It is not surprising that in our town in those days there was no demand for Meredith, nor that Hardy, who had just begun to write, was still unknown. But that Howells' two novels published before 1875 were not there is inexplicable: after all, Howells had one time been a reporter for the local paper, and in another decade was to be the town's chief boast. In 1875 he must not have won reputation enough to make him seem a safe investment.

The American fiction in the library included many of those works classified today as forerunners of realism, as well as those now condemned by our sterner critics because they pretended to be realistic and were not: Holmes's *Elsie Venner,* the stories of Mrs. Rebecca Harding Davis and Mrs. Stowe, Bret Harte's *Luck of Roaring Camp,* T. B. Aldrich, and all of Eggleston, from the *History of Metropolisville* to *The Hoosier Schoolmaster.* One can imagine easily the ladies of the Board of Managers buying those particular books; the few sentimental and sensational titles are harder to account for: either they mark a definite concession to public taste or they were given to the library: the works of Mrs. A. D. T. Whitney, Wetherell's *Wide, Wide World* and *Queechy,* and anonymous novels like *Ought We to Visit Her* and *Cast Away in the Cold.* The literary historian might find a suggestion as to what foreign influence was acting on American literature: there is a foreshadowing of future development in the contents of the "Leisure Hour" series: French and German romanticism are represented by translations of Auerbach and Cherbuliez, and Scandinavian and Russian realism by Björnsen and Turgeniev. One who is not a literary historian but is simply interested in the town may wonder whether Miss Allen or Miss Ewing or Miss McCracken was responsible for the purchase of those particular books, and may also wonder how often the Björnson and the Turgeniev were read.

Mixed and mingled in the catalogue, as they presumably were in the bookcases, are adult and juvenile fiction. Children, like grownups, chose their books from the catalogue, or pointed to the desired volume as it stood on its shelf. If children in the 1870's chose their books on the same principle as children of later generations—"Another by the same author, please," pointing to the next work in the case—they must have encountered some surprises and disappointments: suppose, because you liked *The Wonder Book*, you decided to try *Twice-Told Tales*. . . . In the whole list there are very few titles that are obviously juvenile. Louisa Alcott is there, of course, and *Robinson Crusoe*, *Tom Brown at Rugby* and *at Oxford*, and what must have been the earliest example of that abomination of the modern children's librarian—the series: four books on various activities of the boys of Elm Island. But perhaps the paucity of children's stories, and their being mingled with adult fiction, was not altogether a bad thing. For maximum enjoyment, certain novels require to be read at an age when the power to suspend disbelief has not been weakened by experience, when it is still possible to have faith in perfect nobility and in total depravity—and when the capacity for being troubled by a high-flown style has not yet been developed. Some of those novels were in our library in 1875, for children to happen upon: *John Halifax, Gentleman; Jane Eyre; Scottish Chiefs;* and *Thaddeus of Warsaw*.

The second catalogue, printed in 1882, is more elaborate in its format; it is much larger, and has a green cover decorated with minute engravings of birds, dragonflies, and urns full of flowers. On its upper margin is written in red ink, "Please leave on the table"; it is the very catalogue whose pages were turned by Mother and my aunt and grandmother and great-grandmother.

In this catalogue the books in each classification are in alphabetical order according to author, and adult and juvenile collections have been separated, so that it is easier to run the eye over the pages and pass judgment. The fiction, for instance, begins with Alden, Mrs. G. R. (Pansy) and eleven of her works. William Black is on the list with nine titles; Blackmore's *Maid of Sker* is there, but not *Lorna Doone*. Some of the inexplicable gaps of the earlier library have been filled: by 1882, there had been added two Bulwer-Lytton, one Wilkie Collins, seven Cooper, two Disraeli, and three Trollope. The ladies kept up to date in contemporary fiction, with comparatively few concessions—such as the works of "Pansy"—to popular taste, The list includes four of the works of Aldrich, one Cable, three Bret Harte, seven Howells (two copies of *Their Wedding Journey*), six Henry James, Wallace's *Ben Hur* and Hardy's *Return of the Native*. To be sure, there are listed a few books like Tourgee's *Fool's Errand* and *Bricks Without Straw*, but the duplication of the Howells book suggest that it was for the latest work of this author that the ladies then left pennies, as later, when Mother was grown-up, it was for the new novel by F. Marion Crawford, and in my day—indicating either decline in taste or expansion of library service—the most recently published Myrtle Reed or Gene Stratton Porter.

Amazingly, in that catalogue of 1882, there are many titles under Juvenile Fiction that I remember: they were still on the shelves in my childhood. Either so few children used the library then that books could stand the handling of twenty years, or they were so loved that they were replaced when they had fallen apart. Besides the Louisa Alcott, and Mark Twain's *Prince and the Pauper* and *Tom Sawyer*, and Susan Coolidge's "Katy Books," there were "Zigzag Journeys" through various parts of the world—very educational, I suppose, though I recall nothing of them but a description of the Lisbon earthquake that frightened me nearly out of my wits, even while it enthralled me with its horrors. There were also those books about the Bodleys—*on Wheels,* and in various places—which seem to me, looking back on them, to have contained the essence of New England; there were the boys' books by Coffin which could stir the thinnest blood: *The Boys of '76, Old Times in the Colonies,* and *The Boys of '61;* and there were books bought for little girls, which little girls loved: *Hans Brinker,* Mrs. Ewing's *Six to Sixteen,* E. S. Phelps's stories about Gipsy Breynton. But with these exceptions, the juvenile titles are strange to me: a fact not to be recorded without a sigh of regret, as over a lost opportunity, for surely it was the best books that were so read to pieces that they had to be discarded.

There is a supplement sewed into the back cover of the

catalogue: there were added to the library four novels by Crawford, the complete works of Cooper in twenty-five volumes, three more William Black, two more Cable, another Hardy, another James, another Howells, and Blackmore's *Lorna Doone*. Again the only concession to what the ladies must have considered low tastes are in the five new Pansies, and *Hot Plowshares* and *Figs and Thistles* by Tourgée. The new juveniles were mostly informative, but *Huckleberry Finn* is there, Mr. *Stubbs's Brother*, Dodge's *Donald and Dorothy*, Yonge's *Daisy Chain*, and a new *Bodley*.

Between 1882 and 1900, the date on the third surviving catalogue, Miss McElwain became the town librarian. Fresh out of high school, a girl of seventeen or eighteen, she was hired by the ladies to take their places and stand behind the desk those three times a week when the library was open. Behind that particular desk she stood for twenty years, and for another thirty behind the new desk in the Carnegie library; so, in the mind of the town, person and institution came to be one. But I am sure, knowing them, that so long as the library was the ladies', and not the town's, tax-supported, they and not Miss McElwain bought the books. In fact, the first boards appointed by the town were composed largely of the same ladies, and they continued to add books that Miss McElwain kept hidden in drawers, and handed out on demand unwillingly or not at all.

With this guardianship of our morals in mind, one glances over the fiction in the 1900 supplementary catalogue and wonders how much of it Miss McElwain could pass over the counter without misgivings: it includes, in addition to the popular novels of the nineties, three volumes of Balzac, two of Hall Caine, Crane's *Red Badge of Courage*, Dumas' *Three Musketeers*, Ford's *Honorable Peter Stirling* as well as *Janice Meredith*, two Gissing, two Hardy, Herrick's *Gospel of Freedom*, five Howells, two Henry James, four Kipling, one de Maupassant and one Meredith, one George Sand, two Sardou, and one Südermann. Altogether it is a mixed bag, bought with eyes in all directions: the popular historical novels for romantic women and children and lazy men; the sentimental and religious tales for those good church people who could not read fiction with a clear conscience unless it had a moral; and the realism for those equal to sterner stuff—the blue stockings of the Woman's Club, the schoolteachers, the more earnest young college graduates.

That this catalogue is only supplementary, containing the books added between 1895 and 1900, helps to explain why there are not more names in it that I remember. It was not long after this that I became one of the most devoted patrons of the library, but in this list of titles are only a few that are familiar: some that I didn't like, and couldn't read, unorthodox as my tastes were: *The Princess and Curdie, The Water Babies, Tom Brown at Rugby.* McGuffey's *Fifth Reader* was responsible for my distaste for *Tom Brown:* one of the prose selections included was the incident of the little boy saying his prayers in the dormitory. . . . Of all my old favorites there are in the 1900 catalogue only Kipling's *Jungle Book* and nineteen of the immortal works of G. A. Henty.

Remembering the Henty helps one to remember the old library. It was a great rectangular room; windows in the side wall looked down behind and beneath the stairs to the alley below; those at the end offered a view of a jumble of roofs, ending with the sheriff's house and the barred windows of the county jail. In the center of the floor was a railed enclosure and the librarians' desk; two rows of round posts, painted public-institution brown, held up the ceiling, and bookcases—tall walnut bookcases with glass doors—stood against the walls all around the room. The children's books were between the first and second windows on the alley side, towering high overhead: the top shelves were not only out of reach—they were out of sight; however much you suspected that those were the best books, you could only hope that Miss McElwain put up there the ones that no one wanted. By that time the bookcase doors were left unlocked; you could squat on your haunches and wiggle your way along the shelves, taking down a book, sniffing as you opened it. You had certain standards to choose by: a book must not only look read, it must *smell* read; if it had been rebound, with its title written on the spine in Miss McElwain's neat round hand, so much the better. Every page should be twice as thick as new, some should be patched with transparent paper, they should give off a certain grimy scent as of a hundred finger tips. Only the good books were read into such a state.

Behind the railing in the center were Miss McElwain and her assistant. The assistant was golden-haired and slender, young and friendly; Miss McElwain was stoop-shouldered and thin, with sharp hostile eyes behind flashing spectacles, her scant hair twisted in a tight bun on the crown of her head. She regarded children as the natural enemies of books; she was quick-tempered and sharp-tongued, and too often the provoker of tears. Every child who came in was on probation: Miss McElwain was no kinder to me because she had charged out books to my great-grandmother, was still helping my grandmother, had gone to school with my mother and aunt, than she was to the most out-at-elbows little colored boy from the East End. She bought the best books as they were written, and put them on the shelves; then, by her acerbity, she discouraged you from reading them. If you persisted, if you liked books more than you feared her, then she forgave you for being a child, and treated you as impersonally as she treated adult patrons. You discovered before too long that she knew a hundred times more about her wares than the golden-haired assistant, and almost before your chin was higher than the desk, you quit your old timid sidling around the corner to Miss Anita. After a longer or a shorter while you realized that Miss McElwain's sharp black eyes were as quick to see something funny as to see a misdemeanor. Henceforth, although she might—indeed, certainly would— speak to you so impatiently as to start the tears, it no more caused a breaking-off of relations than it would have done had she been your teacher. Best of all—and in the end it was this that counted —if you had any intellectual curiosity, she fed it as completely as she could, with unflagging zeal. Not one of the distinguished men gone out from our town—poet, archeologist, chemist, historian—but got his first help from Miss McElwain, and has been ready to say so.

It was as an object of mirth that I first discovered her sense of humor. My reading tastes were peculiar, and had for a long time been laughed at by my family. I read the same books over and over, just as I always ordered a chocolate soda: what was the sense of running a risk with something new and strange, when you knew you liked chocolate sodas? *Coquo and the King's Children* Miss McElwain charged out to me again and again, with perfect gravity: from her manner I assumed that she hadn't noticed. Then once, Mother was with me: Miss McElwain caught her eye and broke into irrepressible chuckling laughter. I was amazed—not hurt, being hardened by my family's mockery—and I was pleased at the revelation of her common humanity.

Often in the following years she must have laughed at me inwardly as I exhausted the current supply of juveniles, or simply became homesick for the old books, and turned to them again. Alcott and Mark Twain and *Master Skylark* I had for my own, and I could go to bed with them every night if I chose. But the "Katy Books" I had to take from the library, and *Hans Brinker,* and other delectable tales that seem to me now most regrettably lost and out of print: *Coquo and the King's Children, The Counterpane Fairy,* and a story about the Wars of the Roses whose title I have forgotten. It was full of mysterious battles in the mist, besieged castles, and stealings-away in the nighttime on horseback, wrapped in cloaks; and it made me so unshakeable a champion of the Lancastrians' cause that to this day my blood stirs when I read Somerset's cry:

> Let him that is no coward nor no flatterer,
> Pluck a red rose from off this thorn with me.

In truth, except for certain family prejudices early absorbed, in favor of General Sherman and the Union army, the Republican party, and the Presbyterian church, I suppose that most of my ineradicable allegiances come from early reading. All of Joel Chandler Harris, and books like *Six Little Rebels,* however much I enjoyed them, broke vainly against the wall my grandfathers had built, and the Westminster Catechism made me

impervious to the glamor of Mary Queen of Scots and Bonnie
Prince Charlie, even in the pages of Sir Walter Scott. But most
historical tales I could read siding heart and soul with hero or
heroine in their devotion to Boadicea, Queen Elizabeth, Henry
of Navarre, William of Orange, Marie Antoinette. There were
only two of the works of Henty that I read with angry disagree-
ment: *True to the Old Flag* and *With Lee in Virginia;* the
incredible heroics of British youth in other volumes were accepted as read.

Henty was about as far as I had got, I think, while the library
was on Greene Street, before the new one was built. In the
early 1900's, the town granted the library tax support; then the
Carnegie grant was obtained, the land bought, and the new
library put up. At first, until you got used to it, the walk for your
books seemed very long. Perhaps that was because you made it
oftenest in the hot summertime; it was in fact only three blocks
farther than Greene Street, and when you had gone to the
woods that way, you had never counted what lay on the town
side of the pastures as part of your walk.

The library was built in the corner beyond the lane, trees
were planted, and the hedge; and presently grass grew over the
yellow clay that had been turned up all around. In those days
the weeds were never cut on that side of Church Street; the
cement sidewalk that lay outside the villa's iron fence burned
with a white glare; its edges were overgrown with grass gone to
seed; feverfew and ragweed tickled your nose; white butterflies
danced on either hand, and grasshoppers rose at your coming
and hurled themselves blindly away, or on you, or up under
your thin summer dress. You shook them off on the library step.
When you left the library you went home down the other side of
the street; there was shade there, and you could read as you
walked, even with circles and ellipses of light falling through
the trees and dancing, blurry-edged, over your page.

It wasn't immediately that you did go home from the new
library: you were no longer restricted to choosing your book and
going off with it. Here there was a separate room for children:
all the way around its walls, beneath the windows, were open

shelves, none so high as to be above eye level; there were chairs and tables, and on the tables magazines, and an old-fashioned stereopticon with slides. You could stay until suppertime if you liked. If you were torn between two books, you could read one of them there and take the other with you. Lovely long quiet afternoons: it didn't matter that it was hot, that Miss McElwain was being tart with someone out at the desk, or that there were pages gone, here and there, from the book you were reading.

Time, looking back on it, seems to have passed very slowly. You walked home from the library a thousand times, with a book under your arm, until you knew every aspect of the way: the color and shape of trees against the sky in every season, the shine of roofs in wet weather, the murk of smoke in the winter —every curbstone, every gate, every door. Slowly your reading tastes changed, and very mixed they became, too, until you went as often to the stacks as to the children's shelves. The Victorian novelists were all in the bookcases at home, but *Ben Hur* and *Quo Vadis* you found in the library, and read them perhaps in the same month you were reading the newest in "The Little Colonel" series. *The Long Roll, Alice of Old Vincennes:* you reached adult fiction by way of the historical novel and romances like *Graustark.* When you started in high school your brain turned to mush suddenly and for no reason, and you read with shameless avidity *Lavender and Old Lace, The Rosary, Freckles.*

I, for one, shall be eternally grateful to Miss McElwain for seeing me through that phase without ever saying what she must have thought. If you asked her whether a book was good, she might tell you, but she never gave advice unasked; she stamped with indifference *The Mistress of Shenstone, The House of a Thousand Candles.* However, the indifference in itself was damning, because so in contrast to her interest when you wanted to read all you could find about the Hundred Years' War when you had finished *The White Company,* or about the French Revolution when you had read *The Scarlet Pimpernel.* You were shamed by her silence. Then, suddenly, that particular phase was ended when by accident you stumbled on Arnold

Bennett, and his women in kitchen aprons seemed more real than women in old lace.

You had long ago outgrown your old starting fear of Miss McElwain; you had learned to approach the desk with clean hands, to take your skates off outside, and to shut the door on the dog. As you grew up you saw her oftener outside the library, too, and she came to seem more ordinarily human. On Sunday mornings your path crossed hers, coming home from church; in the spring when you rose at dawn and started for the woods before breakfast in order that you might be the first to find violets in bloom, you were likely to meet her crossing the pasture, her field glasses slung by a strap over her shoulders, coming from a bird hunt. Because of that—because you so often saw her slipping along the edge of the cattails in the swamp, or through the alders by the creek bank—you came to assume that she must know all the flowers and grasses and trees as well as the birds, and so you brought to the library desk wilted leaves, stalks, and blossoms, and held a whispered consultation over the litter. She didn't always know the flowers, but at least she knew the books to look in, and found them for you on the shelves.

Time passed, but except for the maple trees which grew up to the roof and over, there was no change in the library. The last of the villa recluses died, the house was empty and its windows boarded up; the new high school was built in front of it, concealing it from Church Street; no one in town kept cows any more, and the pastures were laid out in streets and building lots; the swamp was drained into a lagoon, and became a park. In the library, assistants came and went, and no one noticed them, particularly: Miss McElwain was there. Her fingers and nails curved back at the ends from much running over trays full of cards; her hair grew scantier and wispier, and she oftener looked over her spectacles than through them; her stoop became so pronounced a curvature of the spine that if you hadn't seen it happening you would have believed her born a hunchback. Before you could realize how many years had passed, it was your small nieces that were being brought to tears by her sharpness, when their chins were hardly higher than the desk—and she, ignoring the tears, was assuring you with delight that she was now serving the fifth generation of your family.

But before that the county had voted to take over the library and to establish branches in the townships. That meant more money, a trained librarian, new methods, and new books. Once the change had been made, you could go to the library and find on the shelves the new novels you wanted to read while they were new, and you could take as many of them as you liked, although Miss McElwain, you felt, disapproved, silently but certainly, when you brought an armful of books to the desk. But except that she never grew quite accustomed to new charging methods, and was flustered to the end of her days by a pencil with a rubber date stamp on its end, she took kindly to the new order: so kindly that the town breathed a sigh of relief and settled down to enjoy an improvement that was without a shadow of regret for old days. The new librarian was in the county, mostly, taking books to branches and to schools; in spite of increased staff, Miss McElwain was at the desk most of the time. Instead of assistants, it came to be librarians who changed: they were young and ambitious and too competent to remain as long as we should have liked in so small a place. But Miss McElwain stayed on.

When she had worked in the library for fifty years, the library board unveiled a bronze tablet in the wall, commemorating her time of service. Fifty years, and a party—and perhaps the happiest day of her life. Tea was served in the children's room; there was a receiving line inside the door, where stood the nieces and nephews of the founders of the library, and Miss McElwain, with her hair professionally waved, and two corsages, one above the other, on her shoulder. The poet and the chemist were there; telegrams were read from historian and archeologist. Everyone in town who counted as a library patron was present, making a hubbub in that room where Miss McElwain had allowed no word to be spoken above a whisper. Fifty years—and a party—and the town congratulated itself: for once, at least, appreciation had not waited for a funeral.

For a while after that Miss McElwain stayed on at the

library. But she fell twice, and broke first her wrist, then her collarbone; she fumbled and forgot; she couldn't hear over the telephone, and wouldn't admit it. She was finally persuaded to retire, and spent the winter going to the moving pictures, which was a new experience for her; she looked forward to the spring, when she could spend all day long, every day, watching the birds. And in the spring she died. She was found dead, kneeling on the floor by her rocking chair, and whether she died praying or not was important to the Methodists, but not to the rest of us, who knew she was of the Elect. Scarcely anyone was at the funeral: it might have been concluded that already the town had forgotten her. I think it was not that so much as that losing her altogether was less startling, less important, than losing her from the library. I hope that it meant something to her that the bronze tablet with her name and the dates of her service should be hanging on the wall. That same plaque may some day be of interest to new generations. Those of us who grew up under Miss McElwain's eye do not need it: so long as we use that library, we shall see her little bent brisk figure moving across the marble floor, snapping up the blinds in the reading room, shaking a forefinger at noisy children.

9. The Opera House

Not too long ago, as years are counted in our town, the old Opera House was replaced by a city hall. After a score of years we have ceased to blink, astonished at seeing a sweep of blue sky which had been filled from the beginning of time by a high roof, corner pinnacles, and a tall pointed tower; but the city hall has by no means taken the place of the Opera House in our affections: the ordinary citizen enters its doors only to pay his water bill or his improper-parking fine; everyone who grew up here knew the Opera House intimately and at firsthand.

The new building is low, severe, rectangular; it is built of smooth white stone; around its base are the correct pyramidal and spherical evergreens, and all the untidy maples have been cut down from along the curb. At night it is floodlighted, and looks more like an architect's drawing than a real building should look. Aesthetically, it is better than the Victorian flamboyance of the old Opera House, but in our town, until we grew used to it, it was like a tubular chromium chair in a parlor full of carved rosewood furniture.

Within its walls are luxurious offices for mayor, city commission, and auditor; a model jail, and police headquarters fitted out with the newest scientific gadgets. But there is no stage and no auditorium. The building has begun to accommodate itself to our air; its white walls are darkening in the murk of our winters, and it is accepted as part of a familiar scene. Perhaps, even, when the image of that corner passes across the mind in revery, the city hall is seen there instead of the Opera House. But in our affections the new cannot take the place of the old.

The Opera House, too, had been erected primarily to house the town's officials; in its first form it was completed in the 1860's, shortly after the war. It was a brick building, two stories high, with elaborate round-arched, almost ecclesiastical windows; it had stone trim and a mansard roof in patterns of variegated slate. The four corners were four square towers, topped just above the roof with four finials to a tower. Both Market Street towers had two doors on the ground floor; and across the façade, above the first-floor windows, was a balcony supported on stone brackets, with a stone balustrade. Police station, jail, and offices were on the first floor; and a hall, with a stage, above. The floor of this hall was level and its chairs movable: it served as well or better for dances than for theatricals, lectures, or political rallies.

Nevertheless, the first of our remembered home-talent plays were performed on this stage, perhaps for the benefit of the widows and orphans of the Civil War. Home-town theatricals had always to be justified in our Calvinist town by the words "In Benefit of . . ." writ large in advertisement and printed program. These first plays were war plays: *The Battle of Gettysburg* and *Color Guard*—melodramas full of sound and fury played by our leading citizens. The heroine of *The Battle of Gettysburg* was the daughter of the president of the United Presbyterian Theological Seminary—a defiance of denominational opinion of plays and play-acting which must have caused some raised eyebrows among her father's people.

For something like fifteen years our play-loving town put up with this untheatrical auditorium, and then in the eighties the Opera House was rebuilt. There were halls enough by that time

—those of the various lodges, and those privately owned—to accommodate balls, sociables, and dancing classes; a little later there was the roller-skating rink up on East Third Street for our "carnivals."

I wonder now whether other towns like this one had carnivals of our kind, or whether ours were unique: church or organization projects which involved everyone who was anyone, and some who were not. The rink was a great wooden barn of a place, all waxed floor, with balconies for observers. For a carnival, booths were erected around the sides and across the back, where there was also a platform for the Statue of Liberty to stand on, holding her torch, and signalizing the end of the evening's entertainment, while the band played "The Star-Spangled Banner." There was ample floor space left clear for an intricate Grand March, which would begin with dignity and end as a breathless romp, and for whatever other dances there were, Highland fling or the Maypole; everyone from old to young, from high to low, was in costume and therefore able to throw off whatever inhibitions encrusted him in daily life. Once—and this was before my time, but it was still remembered when I was small—the floor was marked off in black and white squares, with costumed townsfolk ranged on them as chessmen, and my grandfather and one of his chess-playing cronies called the moves from opposite balconies. Once—and this my sister and I both remember, although she was but five and I was seven—the Ladies' Aid of the Presbyterian church had a "Trip Around the World," the well-crowded booths being each a country. My other grandfather, not the home-town one, had been to Japan not long before, and had brought to all the females of his family Japanese kimonos of soft silk, heavily embroidered, and boxes of Japanese hairpins: fascinating trinkets . . . I remember the butterflies set on tiny springs at the ends of the long pins, so that they quivered with every motion. Because of these authentic costumes, Mother was to be the Empress of Japan, and my sister and I were to be (namelessly, so far as the program was concerned) Japanese children. And the day before the first evening of the carnival we both of us came down with the measles. All we saw of the "Trip Around the World" was Mother in her costume, standing at the foot of our bed to show herself: our pretty black-eyed mother, looking fantastically unlike herself with her black hair high in smooth rolls and all the butterflies quivering. . . . The "Carnival of Authors" is the one I best remember: I was all of ten that year, and my name was on the program as a Maypole dancer—one of a multitude. The affair was "gotten up" by the Woman's Auxiliary of the Y.M.C.A. for the benefit of that organization; it is pretty well dated, since among authors like Scott, Dickens, and Schiller (all the Germans in town, second and third generation, young and old, were attached to that booth, made up as characters from Schiller's plays) were Churchill and Ralph Connor: in those days Richard Carvel and the Sky Pilot were as recognizable as Mary Queen of Scots, Wilhelm Tell, and Pickwick. Carnivals went on for three nights, so that everyone would have a chance to go, and everyone went all three nights, not willing to miss the fun of strutting for a few hours in costume. Men particularly seemed to enjoy playing at being someone other than themselves, in powdered wigs and knee breeches, or kilts and plaids, or Civil War uniforms.

That was all a long time ago; the rink is gone and forgotten, and I suppose there has not been a carnival for fifty years. And all this has nothing to do with the Opera House, except as verification of the fact that what the town needed, even as long ago as the 1860's, was not another hall, but a real theater.

When the Opera House was altered in the eighties, it was given an added story. There was still a mansard roof; the corner towers were capped with short peaks, and their doors changed to windows. A wide entrance was opened in the center of the Market Street side; above it the stone balcony was retained, but one great round-arched window replaced two smaller ones, and from the eave over the arch rose a new taller tower crowned with a lightning rod. As before, the roof had a wide overhang, supported on curved brackets like those that held up the balcony.

Stone steps, barred by a locked iron gate, led straight up through the new entrance to a landing, where there was a door on each side and the ticket window ahead. Beyond these doors lay the new theater, with a steeply pitched floor, a railed-off dress circle, an orchestra pit, and a mammoth stage. Over half the auditorium slanted the balcony, supported by iron posts whose imitation capitals were cast-iron acanthus leaves—a regrettable Victorian attempt at Corinthian ornamentation. Above the balcony, climbing right to the roof with its dormer windows, was a steep gallery.

In the center of the proscenium arch, in an oval frame of laurel wreath, was a portrait of Shakespeare, bland of brow, benign of expression. That picture survived to the end, but the drop curtain was forever changing. Sometimes it was painted with a fanciful landscape: trees and a bridge, or a village street; once some local artist reproduced on it the falls of the Little Miami at Clifton, duly labeled. Another time, during some fit of commercial-mindedness, it was made up like a crazy quilt of the names and addresses of local merchants.

Those of us who grew up when the Opera House was the rather shabby scene of local-talent performances find it hard to believe that long ago great actors and famous lecturers stood before those footlights, but surviving programs prove that the proud stories of yesterday's citizens were all true. Whitelaw Reid came home from New York to open it after the remodeling had been completed in 1882, and flattered the town by calling the occasion the proudest moment of his life. And after that Patti came to sing, Joseph Jefferson acted *Rip Van Winkle,* John E. Owens appeared in *Solon Shingle,* and Maggie Mitchell in *Fanchon, the Cricket;* Laurence Barry was Richelieu one time and Uncle Tom another, and Frederick Ward gave us *Richard III.* In the days of the great minstrel shows, Coburn and Billy Emerson brought their troupes to town—long-anticipated annual events.

Long before I can remember, important actors had ceased to include small towns on their road trips. When some extraordinary cause brought a famous company to the Opera House, we looked forward to it for weeks, and talked about it for as long afterwards. Sousa's Band played for us once, maybe more than once.

In the season of its popularity, when I was in high school, a performance of *Bought and Paid For* was given in the Opera House by a New York company that found itself with a free night between city stands. But *Bought and Paid For* seen from our familiar dress-circle seats was shocking to an audience that could have witnessed it without a blush in Cincinnati: those present were a little shamefaced about it afterwards, and did not discuss it much.

When I was a child, the shows that came to the Opera House —and shows of a sort did come, one after another—were not attended by the same townspeople who would go to the city to see Sothern and Marlowe, or Maude Adams in *Peter Pan*. It was mostly burlesque companies that still found it profitable to perform at country opera houses—or the troupes that acted melodramas like *East Lynne* and *Ten Nights in a Barroom*. Of course we were never permitted to go, and could only study the playbills hopelessly, and wonder. On each side of the wide front entrance was a tall billboard where bright placards were pasted up so long ahead of time that before the date arrived they were scarred by the stones hurled at them. Sometimes they pictured grinning blackface minstrels in fantastic garb, hats cocked, canes lifted. Every year as it rolled around brought *Tempest and Sunshine,* and one board would show a blonde angel with sunny curls, and the other a dark beauty, sullen and lowering. Most interesting and most puzzling were the high moments of melodrama as they were portrayed for us. The actors were caught by the artist either at the moment of murderous assault or just afterwards, when a bleeding corpse lay on the ground at the villain's —or the hero's—feet. These were gory pictures, and we believed when we were young enough to have faith that they reproduced in every detail exactly what took place on the stage. "What did they use for blood?" we wanted to know; fortunately for our illusions, we never got inside the doors to discover that there was no blood at all.

Most years more than one *Uncle Tom's Cabin* came to town. Then, one board would show Uncle Tom under the lash, the other Little Eva in the arms of the angels. We studied these pictures under the patronizing tutelage of friends who had seen the play last year and would be allowed to see it again: *Uncle Tom's Cabin* was a classic, and educational. Unhappily, my father did not consider it a classic, but a dreadful falsification, and Mother, having seen the flood of tears that washed my face when I read the account of Uncle Tom's death in the book, believed that I was too impressionable to be exposed to a representation of the scene. Remembering my frustrated longings, it seems to me now that what I wanted most was to satisfy my curiosity as to the mechanics of the play: did bloodhounds actually chase Eliza across the stage, and what were the ice floes made of? Were the angels around little Eva's deathbed suspended on wires, and did they look like flying? And could they really show a soul on its way to heaven? My friends were more than willing to enlighten me on these points. I wanted to satisfy my own curiosity, but no doubt Mother was right: had I gone I should have forgotten, in painful response to the sorrows of others, all that I thought I wanted to know, and cried myself sick.

A performance of *Uncle Tom's Cabin* was preceded by a parade: Topsy (or even more than one Topsy) cakewalked through the dust of our streets; Eliza in a shawl carried her child in such fashion that we could not tell whether or no it was really a baby; Little Eva rode in a pony cart: a Little Eva with dubious yellow curls, in a blue velvet dress with a tawdry gold-lace collar. The parade meant something to me, but not so much as the fact that one of our friends lived on Detroit Street behind the Opera House, just across the alley from the stage entrances. One of these opened on the freight elevator, where battered trunks were taken, and small packing cases. Upstairs was a door like a barn-loft window, with a beam and a pulley above it. When a show came to town, the pulley was rigged with ropes, and stage sets were hoisted up, one by one, after they had been unloaded from the dray which hauled them from the depot. If we went to Ruth's bedroom and hung over her window sill, we could peer in, past the rope, to the mysterious depths of the stage. I cannot remember that we ever saw anything more exciting than stage-hands, but there was always a chance that we might, if we watched long enough—and besides, even sweating, swearing stagehands had a shadow of the glamor inherent in all things related to the theater.

My acquaintance with the inside of the Opera House, from the dress-circle side of the footlights, began with lectures. The lyceum tradition lingered on in our town long after the theatrical one had died. It had declined, of course: early lecturers were Bayard Taylor on "Ancient Egypt," Wendell Phillips on "Lost Arts," Anna Dickinson on "Women's Rights," General Lew Wallace on "Turkey and the Turks," Robert Ingersoll on "The Home," Conwell on "Acres of Diamonds." (It would be interesting to know how our conservative citizenry responded to Anna Dickinson and to Robert Ingersoll, but no one remembers, and there is no record to turn to.) Lecturers were still brought to town in the early 1900's by local organizations hoping to make money, but for the most part they were presidents of nearby colleges speaking on historical subjects that ranged from "Ancient Rome" to "Lincoln the Man"; or they were returned missionary archeologists, with lantern slides of their diggings, to prove that the walls of Jericho had tumbled down, or that Sodom and Gomorrah had been destroyed. Or it was Senator Foraker, there to tell us—without charge—what we already knew: that the Republican party could do no wrong.

And then, every year, Lyman H. Howe came, first with lantern slides and later with moving pictures, to show us the glories and the terrors of the world. I think it must have been Howe who lectured on the eruption of Mount Pelée. On a sunshiny winter afternoon all the school children were marched to the Opera House, two by two, to listen. I could not have been more than eight: the grisly details of what happened on the Island of Martinique, with pictures, are not perfectly suited to a child of that tender age. Even in our safe flat Middle West, with no volcano within several thousand miles, I could not be sure for a long while that the earth would not betray us; I had nightmares for weeks, and have still a clear recollection of all the horrors.

Throughout those years, the Opera House continued to be the scene of political rallies, temperance lectures, band concerts, magicians and hypnotists—and above all, of home-talent shows. For these a professional director was hired; he insured the success of the performance by enlisting always as large a cast as possible, since friends and relations of the actors would feel compelled to buy tickets. It was in the role of friends that my sister and I attended such plays. Other children knew the Opera House backstage long before I did: they were *in* things. My father had strong views on the propriety of a lady's performing in public (or anyone who was going to be a lady, he hoped). When the dancing class was requested to furnish a ballet for some benefit performance, we were left out and forlorn during all the weeks when they were rehearsing the daisy chain or the Indian dance on the Opera House stage. Even worse, we felt conspicuous in our dress-circle seats on the night of the show: how could the rest of the audience, seeing us there, know that we had been asked to perform, and had not been overlooked?

Of course the whole family attended all home-talent productions. *The Mikado,* as sung by the Music Club, was even funnier than Gilbert and Sullivan could have hoped it would be. But the most uproarious occasions were the semiannual Elks' minstrel shows. The end men, famous for a generation, were the roly-poly janitor of the courthouse, and the printer who would have been on the professional stage had not his mother been so strict a Scotch-Irish Presbyterian. He was tall—a six-footer; once, when reciting "Woodman, Spare That Tree," with gestures, he split his black tights at a critical spot; another time he performed a hula dance in long winter underwear and a grass skirt, and his wife, caught unprepared by the spectacle, rose in wrath and departed forthwith. But we hold him in loving remembrance not for incidents like these but for his genuine mirth-provoking talents.

The most important function of the Opera House was to provide a setting for commencements, both white and Negro, and for the senior-class plays. High school seniors, in those days of pompadours, shirtwaists, and long skirts on the girls and of dark suits, high starched shirt collars, and neckties on the boys, seemed completely grown-up, and we watched them with awe year after year as they came and went at the Opera House, nonchalantly clattering up and down the fire escapes. Of all the plays, I remember only *The Cricket on the Hearth* and *The College Widow,* because those years there were seniors whom I knew: neighbors or older sisters of friends. Class plays seemed a trifle less wonderful after we were in high school, and knew the older students all too well . . . until, finally, our own turn came, and then the Class Play—being *in* it—was all we had ever dreamed it would be. And at last I was one of those who knew the Opera House from top gallery to under-the-stage, from the loft window with its pulley to the cubbyhole where the ticket seller stood.

Not that I was altogether lacking in stage experience: there had been Sunday-school entertainments since I could remember; there was the fifth grade's production of *Hiawatha* in the school auditorium, when I was borrowed from the second grade to be the rabbit: I scuttled across the stage on all fours, the audience shouted with laughter, and I could easily have died of humiliation. There were the Friday afternoon Program Meetings of the English classes, and above all there was the Third Street Dramatic Society, which wrote its own plays, or arranged them, and which performed in our back parlor. The membership of the society included all who lived on two blocks of our street and were old enough to speak plainly and do as told, and were not so old as to have jobs in the summer, when the society was active. The audience, who sat in the front parlor, included parents, grandparents, aunts and uncles, and such childless neighbors as could be induced to attend by, we thought, our writing the word "refreshments" conspicuously on the invitations that we sent around.

All these were makeshift devices: they hardly counted at all when measured against the Class Play. We were modest in our aspirations; we chose to give *Little Women;* where the dramatic version was not close enough to the book, we revised it to suit ourselves. Laurie proposed to Amy in a swing, that being the next best thing to a boat that could be put on a stage. The play— our play—included a performance of one of Jo's own tragedies, and a ball at the Laurences', where the Virginia reel was danced—these interpolations being for the purpose of providing every member of the class with a speaking part, however small. We ended with a scene in Plumfield orchard. For days in advance, we wired bits of pink paper to dead branches; when these were set up, we had achieved a creditably realistic imitation of an apple orchard in full bloom. For the March family living room, there were stairs—real stairs, banisters and newel post all complete—which went up against the back wall, with a door at the top, and backstage a platform with a ladder to the floor. That staircase was an achievement: the boys had scoured the town and had finally found one removed from a demolished house, but not yet destroyed. Halfway up was a window where Jo, carrying the dying Beth upstairs, paused for a moment long enough for Beth to ask plaintively whether it was a robin that she heard outside. Unfortunately, on the great night, as the sisters stood listening, the sad question was answered by one of Professor Cox's colossal, roof-shaking sneezes. The audience guffawed, and for Beth, at least, the evening was ruined.

For weeks before June, we lived in the Opera House. We went through the motions of ordinary everyday life during other hours: we ate and slept and even attended our classes, most of them, but except when we were in the Opera House, we were all of a fever to get there. We would go pounding up the front stone steps, slam through the noisy door at their top, and race down the aisles. From the orchestra pit a short flight of steps at the left corner led to the stage; in the right corner, a door so low that you needed to squat to crawl through it opened on other steps which took you down to the property and dressing rooms under the stage. From this dark cavern of a floor another flight of very narrow and precipitous stairs led up to the stage. Because it was so involved, and required so intimate a knowledge of the building, this was a favorite path to the spot where you were supposed to be at "three-thirty sharp." But if you preferred, you could enter by any one of four fire escapes: on the Detroit Street side, to the orchestra or the balcony; in the alley, to the orchestra floor again, or farther back, slanting up past the barred window of the jail, to the stage. If the outside door to the freight elevator was unlocked and the elevator on the ground, you could haul yourself up on it by pulling on the rope; this seldom happened, and never if the teacher who was directing the play was on hand, for when the unwalled elevator was on the ground, it left a gaping six-foot hole in the backstage floor.

Year after year the same teacher directed the class play, yet she preserved not only her sanity, but her kindness and her impartial liking for us all. I marvel at it when I remember not only how interminably many times we repeated every scene, but also how often a cue was missed because an actor was exploring the gallery, or looking out over the town's roof tops from a fire escape, or had gone up the ladder to the platform before the light-control board, or to the top of that other higher ladder to the flies and was walking around the catwalk in those dim cobwebby regions whence you could look far down to the stage below. Even girls not given to exploration were likely to have taken seats somewhere in the dress circle where they could put their heads together and carry on their "he said" and "I said." Or they were paired off with boys in dark corners backstage, where unused flats were piled against the walls.

Not many years after we were out of school the state fire marshal on one of his inspections condemned the Opera House as a trap, but finally compromised with the town by nailing shut the gallery doors. School plays continued to be given there until the new high school with its stage and auditorium was ready. Then for a while the old stage was not used at all. But at about the same time that the fire marshal came again and nailed up the balcony doors, a community little theater was organized and the Opera House came into its own once more. No fee was charged for its use so long as the janitor was paid for heating and cleaning it; the money thus saved could be spent on royalties and costumes. We were not afraid of fire: we knew the building too well, every splintered board, every crooked step, every ragged rope: it would have been like expecting a friend to betray you. By that time it was not thought worthwhile to lock the iron gates across the entrances, or the doors at the top of the steps, or the fire escape doors. Anyone could enter, and anyone did, at all hours of the day or night. When play rehearsals were in progress, everyone on a committee—publicity, or costumes, or properties—felt free to drop in and offer suggestions. Even the janitor leaned on his brush and listened and criticized. When the play was given there were few in the audience who had not seen it, or parts of it, once or a dozen times, but no one stayed away on that account.

The Little Theater was a serious organization; probably better plays had not been better acted in our town since the early days of the Opera House than those that were staged there in the late 1920's and early 30's: *Hay Fever, Dover Road, Craig's Wife;* our one-time end man, who must then have been in his sixties, was as moving in his part in *The Swan* as he had ever been funny as a minstrel. For a role in *East Lynne* someone found for us a superannuated politician (a Democrat of the Bryan school) who lived in the southern part of the county; no one was ever more delighted to have a part in a play, but he could not at first understand that we were making a mockery of the old melodrama; he could not believe we would so desecrate a classic, and when he was finally convinced, he would have no part in it but continued to play his role straight; no old-style Shakespearian actor was ever more orotund and bombastic than he, using for its full effect the rich voice of the high-flying political orator, pulling out all the stops of the organ. The play as given was far funnier than—we hoped—he ever knew; or perhaps the applause that followed his scenes convinced him that he had been right and the rest of us wrong.

For most of us, one of the pleasures of helping with the Little Theater lay in the revived associations with the Opera House. One artist member painted a new drop curtain; others evolved new sets for each play out of the old torn and grimy forest or garden or parlor or street scenes. And always there was a kind of amused affection for the very thing that was being wiped out by a sweep of the paintbrush. That this was so was proved, I think, by the fact that the Little Theater did not survive for long the demolition of the Opera House, in spite of the passion for acting that still stirred the hearts of the printer, the postmaster, various lawyers, stenographers, and clerks, and members of the women's clubs. It is true that the high-school auditorium was not altogether satisfactory in various ways—still, it was partly because being in plays, or helping with them, was so much less fun there than in the Opera House, that interest dwindled until the organization was allowed to die.

Perhaps the Opera House would not even yet have been replaced had not the fire marshal made another final trip and nailed the front doors shut. Quarters on the ground floor—jail, police station, municipal offices—had long been worse than inadequate; they were indecently crowded, shabby, and unsanitary. But they might have been endured a while longer if the Opera House had been usable: even the policemen liked occasionally to take part in a play.

For a long time our young and intelligent police chief had used what modern scientific methods he could, without equipment, but in spite of his endeavors there hung about the old police station a flavor of the days and ways of Chief Smith and Officer Tarbox. Chief Smith was a heavy-set, easygoing man who wore a faded soft hat and a crumpled uniform. In his time there was an awning over the station door and window on Detroit Street, supported by iron posts set in the curb. The chief sat under this awning, his chair tipped back against the wall, feet dangling, arms folded, hat over his eyes, his dog asleep at his feet. Topsy was no trained and effective adjunct to our police force: she was a small curly-haired black dog, friends with everyone who could call her by name. If she justified her existence at all it was by chasing cats away from the police station. Chief Smith, a paternally minded man with eleven boys and girls of his own, was principally valuable to the town as a retriever of lost or runaway children. Officer Tarbox, a thin little man who was almost extinguished by his big gray helmet, played detective to his heart's content, without any manifestation of jealousy on his chief's part—or any encouragement, either, one supposes. If he did not carry a microscope in one pocket and a dark lantern in the other, we thought that he did, and we knew that he swung a truncheon from his wrist. One saw him in back alleys at odd hours, peering around corners—and when George Barr McCutcheon's *Anderson Crow, Detective* was published, the town wondered if its author could possibly know our Mr. Tarbox. The most capable member of the police staff was the immense burly Negro, Officer Simms, who enforced law and order in the East End. He entered into frays that no white man would have dared approach, and brought the offenders to jail. We used to watch on such occasions from some discreet vantage point. The patrol wagon would stop before the station and unload, with an accompaniment of thick and unintelligible cursing. Presently, we would slip down the alley and peer between the flat iron slats that latticed the jail door. The cell was dark: too dark for us to see much except sodden figures huddled in a corner or lying on the bench. By that time maledictions had turned to prayer, groans, and lamentation: shivers ran down our backs as we flattened our noses against the jail door and hearkened to the cries to heaven for mercy on a soul in the depths.

It was freely predicted among us that some day Officer Simms would meet his end at the hands of some vindictive Negro who feared him. He went his way for many years—long after Mr. Tarbox had died, and Chief Smith, and his successor Chief Graham—contemptuous of wrongdoers, by his very bulk inspiring awe where he walked. But in the end, on a dark winter night, he was knifed and left dying in an East End alley, and the town lost one of its incorruptible, fearless, and faithful servants.

Our most amusing crime stories, which center about the police station and the mayor's court in the Opera House, have to do with the troubles of our colored citizens. There was for instance the cold winter night when Jim Towner was shot. The Brackett family, huddling around the red-hot stove in their shack, heard the stealthy footsteps of a prowler on their front porch. One of the sons picked up his rifle and fired what he intended as a warning shot in the direction of the footsteps. But so flimsy was the wall of their shack that the shot took effect. A cry and a fall on the porch frightened the Bracketts more than the footsteps had done; eventually they screwed up their courage to investigate and found Jim Towner dead on their steps. Jim had been out of the penitentiary only a few days; various of his associates had been in and out of prison, too. It was not to be supposed that they would take the slaying lightly, or pass it over. The Brackett boy took off for the police station at a dead run and arrived there, terrified, breathless and panting, before the police knew that anything had happened. He begged to be locked up. After investigation the next day the officers of the law, convinced that the homicide was accidental, would have released him had he not begged and prayed, wept and pleaded, to be kept there safe until his family could make peace with the family of the deceased. That night our local paper carried a message in the Personal Column, expressing the profound regret of the Brackett family for the unfortunate accident, assuring the Towners that they had never felt for them, and particularly for Jim, anything but the warmest affection and friendship. Apparently, this Agony Column apology was accepted: there was no sequel to the shooting.

Not all our laughter has been at the expense of the East End. In the days of Chief Graham the city racketeer came to our town—and departed, his departure leaving us shaken with mirth. He appeared not on business but to see a local girl whom he had met in the city; if, against his own background, she had not recognized him for what he was, she did when he entered her mother's parlor. After some dispute, when he refused to go and leave her in peace, she called the police. Chief Graham himself answered the call; he was a tall, white-haired, white-mustached Irishman, immaculate in his uniform, very martial in his bearing, and in appearance a credit to the town. He drove the police car down to the house on Main Street and invited the offending stranger to get in the back seat and ride up to the station. The stranger entered the car without demur, but the next thing Chief Graham knew, he was driving south out of town as fast as he could drive, with the end of a gun cold against his neck. He drove on for forty-odd miles before he turned off the road and wrecked his car in a field. We were never quite sure whether this was accident or cold resolution, but gave him the benefit of the doubt. The man with the gun took off across the field, and Chief Graham, already red about the ears, sought the nearest telephone.

The last mirth-provoking episode involving our police force occurred in the days of the later capable young chief, but before the new city hall was built. The Garden Club, which worked season in and season out to beautify the park, began to miss shrubs: at sunset a lilac bush or a spirea would be at home on its bank; in the morning there would be only a hole in the ground. The policeman ambushed to catch the thief reported no sight of him, although the disappearances continued. The Garden Club finally, in despair, hired its own watchman, who caught the policeman who had been set to catch the thief. He had just bought a new house, and was improving his grounds.

Nothing like that can ever happen, surely, with a police force acclimated to its new surroundings, which have the atmosphere of a surgery, all white cold science—glittering with apparatus— not subject to human weaknesses. The new jail is spotless, even comfortable, in comparison with the old unsanitary hole, but offenders locked there must feel an implacability in the stone walls that was foreign to the worn mid-century bricks. And I am sure that no children learn at firsthand of the dire consequences of misbehavior by peering between iron slats and listening to blood-curdling moans and groans and curses.

The new building is something to point to with pride, if you are entertaining guests from out of town. On such occasions you do not admit that you are still walking around it as you walk around a handsome new piece of furniture in your house, hardly accustomed enough to it for homely usage. And of course you do not admit that you miss—that you always will miss—the ugly old Victorian Opera House.

10. The Railroad

Trains have always been a part of the daily life of everyone in our town. We boast a distinction shared by no other county seat in the state: down our principal street, past the city building, the courthouse, shops, bank and newspaper office, runs a railroad track. Passenger trains came that way not too long ago. When stopped on a corner as one went by, we looked up indifferently at the faces pressed against coach and Pullman window to peer out curiously at the street scene, its life slowed to a standstill. Giant locomotives pulled those trains. A stranger on Detroit Street who saw for the first time a juggernaut of an engine bearing down on him from beneath the courthouse elms must have felt somewhat as he would if he had met an elephant on a garden path. Now the only accommodation for passengers to and from our neighboring city to the north is a one-car diesel unit known locally as "the doodlebug." But there is still freight traffic, and those long trains are pulled by heavy diesel engines that crawl through town as cautiously as their predecessors did.

This idiosyncrasy, which amuses or annoys us when we think of it, but which is ordinarily forgotten by the accustomed mind, we owe to the cupidity of our forebears. When the first steam roads of the 1830's and 1840's proved their practicability, every little place that could raise the money built a line to the nearest city. Our town, halfway between Columbus and Cincinnati, became the terminus of a road from the state capital, and a stopping point on a line from Cincinnati to Springfield—a junction for travelers who wanted the shortest route from Cincinnati to Columbus. The Little Miami road was chartered in 1836 for commerce "in or near" Springfield and "thence down the valley of the Little Miami River to the city of Cincinnati." Our town was the first of any size south of Springfield; so certain were the citizens of that day that prosperity would dwell in the very shadow of the passing steam engines that a first-class argument as to the route of the Little Miami was settled only by the donation of a lot on the corner of Second and Detroit streets for a station, and it was legend in our time that property owners on the courthouse side of the street paid a bonus to have the tracks laid closer to their gutter than to the gutter over the way—a particular advantage to John Hivling, whose hotel, bank, and store lined the block between Main and Second streets.

When the first train passed through, the folk who assembled to cheer for progress were so in awe of their own creation that they stood not in front of the station nor anywhere on Detroit Street, but up on Main Street in front of the courthouse, half a block away from the line: they were not at all sure the engine would not fly off the track, or explode and blow them to destruction. Yet in those days, when cars were stagecoaches built to run on rails, and engines had smokestacks like the kitchen stovepipe topped with a funnel, there was nothing so very outlandish in the sight of a train in the heart of the town. A modern engine, however slowly and cautiously it proceeds, shakes the walls of buildings along the way, and rattles their windows; in the days of the steam locomotives the lower branches of the courthouse elms tossed frantically in the blasts from the squat smokestack.

The railroad to Columbus was built in 1850, and it was then that our town became the stopover point for travelers who wanted to go northeast or southwest across the state. Those were proud days for us, those few years when Daytonians who wanted to "take the cars" had first to come here by stagecoach in order to catch a train. Old letters of Dayton legislators prove how great an improvement even that trip was: in the decade before the rails were laid to the capital, they wrote their wives of their safe arrival at the Neil House, deposited there by the stagecoach after a night-long ride in zero weather, bundled in overcoat and lap robe: a trip that must have been almost pure torture, even when made, as once noted, in the agreeable company of Governor Tom Corwin "and his lady." In the fifties their letters describe the short preliminary ride to our town by stage, the night spent either at the hotel where the coach stopped, uptown, or at the "depot" hotel—and then the morning trip by train to Columbus.

In the same year that the Little Miami's "uptown" station was finished, another, "large and convenient," was built on the south edge of the town, at the junction of the two roads. The lines became one in practice, and trains ran through from Cincinnati to Columbus without transferring passengers at the junction. Inevitably, as time passed and the early short one-town-to-the-next railroads were amalgamated, our two lines were linked to a larger system (the P.C.C. and St. L., familiarly known in our childhood as "the Panhandle") which in its turn was taken over by the Pennsylvania. The stations and tracks of our original lines were leased "in perpetuity" by that railroad, and became part of its main line. (Descendants of those citizens who subscribed to stock in the Little Miami road in the 1830's, in order to help secure its construction, have reason to be grateful to them: so long as the Pennsylvania exists as a corporation and runs its trains, it must pay for the lease of the Little Miami, which in turn continues to distribute dividends to its stockholders as unfailingly as it has done for well over a hundred years.) But the Little Miami, which in the beginning had been ambitious of reaching Lake Erie on the north, never built its tracks beyond Springfield; hence that line declined to branch status, used only to bring here such passengers as wanted to make connections in our station with one of the many Pennsylvania trains going south, east, or west.

Had that Detroit Street track been a part of the main line we should have found it intolerable long ago. Now there is so little traffic on it that we are almost surprised ourselves when we are reminded by the sight of a freight train crawling down Detroit Street that the right of way is still there. And since the Opera House is gone, the one train that we always considered an unmitigated nuisance would no longer be so—even if it still ran. That train puffed and snorted and rang its way through town about nine o'clock in the evening, and since the walls of the Opera House were not more than twenty or thirty feet from the track, many an actor from the days of Joseph Jefferson on was brought up short in the middle of his most dramatic scene, stunned by the noise and his inability to make himself heard. When we were young, the building was old and decrepit, its walls shaken as by an earthquake when a train passed, and nothing spoken on the stage during that interval could be audible beyond the footlights. Fortunately in its last years, when the Opera House was used almost exclusively for home-talent performances, rehearsals enabled the cast to provide for those moments—to fit the time of the train's passing as neatly as possible into the drama, so that the necessary full stop need not come at the most tense or the most passionate climax of the play.

The railroad was always as considerate as possible of the town's feelings. Every engineer leaned scowling and watchful from his cab window as he crept down the street; if in spite of the incessant clangor of his bell, a parked automobile stood athwart the tracks—as sometimes happened on a busy Saturday night—he stopped his train and rang insistently until its owner woke up and came and rescued it. When we were children we knew all the engineers. We laid crossed pins on the track when we saw a train coming, and picked them up afterwards, flattened into the semblance of a minute pair of scissors, or we played a game of standing as close as we dared to a freight train, touching every car as it passed. Once upon a time, when the New York Central line north of us was washed out by a flood, that road borrowed the Pennsylvania tracks. The first New York Central engineer to use them drove his train fifty miles an hour through the town, scattering startled and indignant citizens as an auto-mobile scatters chickens. The police, who reached the station in time to arrest him, were not soothed by his explanation that he did not know the town was there until he was halfway through it.

The original franchise of the Little Miami, whose terms were to stand a hundred years, required not only that the railroad build a station on the donated lot uptown, but that all the trains going that way stop at its doors. Built in the same years as the main station, it followed the same austere pattern: rectangular, flat-roofed, with overhanging eaves, and on all four sides, flat pilasters alternating with small-paned windows. In our childhood its second floor was the home of the stationmaster and his family: the building stood in its green yard, with tall trees and an iron fence like any private dwelling. Seldom did anyone board a train from its doors, and so eventually it was closed: the franchise had required the building of the station and the stopping of the trains, but had neglected to state that the station must be kept open. For several years we were treated to the spectacle of a train's pausing, as if in salute, at that corner where burdock grew in the uncut grass, where the untrimmed branches of maple trees hung nearly to the ground, where the building itself stood blank and deserted, with shuttered windows and locked doors. The original deed of gift to the railroad had stipulated that at the end of the hundred years, if the railroad no longer needed it, the lot should be returned to the heirs of the donor. When that time came and a new franchise was written, the railroad's lawyers sought out the scattered heirs. They sold the corner, another landmark was razed, the trees cut down, the ground black-topped, and we had another parking lot.

That uptown station was never really important. The main station—the "Depot"—was. To reach it you walked south on Detroit Street as far as the overhead bridge which carries the track from the east; just this side of the bridge you turned sharply to the right and climbed a steep hill. The station platform is a paved-brick area that in these latter days seems even vaster than it did once upon a time because it is so empty. It is a flattened triangle in shape, with the freight depot in one acute angle; the passenger station, with its baggage rooms, express office, and restaurant, in the other, at the far end; and a waste of sunbaked bricks between with, toward the last, not even a baggage truck standing waiting beside the track. The two buildings were of the same pattern, the one a small rectangle, the other a large flatiron, narrower at the ladies' waiting room end; both were severe of line, the bricks old and worn, the only ornamentation the flat pilasters between the windows; they were matched in style except that the passenger station had around its four sides a wooden awning supported on iron brackets, too high to be an effective protection against rain and snow.

When we were children, in the great days of railroading, our town was division headquarters; the station was a bedlam of activity, furious with train-dispatchers, telegraphers, superintendents, train crews, shopmen, and section gangs. All day long, famous trains stopped there for passengers coming and going: trains that no longer even acknowledge our existence as they slip past the platform. Then, we were ashamed of our station, its age and griminess and outmoded architecture; we believed that we deserved better of the Pennsylvania, but we allowed ourselves to be put off with promises—next year, or tomorrow. Now the day when there was need of it has passed: along with roundhouse and coaling dock, the old station has been torn down; passengers must content themselves with a corner of the freight depot. Thirty years ago the station was merely an eyesore, wornout and dirty; before it was razed it had become a monument, and we were outraged by its loss. We were proud because it was over a hundred years old, and we published its picture in the paper on suitable anniversaries. In these photographs the building looks as austerely, even grimly, dignified as in the steel engraving which portrays it as it was in the 1860's. But in the earlier picture it is the center of an historical activity: a minute engine puffs white smoke through a funnel; the train behind it is a trooptrain, and the car windows are full of tiny faces under forage caps. On the platform are hoop-skirted ladies behind board-and-trestle tables laden with food. The caption explains the scene: "General Hooker's Corps Passing through X—Route to the West."

Again in World War II, trooptrains passing through and soldiers' families traveling after them woke our station briefly from its slumbers. But after the end of the war it was once more deserted, the ticket office closed for most of the day. Until the government began recently to truck our mail to Dayton, the mailboxes on the depot wall, "North and East-Bound Mail," "South and West-Bound Mail," were more frequently the objective of our citizens than the few trains that served us still. A long while ago the letters mailed at the station were dropped in the boxes around seven o'clock in the evening. Even then we were too sophisticated to walk to the station just to see the trains come in, but on a fine summer evening letter-writers waited on the platform to admire the east-bound limited while it stopped. Small boys would squat beside the engine, hands on knees, to study piston and driving wheel, and would talk like experts of "Pacific" and "Atlantic" types of locomotives. Nowadays if small boys are at the station at all, they stand back and watch the streamlined diesels whip past them.

Familiar and everyday as the railroad has been to everyone in town, it has always been most intimately known to those who live on our street, which is the street nearest the station on the north, and to those who live on the near edge of Spring Hill, to the south. We have no "wrong side of the tracks"; Detroit Street climbs the hill beyond the overhead bridge and leads to the residential south end. Just beyond the station and the many lines of track is an iron fence, and behind the fence a lawn sloping steeply up a hill to the Arnold house on its crest. Our attic windows face the windows of this house from as far away as the equivalent of four blocks; in between are the creek bottoms far below and, on a level with our ground-floor windows, the railroad station.

Between us and the station lay our own back yard, a few back yards of houses on the side street that came to a dead end at the creek bank, and, on the bottom land between the two branches of the creek, half a dozen shanties planted crookedly in a tangle of weeds and willows. We were never out of earshot of the trains; we fell asleep to the familiar tune of panting short-breathed switch engines. We knew the wrecking whistle as well as we knew the fire bell. From the attic windows, where one could see over the willows along the streams, the whole station lay in view, from the water tower at one end to the roundhouse and the coaling dock at the other.

We always mailed our letters there. Even if we went the long way round, by Detroit Street, we were closer to the station than we were to the post office, and by the back way it was only a few mnutes' walk: along the side street to the first branch of the creek, down a rotten flight of wooden steps that clung tipsily to the high bank, over a narrow footbridge of planks as rotten, with a shaky wooden handrail, along a cinder path past the crazy tumble-down shacks that made up the Bottoms, past the gasworks, noisy and odorous, that polluted to a scummy green the waters of the creek branch on which it stood . . . then finally up another flight of steps—shorter but more precipitous and rottener than the first, splintered, black with ground-in coal dust—to the trestle that carried the track slantwise from Detroit Street over the low ground and the farther creek . . . along the trestle to its end, and across a double track to the station platform.

In our very early years it was an adventure to take the back way to the station, with its brief passage through the underworld of the very poor—unlucky or shiftless—who lived down in the Bottoms. Half-frightened, half-fascinated, we stared sidelong at unkempt dooryards, through broken-windowed doors. One child who lived down there somewhere with her grandparents I was briefly acquainted with: we started in the first grade together. Incomprehensibly to me, her family owned no clock; after the six-thirty mill whistle blew and the grandfather had gone off to work, they could only guess at the time; the little girl, scrubbed and tightly pigtailed, in clean limp garments hanging to her ankles, would turn up at our back door somewhere between seven and seven-thirty to walk to school with me, and would wait in the kitchen, mute, round-eyed, motionless on Grandma's rocker, while we ate our breakfast. My grandmother knew her grandmother: "A good woman," she would say, or "A nice old lady," and she would tch'k, tch'k, shake her head and add "And now those children to raise." Because I was so small then I never knew just which place was theirs; the child sometimes stopped afternoons to play with me, but I never went there. Long before I was old enough to take the back way to the station by myself, that family had moved away and out of my knowing—I hope to some better place and fortune. I never knew anyone else from the Bottoms while it remained the slum it was in those days.

When we were very small we never went to the station by the back way without an adult hand to cling to: the steps up the railroad embankment were set so far apart that short legs could scarcely reach from one to the next—and at the top you stepped out on to the naked trestle. As we grew older this half-real, half-made-up horror of the shacks, the gasworks, the trestle, faded out. We played hide-and-seek and run-sheep-run along the creek banks, under the footbridge, and as far as the sawmill up near Detroit Street. We were then oblivious of the smell of the gasworks, and did not dislike the rank growth of ironweed, goldenrod, black-eyed Susans, and sunflowers. We mailed the family letters when we could be trusted to walk the trestle and cross the tracks alone. We saw the gasworks replaced by an electric-power station, and the creek water run clear again; we saw the shanties torn down and a neat row of fresh-painted cottages built in their stead, each with an immaculate garden—each with an owner who could afford to "keep it nice" and buy a clock for its walls. And one couple who came to live there after I was grown we knew well: country-bred, they produced in that rich bottom land not only the most beautiful flowers in town, but the most succulent vegetables and berries, and brought them to our front door all summer long. . . . When the wooden steps and footbridge gave way to concrete, with handrails of iron, we had already outgrown what had been one of our favorite diversions: sitting on the rickety bridge railing, trying which of us could come closest to spitting through a crack between the boards into the water beneath. The other steps, up to the trestle, were never replaced. The last time I went that way they had disappeared as if they had never been, and I had to scramble up the stone abutment through the blooming elderberry bushes growing there.

Through all these years of change and improvement in its neighborhood, the station remained exactly as it had always been, only its accretion of coal smoke and soot growing darker and thicker as the years passed. Along with other townspeople we continued to use the trains as we had always done. When we went to Cincinnati we rode down on the "accommodation," and stopped at all the crossroad hamlets with the bucolic names: Spring Valley, Roxana, Blue Ash, Twelve-Mile Stand. We traveled by train to the nearest city for a day's shopping, although there was an interurban electric-traction line which was cheaper. We were closer to the station than to the traction office, the train trip was only twenty minutes long, and was more comfortable than the hour's ride on the interurban; these were adult justifications for the extravagance. To us children the train was far more exciting than the electric car: the railroad went to faraway places; the dust on the window sills, which we were not to put our hands in, or our elbows, might have been the dust of St. Louis or New York. Not one of our brief trips proved to be an adventure, but we could always hope, when we climbed the car steps, or pretend. In our station in the morning, anyone who saw us might believe that we were going halfway across the continent. In the city depot in the evening, we might have been— we hoped we gave the impression of being—experienced travelers in the middle of a long trip, taking advantage of a wait between trains to stretch our legs and breathe a little fresh air.

Without a word spoken between us, my sister and I joined in this Experienced Traveler game. Blasé and indifferent, we paced back and forth between the benches of the waiting room, surveying with something like contempt their occupants: nervous old ladies on the edges of their seats, clutching handbags and umbrellas; immigrants crowded huggermugger in the midst of their bags and bundles, some of them silent and dazed, some of them talking in a thick foreign tongue and with lips, hands, and shoulders. We watched and listened; we kept a wary eye on the clock, but never started for the door until the train-announcer came in with his megaphone. We had heard his call so often that its words and tune were as familiar to us as "The Star-Spangled Banner": "*Penn*-syl-*van*-ya lines *e-e-east! Co-lum*-bus, Pittsbur-r-rgh, *Har*-ris-burg, Phila-*delph*-ya, Washing-ton and New York! *All* points *east! Penn*-syl-*van*-ya lines *east!*" Unhurriedly then we strolled to the gate, leaving our elders to follow with their bundles. Only the gateman who punched our tickets at the barrier could know that our destination was short of Columbus —or of Washington or New York.

Once on the train we let that game drop and forgot any possible onlookers. From that moment we separated each into her own world. When a seat had been turned so that the four of us could sit facing each other, my sister and I were permitted to take the places next to the window, where we glued our noses to the sooty glass. When the train had pulled out of the station and on the outskirts of the city gathered speed, there were any number of games that could be played in the delightful privacy of the mind. The clackety-clack of wheels on the rails was a powerful stimulant. In whatever distant country you chose for the moment to be traveling, the train would be making just that noise. The landscape outside the window—if you were good at pretending, for it wasn't much like the pictures in the geography —might be the fields and the trees of England or France or Italy: you might be coming soon to London, or Paris, or Rome, or Venice.

Or you could be more easily convinced, more completely absorbed, pretending that you were coming home again after years of absence. "I remember this curve here by the old canal, and the way the track climbs until you look down on the roofs of those shacks and their dirty back yards, with the clothes hung out to dry. How queer it makes you feel, when you remember it all so well. It is the same as when you were young: if you close your eyes you can think what comes next: the long trestle bridge, the river, the island in its center covered with scrubby willows and alders, under water every spring."

Of course you were not, in your mind's eye, coming home in a day coach but in the most august of Pullmans; you were rich, which was of minor importance, and famous, which was very important indeed. People recognized you, and stared; when the train slowed and the porter came for your bags, they wondered audibly: "Wy should she be getting off here, in this funny little town?" And someone knew: "Oh, that is where she grew up." And you got off the train, smiling with tolerant amusement at the flurry you had created, thinking how often, long years ago, you had descended at that station, which hadn't changed, not a particle—and how in those days you had never dreamed that you would leave the town, for so many years, for such strange faraway places, and return famous. . . .

I have a good memory, and I have never believed much in the little-did-I-dream affectation on the part of the great, the near-great, or the not-so-very-great. There is nothing much, probably, that any he or she did not dream as a child, although it is likely that in each case, as in my own, the dreams covered so much ground so rapidly that they saw all desirable ends attained by the age of twenty-five, and left the other two-thirds of life a complete blank.

The journey to our town took just twenty minutes. The imagination travels so much faster than any train that those twenty minutes could cover several lifetimes (up to age twenty-five), each different, although fame was gloriously achieved in each— all reviewed carefully and lovingly by the traveler coming home after many long years. It was only when we stumbled off the day coach to the pavement of our own station that I would be jerked back to the present, and became again a weary child with grimy hands, fuzzy pigtails, and hair ribbons like shoestrings. On that station platform we had to wait to cross the track, if we were taking the short cut home, until the train, having discharged its passengers, could back far enough for the engine to fill up with water. Those were the longest moments of the day. There was no pretending then; there was only impatience, until finally Pullman cars were pushed back, and the dining car, day coaches, mail car, express and baggage cars, and, at last, the engine. Then you could look across the creek bed and the Bottoms, above the treetops, and see your own roof, your own chimney and the attic windows, and know that the house was still there and that all was well.

In not one respect have those long-ago dreams been prophetic: even the station is no longer there. As for returning home famous at any more likely age than twenty-five—if it had happened, there would probably have been no one there to see. Even the friendly folk who were for many years part of the station scene have been gone for a long while. Today Noah would not be the porter on your train, nor Billy Golden its engineer; Miss Toohey would not be in the ladies' waiting room even were it there, nor Ike Emery behind the ticket window.

The trains themselves are different. Not only have the steam locomotives been replaced by diesel engines: express trains have names, like steamboats, and never stop except at the request of local millionaires. The trains with which we were once familiar and which had their own definite characters were known to us by number; Twenty-One, particularly, had as distinct a personality as any trans-Atlantic liner. Twenty-One left New York in the afternoon and arrived early in the morning; it was the favorite coming-home train of our part of the world. It brought us back from college for our holidays, and from New York in the days before that city was within easy motoring distance. Even before we were grown to traveling age, we knew Number Twenty-One: when it came puffing into the station, easily audible from our dining room, we knew that it was time to be starting for school. Or on cold winter mornings when it was exciting to believe that Providence had singled us out for something special in the way of ice and blizzards, we would listen for that peculiar shrill sound that steam whistles make in zero weather; not hearing it before the school bell rang, we would start out into the day telling each other, with satisfaction, "Ol' Twenty-One's late today: couldn't get through the drifts, likely."

Noah was the porter on that train; he was a Negro from the East End whose last name I have long since forgotten. But I have not forgotten how pleasant it was to be recognized by him

—first as a child in our own station, then as an adult in the Pennsylvania Station in New York. He knew everyone from his native town; he never failed to speak to a fellow citizen who came down the steps in New York and passed him on the way to the Pullmans. "Howdy, Miss!" he would say, and with a smile that showed all his teeth would lift his uniform cap: "Goin' home with us? How's your Pa? Ain't carried him for a long while." His delight was flattering; it was heart-warming to be called by name and rescued from the anonymity of that station's incessantly thronging crowds—and Noah's friendliness was all genuine, since no one ever heard of tipping the train porter who had charge of the day coaches. And now Noah is dead, and there is no one to recognize you in the New York station if you should ever go there again.

Of all the engineers we knew Billy Golden best, since he carried us to the nearby city or back again. When we stood on the station platform in the evening, waiting for the train to back out of our way, we watched to see if Billy was in the engineer's cab. If he was, he leaned out, his grimy face beaming, and waved a gay farewell. Billy's was the most sought-for run on the division: Columbus to Richmond, Indiana, and back again, then a day off. On his off days you would see him uptown in front of the cigar store, immaculate in dove-gray suit, a spotless derby on his silver hair, a cane in one hand, a rich Havana in the other, his round florid face glowing with satisfaction. He was more nearly the perfect picture of the millionaire than anyone else in town. But Billy retired a long while ago, and moved to the city.

And Miss Toohey has been dead for more years than I care to remember. It was Miss Toohey, in charge of the ladies' waiting room, who made the difference between our station and those of all the other country towns scattered east and west along the route.

Our division of the railroad was manned almost exclusively by Irish Roman Catholics. This may have been true of every line in the country or it may have been true only locally. Why it was I do not know, but can guess that after they were brought here as cheap labor to build the line, they stayed on to run it. From section hand to engineer they were Irish in origin, and lived, most of them, in the West End in the crooked streets behind the Catholic church. Miss Toohey was one of them, although there was nothing conspicuously Irish about her except her name. She had a grandmotherly air: you could see at a glance that she was kind, capable, and would stand for no nonsense. She was a tall woman, sanguine of complexion, blue-eyed, spectacled. Her sandy hair, which faded into silver as the years passed, was parted in the middle, plaited, and twisted into a flat bun on the back of her head. Her dresses were black, her skirts long and full. She always wore a white apron—the sort distinguished by our elders as "sewing apron," made of lawn or dimity, with ruffles and wide starched strings.

When Miss Toohey ate or slept is a mystery: she was always at her post in the waiting room. This her domain she kept as meticulously as my grandmother kept her parlor, and everyone who used it behaved as circumspectly as she would have done in that awe-inspiring room. No chewing-gum wrappers, no peanut shells, were dropped on Miss Toohey's spotless floor. Her broom was brought out for one scrap of paper, and her dustpan emptied into the stove; no word was spoken, but the offender went outside to finish his lunch on the platform. Benches lined the room on three sides, and usually one of them at least was occupied by Negro women and their sprawling, wide-eyed, spick-and-span children. Beneath Miss Toohey's eyes they did not put their feet on the benches, nor talk above whispers. A splint-backed rocking chair stood between the stove and the windows; this was Miss Toohey's chair, but she never failed to offer it to a woman with a baby in her arms. Or if the baby was fretful and the mother weary, Miss Toohey would take the child and stand with it at the window, where they could enjoy together the excitement of a switch engine's passing. On a winter day she would hold the baby close to the stove, warming its hands, wiping its nose. The old-fashioned pot-bellied stove stood in the center of the room, and on zero days and nights when all the trains were late, Miss Toohey kept it glowing red-hot, handling her coal bucket with precision and accuracy, never dropping so much as one small lump of coal on the sheet of zinc the stove stood on.

Whereas the ticket agent knew the trains theoretically, from the timetable—where they should be and when—Miss Toohey knew them practically: she called them by the name of the engineer in charge, and she could tell you not only how far along Pat or Tim had come on his way but why he wasn't farther, and how long it would probably take him to pull his train in. She was alert to every distant whistle, and when she heard one, knew just where it was blowing. She never thrust her information on a fellow townsman, whose acquaintance with train whistles presumably equaled hers, but to a stranger she would say quietly, "Columbus, Miss? That's your train whistling. It'll be here in about four minutes." Then she would meet your eye and smile as to one sharing a superior education. You would say, not unwilling to show off, "Trebein crossing?" And she would nod and you both would listen until you heard the bell as the Market Street gate was lowered. Then it was time for you to pick up your bags and go out to the platform. Miss Toohey could guess from the hour of your arrival at the station which train you had come to meet or to take; if it were not on time, her advice depended on where you lived in town. To us she would say, "Cincinnati? Danny's half an hour or forty minutes late this morning; you might's well go home and be comfortable. If he makes up any time you can hear when he whistles for the Jasper crossing."

I do not know how long Miss Toohey had been in charge of the waiting room before I was grown-up enough to notice her. Her figure has its place in my early memories, tending the stove in the winter and in summer standing in one of the screened doorways, occasionally opening it a few inches to brush the flies out with a swish of her apron: my grandmother's gesture exactly. Age did not change her much: she was there, exactly so, through all the years when I was going to college and after I was home again; she was there until forced by her last illness to give up. On the morning of her funeral I knew for once for whom the Catholic bell was tolling. After that the ladies' waiting room seemed an empty and desolate place. Miss Toohey, happily, did not live to see the day when the railroad began to neglect us. It would have broken her heart could she have foreseen that her job would end with her; that the ladies' waiting room would be so little used, so frequently locked, that it could be left to itself, untended. And that the station itself could be torn down and never replaced would have been beyond belief.

Miss Toohey could not have imagined the station looking as forlorn as it did toward the last. To reach the ladies' waiting room, you walked the length of the platform, past the baggage room, past the lunch counter, past the men's waiting room, past the ticket office. Since each of these compartments ran the width of the building, with doors and windows in both walls, whoever passed could stare in. For a number of years you stared at empty space. Even the ticket office was locked except when one of the two or three local trains was due. The lunch counter stayed open, but its mounds of grayish buns, its hard yellow cheese under a glass bell, its battered coffee boiler, had all the look of having been petrified by some wicked enchantment.

The building across the tracks and above the creek, that was once the railroad hotel, became so decrepit before it was finally torn down that a push would have sent it tumbling down the bank into the water below. It long housed a restaurant run by Tom Taggart before he went on to French Lick, fortune, and the bossing of Indiana Democrats. In those days when Tom was running the station hotel, there was a four-o'clock-in-the-morning train to Cincinnati, much favored on Monday mornings when the boys who worked in the city had to get back to their offices after a week end at home or visiting their girls. The interminable hours after the last good night must be spoken to the girl, and before the train could be hoped for, were spent in the hotel restaurant. Fifty or sixty years later those men remembered and spoke gratefully still of Tom Taggart's coffee—not because it was good coffee but because it kept them alive.

The boys who come to town now to do their courting drive their own cars. They never think of the railroad; it is not in anyone's mind as a possible means of transportation. A generation has grown to manhood whose members have never set

foot on a train. Their families have driven their own cars everywhere; children have been brought up in automobiles. The difference that this must make in their store of experience, both real
and imagined, is hard for one of my generation to estimate. Not
to know how exciting it is to step on a Pullman, never to have
seen the end of your own train whipping around a curve behind
you: one cannot imagine it. And how does a woman learn now
when she has irrevocably crossed the line between youth and
middle age? I knew it on that morning when the Pullman
porter addressed me as "Madam" and not "Miss.". . . It is impossible to conceive of the lack in oneself or another of certain
expanses of memory; one of these is that expanse so richly filled
with recollections of the railroad, the station, and all the trains
one rode on. Such a blank in the minds of following generations
we must needs lament, as no doubt our great-grandfathers lamented over those victims of progress who grew up knowing
nothing, remembering nothing, of the stagecoach.

Here must be, as a result of the absence of any awareness of
the railroad, an old loyalty lost. Perhaps "loyalty" is an unreason-
able word; perhaps "prejudice" would be better—but it is a harm-
less and an amusing prejudice, that which one feels for the railroad of his childhood. No one of my generation grew up in any
county seat in America without consciousness of a certain relationship between himself and the railroad: a sense of favors
given and received, a loyalty on his part, not to a corporation, a
thing of stocks and bonds, dividends, directors, capital, not even
to the visible creature, the thing of engines, cars, and cabooses,
of tracks and ties, but to a kind of spiritual entity, The Railroad,
indefinable but real as any breathing being.

Of course one felt this only for one's own road. In a large
part of the country it must have been the Santa Fé that called
forth this loyalty, and in another the Union Pacific. There were
those who championed the New York Central and were honestly surprised to learn that other people, even when there was
a choice, rode on other roads. So anyone who grew up in our
town in the first decades of the century conceived of the country
as divided into two parts: one served by the Pennsylvania; the

other, benighted if larger, served by all other necessarily inferior roads. It was absurd, even grotesque, but it was indelibly stamped on the mind. Whenever in your imagination you accompanied the hero and heroine of your reading up the steps of a Pullman, the car was the gleaming dark red of the Pennsylvania, even when knowledge of geography blanked out the familiar keystone on the engine. Since it was Pennsylvania whistles that echoed distantly through the nights of your childhood, it was that whistle and that one only which held for you always the proper quality of eeriness when it came to your pillow through the dark.

You mourn the loss of that whistle—the voice of longing in childhood, of nostalgia later—when the bellow of a diesel engine reverberates through the town. Strangely enough, just recently, through what necessity or by what choice only The Railroad can know, there have been steam engines sounding their whistles, ringing their bells, pulling their long trains past our station. Familiar as the sound has been all your life, you take no notice at first, or even until after the whistle has blown for some country crossing; then, hearing it in retrospect but not quite believing, you listen for it again—and not thinking, just hearing, you are back in time, in the long ago past. Particularly if it sounds at night, almost as if in your dreams, you are not remembering but being, for a brief instant, a child: feeling the pull, knowing that you will one day follow that call, but all the while unconsciously confident that when you do those who stay at home, and home itself, will never change, will always be awaiting your return. The instant passes, leaving you half-sad, half-pleased. Listening for one last echo of that whistle from the distant train, you are sad almost to tears because of the changes there have been: because those who stayed at home are gone now and the best of them gone forever. And you are pleased because that sound is after all still to be heard occasionally by today's children, if they will but hearken. For surely no child's imagination can ever be stirred by the horn of a diesel engine as yours was once stirred by the last faint sound of a steam engine's whistle dying away over the curve of the world.

11. Covered Bridges and the Doctor

Almost every village has its antiquarian and historian, whose inescapable fate it is to be humored, put up with, loved and laughed at by his fellow townsmen. In literature the antiquarian is a dismal figure, modeled perhaps on the "Character" by John Earle in his *Microcosmographie:* "He is one that hath that unnatural disease to be enamoured of old age and wrinkles, and loves all things (as Dutchmen do cheese) for being moldy and worm-eaten. . . . He loves no library but where there are more spiders' volumes than authors', and looks with great admiration on the antique work of cobwebs. . . . His grave does not fright him, for he has been used to sepulchres, and he likes death the better, because it gathers him to his fathers." This paragraph suggests, for one, the elderly scholar Casaubon of *Middlemarch*. But one cannot believe that living antiquaries have been so unhuman. Sir William Dugdale's researches into the history of Warwickshire may have amused his friends, and his comrades-in-arms must have thought him more than mildly eccentric on that day when he removed himself from the battle of Edgehill, that he might note its details and map them accu-

OHIO TOWN

rately for the future historian, with a mark where every dead man fell. But Sir William was richly rewarded for his love of an older England, and for his loyalty to his king. His contemporary and Earle's, Sir Thomas Browne, was as widely read an author as any of his time, and there is no suggestion anywhere that anyone thought the less of him as a physician because he was moved by the Roman funerary urns disinterred near Norfolk to write that most eloquent and melancholy essay: *Hydrotaphia; or Urn Burial.* Today a local—and less eloquent—antiquarian is likely to find but a handful of sympathizers, and those without power to bestow rewards. It is only because enthusiasm is contagious that he sometimes accomplishes more in the way of monuments erected, reputations restored, and traditions preserved than would have seemed possible—or than is acknowledged until after his death, when his work is recognized as having a certain value.

These services have in the past been performed for our county by one of our mail carriers and two of our physicians—all men whose vocations took them up and down our streets, so that it was natural for them to notice change and compare past with present. The postman after his retirement continued his researches, added to his hoard of old photographs, and could always supply pictures and information for such occasions as anniversaries, homecomings, and cornerstone layings. The two doctors exacted from their friends assistance for their projects and in their investigations: they not only worked at their hobby, but set others to work also. It is largely due to Dr. Ben that we have a museum. But he turned to antiquarianism only toward the end of his long life, whereas Dr. Will had been concerned with the past since long ago, all through the years when I was growing up. He was one who had always been "strangely thrifty of time past." His thoughts, when they could take a holiday from pills and prescriptions, were bent upon it, and his endeavors, when not concentrated on the cure of disease, were devoted to the preservation of such relics of an earlier day as had so far been left untouched. It is not surprising that a physician should combine with his profession the activities of a Dugdale, for no one can be more knowledgable than a country doctor about all the roads to the four corners of a county. Day after day, week after week, he sees every difference made by the seasons in every field and every hill, and notices every change brought by the years to the roads that wind between and among them. And no man has a larger or more varied lot of acquaintances to interest and to influence. Dr. Will was too well liked not to be listened to with respect; his friends may have heard more than they desired of Indian and pioneer, but to oblige him they would drive farther than it perhaps seemed worth to look at tumble-down mills, weed-grown burial places, and excavated mounds. He knew all that had happened on every obscure road in the county, every stream and every bit of woodland; he was eager to share his stories, and expected his audience to feel as he did about the vanished generations.

Although Dr. Will suppressed all sentiment in the exercise of his calling, he gave way to it when he turned to his avocation. He was very tolerant of dead men's—particularly dead Indians' —frailties, and he thought last century's landscapes more beautiful than last spring's. But he was realist enough to admit that remonstrance would be vain when it was progress that threatened the surviving features of that older scene. He did not hope that because they were antique and picturesque the county's covered bridges would be spared when their purpose could be better served by iron and concrete. Years before the revived interest in covered bridges, he prevailed upon one of his friends to photograph for him all those left in our countryside. He wanted the pictures for his collection of mementoes of the past. There are far fewer of the bridges standing now than when he had the photographs taken. That the last score of them were not demolished before he died is true only because with us in those years time moved slowly and change came limping after.

These last wooden bridges are not on the hard-surfaced "pikes" that proceed from one county seat to another. A few are on fairly important highways, but for the most part they are in the back country, where farmhouses are scattered among the hills and the woods, and the only road that finds them out is one that follows a river or a creek along that bank where bottom lands are widest and, when the roads were first made, afforded the most room for a traffic of hay wagons and threshing machines. The way stays close by the stream, but except at brief intervals the water is hidden behind a barrier of willow and sycamore trees. The river is slow-flowing, heavy with silt, and often the color of its mudbanks, but still it can reflect the sun in bright occasional glimmers that dance between the branches when the wind stirs the leaves and lifts them aside. Wherever the stream is deepest and darkest a forgotten gristmill is surely to be discovered —not seen clearly, but apprehended as mass and shadowy bulk behind the willows—even its roof line not quite defined through the density of the foliage. In the spring rains, when the snows melt, such a road is likely to be flooded for a few days or a week. The river spreads thinly beyond the sycamores, it creeps through the wire fence that lines the roadside ditch, and by the fence it is raked clean of its scourings of straw, bleached cornstalks, and dead branches. It pours into the ditch, fills it, and foams out across the level. When the rains have stopped and the flood subsides, it leaves water behind it in chuckholes and hollows, but washes the dirt surface away from every curve, so that here and there the rocky backbone of the road is left exposed. Farm trucks and tractors labor through the mire, and their wheels turn the mud back in ridges. The sun comes out and shines steadily for a week or a month, and the ruts bake hard as iron, then slowly disintegrate into dust that rises at a touch and drifts down again on the weeds, on the willows and the sycamores, subduing them all to its own color. A road like this was not built for anyone in a hurry. It follows every curve of the stream, and when the flat space narrows so that it must cross to the other bank, it approaches the covered bridge at a right angle and then, without any wide graded curve, turns abruptly and disappears into the dark mouth of the tunnel.

Covered bridges belong to the day of the stables long since vanished from our back yards. The same principles of construction were followed in both: the walls were built of wide boards set upright, the shingled roof was pitched low above beam and rafter, floors were broad planks of wood so soft that it wore away in dust and splinters. Today one can walk into a covered bridge and remember the warm dry smell of an empty hayloft. If a sunbeam has found a crack between the shingles, then in the path it takes between the rafters there float visibly in the undisturbed air a million million dust motes. In either side, through cracks between the boards, glimpses of the river may be caught: the branch of a tree and its shadow on the water . . . a rock and an eddy . . . a still pool in the curve of the bank.

Because of its difficulties, a river road is more suitable to horses than motors. Because of its associations, a covered bridge seems to be haunted by echoes of the slow clomp-clomp of horses' hooves on its splintery floor, the squeak of wagon wheels, and the light rattle of a buggy. Nevertheless it must be crossed by men who drive cars: farmers and those who communicate with them: mail carriers, doctors. . . . Many automobile horns have wakened echoes high in the gloom in the peak of its roof. Doctors were the first in our community to hazard the purchase of automobiles; they were justified in their extravagance in the eyes of our conservative citizenry by their need for rapid transportation over the distances they must cover. Some of those early cars are still mentioned in reminiscent articles in the newspaper: Dr. Sam Wilson's Stanley Steamer, and Dr. Will's towering red Buick that was memorably identifiable—he could not visit a patient unobtrusively: his call was noted up and down the street, up and down a country road. But when Dr. Will's horn sounded on a covered bridge in the last years before he died—long after the days of the red Buick—it was when he was driving not as a physician but as a historian, as on the day when the snapshots were taken.

He retired in, I think, 1925 or 1926, insofar as he was allowed to retire by patients who felt that they had a claim on him. Even after he had turned us over, formally, to the protégé who was installed as a partner when he had finished his internship, Dr. Will could not break the habit of a lifetime and stay away from his office. His patients could find him there almost every day, although they knew better than to expect him to obey a summons to their bedsides. It is to be hoped that he was touched and flattered by their insistence on his personal attention when they had the luck to catch him at his desk; he could have found little compensation otherwise for the distraction of his thoughts from his ruling passion.

No one was more selfish in this respect than I; I was reluctant to take even a cold in the head to anyone else. It is amusing that it should have been so, since there had been a time, when I was small, when I crossed the street rather than pass his door. I did not dislike him personally; he had no personality in my eyes: he was The Doctor, and I had a horror of doctors. I tried desperately to conceal all minor ailments, and fought like a wildcat against putting in an appearance when he rang the doorbell. Whatever had happened to make me feel so violent an aversion lies back beyond the margin of memory, but I recall well enough the emotion and its effect on my behavior. His was one of the old houses built squarely against the edge of the sidewalk, after the Pennsylvania fashion, the steps leading to whose doors occupy a third or more of the width of the pavement. A child walking there will take the steps in his stride—a leap up, a hop and a skip beneath the doorsill, and a jump down. An adult maintains his dignity and conserves his energy by going round them. I never skipped across the doctor's steps; neither did I circle them: I crossed the street for the length of the block. I was not afraid that he would reach out and snatch me in, but I was literally sickened by the smell of iodoform or carbolic acid that came out of the open door in summertime in waves, and that hung about the threshold even in winter.

I think I must have been almost grown-up before my feet failed to quicken as I passed his steps, but when I was only six and a half, I suffered one of those accidents which make all but the luckiest or most carefully guarded children recognize the need for doctors in a calamitous world. I tumbled off a high pile of boards and had to have a cut lip sewn together again. It was a public performance, but whether or not I attracted general attention I have no notion: there was room in my consciousness for myself only, my mother, and eventually the doctor. The town worthies had assembled with all the school children and their teachers to lay the cornerstone of a new school building. Fascinated by the Masons' little white aprons, I lightheartedly ascended a pile of lumber, that I might see over the heads of my seniors. As the ceremonies progressed, I forgot the precariousness of my position, and some careless movement set the timbers sliding and brought me to the ground in the midst of them. I remember the treacherous shifting of the wood beneath my feet, and nothing after that until my mother, who had been found for me in the crowd, had me by the hand and was leading me uptown. I went roaring down the street like Tom the Piper's son, not because of any pain I felt, but because of the blood that streamed horribly red over my white pinafore. We walked hand-in-hand to the doctor's office, and I bellowed and bled all the way.

Dr. Will was a young man in those days, not so very many years older than my father. He was called by his first name to distinguish him from his brother who was also a physician—after the country custom when the practice of medicine engages more than one member of a family, and there is the "old doctor" and the "young doctor." Young Dr. Will, then, lifted me, still crying, into his chair. At this distance in time I can admire and be grateful for the art with which he quieted a terrified child while he sewed the cut so skilfully that the scar has never been too apparent. Of the operation I remember only my mother's tremulous "Will it have to be sewed?" and his unflurried "Oh, a stitch or two"; someone's promise of an ice-cream soda if I would hold still; and his improvisation of a bandage—a bunion plaster held in place by adhesive tape—which he coaxed me into thinking very funny. I was not taken home from his office, but to the nearest drugstore. My spirits were completely restored by the soda, which was by no means an ordinary treat, and by the conspicuousness of the bunion plaster, which for some reason made me feel heroic.

I may soon have forgotten how my terror subsided when I had been put in his chair and hoisted to the level of his face—his kind, calm, even amused, face—but the experience was not without its effect. I was not exactly glad to see him when I had a bilious attack, or when I was dragged to his office to have my swollen hands bandaged during the annual bout with poison ivy; I continued to tell him, as I refused to sit on his knee, "I don't like doctors," not caring in the least whether or not I hurt his feelings—a possibility to which I was ordinarily sensitive, since like most children I exaggerated the value to its recipients of my affection. But when in health, I was willing to acknowledge him as an acquaintance, even to laugh at his jokes, and I no longer shied away from his friendly advances like a startled colt. I saw him often uptown in the neighborhood of the courthouse, and once ran into him literally: I was skating backward, along in front of the drugstore, in order to engage more vehemently in the argument I was carrying on with some forward-moving friend; I was brought to an abrupt halt against his bulk and his steadying hands on my shoulders, his laughing "Whoa there, Sister." He could have avoided me, I know, but he loved to tease. . . . One frequently saw the town's doctors on the street in those days—in the drugstore, the post office, the banks, coming and going. How else could one have known them all by sight, as a child—those who were not neighbors, fathers of friends, or Presbyterians? Now one never sees a doctor on the street—never. They have their offices far away from the center of town, and secretaries to look after their mail. When I was small, they all lived or had their offices within a few blocks of the courthouse, they kept their own books, and they would not have dreamed of hitching a horse or trundling out a hand-cranked automobile to go so short a distance.

It was not until I was seventeen and grown-up (or thought so), when I had typhoid fever, that I first submitted cheerfully to being medicined, and could give Dr. Will an amiable greeting even from a pillow. Mine was the lightest possible case in a summer when there was a serious epidemic. Perhaps I am unique in having felt that the pleasures of typhoid outweighed its pains. Incurably lazy, I did not at all mind staying in bed, and besides, although I had felt wretched for a week or so before I gave in, I did not afterwards suffer. The conventional adjuncts of illness —flowers and delicacies to tempt the appetite—were missing: it would not have occurred to anyone to bring me flowers in August, when our garden like everyone's was riotously in bloom, and delicacies of course I could not eat. Other compensations were numerous. Because I had always been what in our town is called "peaked," everyone expected the worst, and I enjoyed the notoriety of being at death's door when I was not even uncomfortable: our most eminent citizens made solicitous inquiries of my father when they met him uptown, and I was flattered by the reports of conversations with people I hadn't supposed knew me by sight. My own friends were not, most of them, afraid that typhoid was contagious so long as you kept at a good distance and touched nothing; they visited me every day. I was indulged in every whim, lest opposition should elevate my fever; that meant that for a month books were fetched and carried for me, and I read to my heart's content. For four weeks I lay in comfort in a room whose windows reached the floor and overlooked the street, so that I missed nothing of the passing scene; I had letters to read and a good excuse for not answering them; I had books . . . and the windows stood open and the breeze fluttered the curtains and the air was sweet with the fragrance of the August lilies which grew in a deep border against the foundation of the house.

Only two elements of those weeks do I remember as painful: the buttermilk Dr. Will insisted on my drinking—I never liked buttermilk and liked it less after so infinitely many quarts of it— and the invasion of my sickroom by my father's Aunt Bert. Never before and never again did she visit us, but that summer she appeared, unheralded and unexpected, on our front porch—suitcase, umbrella, and all. So long as I was not really sick, my mother's standards of hospitality forbade a hint that some other time might be more convenient; Aunt Bert for her part was convinced that her arrival was providential, she could be of so much help. Always a cultist, she had at that time taken up New Thought. Standing at the edge of the back porch every evening, inhaling deeply, she *willed* me well. (Father always said that what she called "that wonderful ozone"—so contributory to her power—was really the pigpens in the Bottoms.) She believed that it was because she had the good fortune to be there that I grew no sicker. Her convictions hurt no one. I should not have been bothered by Aunt Bert had she let it go at *willing*— but she went farther, and insisted upon exercising my legs. I submitted meekly: I had been brought up to be polite to guests, particularly elderly members of the family. I did not like it; it was humiliating: every morning my covers were thrown back, and Aunt Bert would take my heels in her hands and put me through the motions of riding a bicycle flat on my back. . . . And Dr. Will betrayed me: he said it wouldn't do any harm, and might even do some good. I suspect that he relished Aunt Bert's oddities: he was a willing captive on those mornings when she lay in wait for him at the foot of the stairs, after he had left me. Before he could get away they had long debates in the front hall or on the porch. Afterwards my family never thought of the time when I had had typhoid without remembering the arguments between Aunt Bert and the doctor, on New Thought and various other topics. She was no antiquarian, but she was an ancestor worshipper, and so they had in common at least an interest in the past—and particularly they were two loquacious people trying to outtalk each other.

That Dr. Will liked me I never thought to doubt; that he took pleasure in his visits at my bedside was obvious. I suppose now that the liking was born of gratitude to me for being so little ill. That summer must have been one of the hardest in his career. The town was full of fever; most of the cases were among his patients and they were all except mine serious, some dangerous, some fatal. He said nothing to me of this, beyond reporting the progress made by those people whom I knew, but I could see for myself how haggard he became, and I remember his face the morning after the night when a neighbor's child had died in his arms. He was the blond, square-faced, heavy-set sort of man who has a look of dogged strength until he goes flaccid with weariness, and then seems fat, lumpish, and double-chinned. He would come like that to my bedside at the end of his morning round. After he had taken my temperature and thumped me a bit, he would drop into a rocker beside me and relax for that brief interval in the day when he could dismiss apprehension from his mind. He was not one to find rest in silence—talk was as natural to him as breathing: in those weeks he told me about the part his ancestors and mine had played in the county's history, about the Indians, about raids, forays, fights, scalpings and burnings, captures and escapes. In his enthusiasm he would forget how tired he was, his muscles would tauten and his eyes flash. At noon, when the factory whistles blew, he would start, look at his watch, rise reluctantly but refreshed and ready for Aunt Bert if she were waiting for him.

I do not say lightly that from that summer until he died we were friends, nor do I claim it as a rare distinction. Few men have had more friends than he. I was, however, among those distinguished by his favor: when he found me in his anteroom, in a chair against the wall, in a line with the oddments of humanity that frequent a doctor's office, he always invited me into the next room, where I could await my turn in comfort, with something more interesting to read than the tattered magazines on the table outside. Except in an emergency no one ever saw Dr. Will without the exercise of patience. This was emphatically so after his "retirement," when he had an illusion of leisure, and felt free to exercise his garrulity on all and sundry. Appointment or no appointment, you waited until he had attended to those who had been there before you—you were lucky, therefore, if you were one to whom the central office was open. In that room leather armchairs stood close to the fender, and a coal fire burned in the grate. On a long table beneath the window were scattered medical magazines and the publications of historical societies. On the walls were steel engravings—"Sherman's March to the Sea" and "The Battle above the Clouds"—and a heterogeneous collection of weapons: mound-builders' stone hammers, flint arrowheads, old muskets and powder horns, and Civil War cavalry sabers. The air was thick with the smell of drugs—he did his own dispensing—and never quite free of tobacco smoke. I have spent many hours there, buried in one of the armchairs, reveling in the horrors of the *American Medical Journal*, while from within came the sound of voices, or the clink of a glass stopper in a bottle neck, and from without, the occasional creak of a chair, the rasp of a heavy boot dragged impatiently across the floor, a sigh, or the noise of a screen door closing.

On such afternoons, when my turn finally came he would draw up another chair, extend his feet, too, toward the fender, and lean back till the leather chair back ruffled his sandy hair. He would sit with his elbows on the arms of the chair, smoldering pipe in one hand, that hand in the other, both palms up, in his lap. His eyes behind his spectacles were sometimes tired and always kind; his smile was benignant as Buddha's. He would say, "I've been wanting to ask you—have you read so-and-so, and how did you like it?" or, "I've finished another chapter of my Indian book—I wish you'd read it and see if you have any suggestions," or, "Here's an old story I just picked up—listen to this." And off he would go, long-winded and repetitive, but so ardent that I would be roused to see with his eyes some unimportant pioneer step for a moment out of the obscurity of the deep woods into history, or some familiar humdrum spot colored to a new significance. . . . At last he would knock the ashes out of his pipe into the grate, and would say, "Well, Sister, what can I do for you? You must have been wanting to see me about something." And he would rise and open the inner door, and motion toward the chair that had been familiar to my bones from the dawn of memory. Then he would forget everything but that he was a doctor.

Dr. Will was a good, all-round, hard-working, disillusioned general practitioner. He was not in all respects the typical country doctor of contemporary fiction. He was not slovenly in dress, but rather a dandy; we knew where we could always borrow a silk hat for amateur theatricals. He was not a boor, uncouth in speech and manner, but a man of education, proud of his ancestors. He never called a spade a spade in the presence of a woman —outside of his consulting room. He was not the village atheist, but one of the Session of the Presbyterian church: as far back as I can remember him as a physician, just so long can I remember him as one of our elders, passing the communion bread and wine, the gravity of his demeanor positively lugubrious in comparison with his everyday geniality. In other traits he more closely resembled the novelists' portraits. He did not seem to take his profession very seriously, and those who liked their physician to be soft-voiced and funereal soon went elsewhere. But if his patients suffered from the bluntness of his tongue, they profited by his honesty. When my grandmother was old and dying of myocarditis, he said, "There's nothing I can do. What'd be the use of my coming every day and just running up her bill?" He believed in heredity; he had time to observe all a family's frailties through several generations (he was practicing before my great-grandfather died, and vaccinated my nieces) and would dismiss from consideration any inherited defects that had not killed a parent or grandparent. He made fun of imaginary ailments, but he depended on your ultimate toughness of fiber, and did not hesitate to frighten you out of your wits when he thought it would be salutary. You counted on his telling you truthfully what he thought, and you could believe that what he thought was true. It is not slight praise for any physician.

Not that I, or anyone, would claim for him more than could be justifiably claimed for the dozen or so old-fashioned general practitioners in our town, every one of whose patients was as fiercely loyal in a dispute over medical virtues as in a political argument. Even Dr. Wolsey had her fierce partisans in a day when women doctors were few indeed, when there was still a felt need, apparently, to look as masculine as possible: her white hair was cropped short under a man's fedora, she dressed always in tailored suits, tailored shirts with four-in-hand ties. Poor Dr. Wolsey, born before her time. Her patients, if loyal, were but few, and she spent most of her lonely evenings at the moving pictures, after that means of disposing of one's time came into being.

Remembering Dr. Wolsey brings to mind some of the other older doctors of that day: old Dr. Dice, long-faced and solemn; the first Dr. McClellan, Dr. Ben's father; and farther back, shadowy figures you only heard of, like the doctor who had delivered your grandmother's children, but who in the end lost all his patients because he became a drug addict, a victim of the laudanum he had at first taken to help him through his grueling days. (His widow went to our church; she became in her old age so vague and tottery that the conviction grew that she had "caught the habit" from her husband.) It seems a pity, now that it is too late, that Dr. Will did not interest himself in the town's early doctors: they too were pioneers, and there must have been stories about them. Only one man is remembered in our county histories as having had an experience worth putting into print: the Ulster Irishman Samuel Martin, who came to this country with degrees from both the Royal College of Surgeons in Dublin and the University of Glasgow, who moved from Pennsylvania to Ohio in 1834 and was practicing here in 1849, the year of the cholera epidemic. Homeless Irishmen who were then building the railroad were the most numerous and hapless victims of the plague; Dr. Martin was physician first and Orangeman second: he fitted out his stable as a hospital, took them in and doctored as many as possible back to health. There may be other tales of heroism as great as this, lost stories of forgotten men, or stories locked from lay eyes in the minutes of the county medical society; it would enrich our store of tradition were some one of the younger doctors to turn antiquarian when he retires, after Dr. Will's example, and hunt them out.

Like many of his profession, Dr. Will was crippled with heart disease long before he was an old man. In the last years of his life, when he was unable to go to his office, I saw him only infrequently. It was rumored among his friends that he was better off unvisited: it exhausted him to talk, and nothing on earth could prevent his talking while there was anyone to listen. I avoided as much as possible the alley that passed close to the end of his sun porch: I did not like to go by and wave to him without stopping. But the alley was a short cut to our house from anywhere in the north end of town, and I went home that way one afternoon in late spring when I had stayed too long at a party. The wild cherry tree in his side yard was in full bloom, a white dome against the sky, its one edge against his roof, the other against the wall of the Presbyterian church across the way. I approached it without a thought of Dr. Will; I was teasing my mind for a descriptive word that would not diminish the beauty of the tree. There are few metaphors, few similes, that do not have that belittling effect, and the mind is bedeviled by the need to find one of them. *The chestnut casts its flambeaux* . . . true and fitting, because the flowers of the chestnut stand straight like flames in quiet air . . . but these? "Cockade?" They were more pliant than that, they dropped, they hung . . ."Tassel" was too limp, and besides had unfortunate associations with draperies . . . I gave it up . . . But how white the tree was, as only the evanescent, the fleeting, can be white: snow, clouds, the bloom on a cherry tree. . . .

Dr. Will rapped on his sun-porch window and beckoned to me. I turned in across his garden, beneath the tree, and found my own way up the steps and along the porch to his corner.

"I've been hoping to see you. I've got another chapter I wish you'd read. It's almost the last. Yes—the book's about done. I've been working on it so long I'll be lost for something to do." He knew, and I knew, and he knew that I knew, that if he finished that book it would be a miracle, but we both laughed. "Trouble is," he went on, "I've found a lot of new material—word-of-mouth stuff—never been printed—came from the Shawnees out West. It ought to go in the early chapters. Would you, in my place, do the whole thing over?"

"Not I. I'd put it in an appendix. Just so it doesn't get lost, but is available to anyone who can use it." I talked for a few minutes as hard as I could, to save his breath, and concluded as I rose to go, "Your wild cherry is lovely this spring."

"Isn't it?" He struggled to his feet. "Come along and I'll give you some to take home."

What could I do but pretend that it was natural to be strolling across his lawn at his side? Beneath the tree I stood with my hands clasped idly before me while he reached for the branch above his head, though every nerve in my body urged me to lift my arms, to rise on my toes and spare him the awful effort. He looked shrunken and sad in the bright spring sunshine, and sharp and thin—brittle—about the knees. . . . Before he was done he had cut off an armload of the flowering branches for me to take home. Across them we spoke the casual *auf wieder-sehen* of neighbors.

I did not see him again. I was away from home that summer and when he died in the autumn. But he did finish his book, and see it printed. He was not an artist; he did not pretend to be: it is as material for artists that the traditions he collected are worth preserving. As a monument to Dr. Will, their publication is superfluous. The town and the county are strewn with his monuments, although his name does not appear on them. Typical were the tablets of bronze at three corners of the intersection of our main streets. The upper half of each was the silhouette of a line of marching soldiers: soldiers in tricorns, with pigtails. Below was the lettering: one said that George Rogers Clark and his men went this way against the Shawnee towns, another gave the route of General Harmar's army from Fort Washington to this point and beyond, the third did the same for St. Clair. It seems an unlikely chance that they could all have traversed this same spot. They had not followed the same road. There was no road. With axes they hacked a way through the forest wide enough for the passage of the small brass cannon that were dragged north to be turned on invisible Indians. If there were any of the same men in all three armies, there was nothing to show them that they had known this place before. These are ignominious episodes in our history that were here recorded: Clark's expedition was fruitless, Harmar's a defeat, and St. Clair's a disaster—still, it is as well that we should be reminded that the land was not won without a struggle. It is a pity, for our pride, that we could not put up a fourth tablet on the fourth corner, but we could not even pretend that Mad Anthony Wayne passed this way. These particular signs were not left standing long; perhaps there are those among us who do not like to be reminded of ignominy, or some pedant may have discovered them to be not altogether accurate, or they may simply have been in the way of those who stand at the curb waiting for the light to change.

But the old Bullskin Trail from the river is marked, and the spot where Simon Kenton ran the gauntlet, and where Daniel

Boone jumped the gorge of the Little Miami River, escaping from the Indians—marked with tablets actually, or written on the maps and in our minds. Signs like these that identify for us certain of the roads and streams in a tranquil landscape are where they are largely through Dr. Will's efforts. It is a pity that he died too soon to have had a share in the establishment of our museum; it was his sister who presented to the county the log cabin of their ancestors, where once Tecumseh had been a welcome visitor, and who with other local patriots supported Dr. Ben in his project for moving the cabin to town and rebuilding it on the museum grounds. But even if the museum will be forever associated in our minds with Dr. Ben, still it is not essential to the memory of Dr. Will as a historian that his name should be on a bronze plaque somewhere, any more than a monument is necessary to him as a physician.

He enriched the town by all the memories he restored to consciousness, but no one can measure what he contributed to its well-being in a lifetime's practice of medicine. It would be as impossible to measure the accomplishment of any of his generation of physicians. They are all dead now: Dr. Ben was the last, and he died, an old, old man, a number of years ago. Their places were taken by their sons, nephews, friends, and by newcomers to town—and some of those men, too, are gone, having died long before they were as old as their seniors. Now there are a few grandsons practicing; otherwise, there are more strange than familiar names listed in the telephone book. These may all be better doctors than their grandfathers and predecessors, and certainly they know immeasurably more—but they seem somehow far less comfortingly omniscient.

Those years are gone when all the members of a family were treated by one physician for every ailment or mishap, from the baby's colic to the elders' broken bones. Now there is one doctor for the children, a surgeon for the sprains and breaks—and even one member of a family may have various doctors for various ills. And the general practitioners who after a fashion take the family doctor's place are always pushed to the limits of their strength: there are too few of them and too many sick people; they must

perforce, whether they like it or not, join together in partner-
ships or groups, hire laboratory technicians and X-ray experts;
they must dispose of each patient as rapidly as is consistent with
effective treatment. The pressure is on the patient as well as on
the physician: aware of the full waiting room, you feel it incumbent upon you to tell the doctor what ails you, to accept diagno-
sis and prescription and get out, without irrelevant chatter about
covered bridges, pioneers, or Indians. If you do break down once
in a while and begin a non-medical conversation, you know—if
you are allowed to go on with it—that it is something the doctor
wants to hear, or at least is willing to listen to; so highly developed is the art of easing a patient out of the office that no one
stays a moment longer than the doctor wants him there.

Not for a moment do you suppose that these doctors are less
human or less kind than those you knew long ago, or that they
have fewer outside interests; you do not suppose that they would
not be leisurely and comfortable were it in their power. If they
had more time, or there were more hours in the day, they might
even be less reluctant to make house calls. They might enjoy
knowing their patients, as Dr. Will once knew his. But those
days will never come again, and if the government steps in, the
situation will inevitably worsen: there will be more people to be
treated, more paper work and red tape, less time for a patient to
become a person. Medicine will be more and more scientific and
less and less human.

Life in a small town with no place in it for the family doctor is
hard to imagine. To lose that tried resort in time of trouble, not
to know that blessed cessation of worry that comes with the
sound of the doorbell, once it has been decided "better have the
doctor in," to be without that faith and reliance: God has been
dropped out of many lives and not left so large a blank. Cures ef-
fected by specialists and clinics are cures by science. Certainly
we need that science, but there is something so terrifying in the
very atmosphere of the clinic, it is so impersonal and so uncon-
cerned in the findings of its tools and its apparatus, that there is
little comfort in it for the troubled human within its walls. The
cures accomplished by the family doctor are partly a matter of

friendship. A catalogue of the emotions known to anyone of my age must include the feeling—an even, temperate, enduring, and unreserved liking—that he had for his physician. An honest review of one's assets will include affection for uncles and aunts and grandparents—if one has been lucky; affection for teachers —perhaps; and affection for the doctor who sewed up the cuts of one's childhood.

When the family doctor is extinct, the feeling will be unknown. When Dr. Will was trying to rescue for his townsmen the memory of the past, it certainly did not occur to him that the place he and others like him had in the community would soon be condemned as obsolete. He would have saved the covered bridges wherever it was possible, because they add to the amenities of the landscape. But the general practitioner adds to the amenities of daily life. There are many who disagree, obviously, since the bridges are coming down, one after another, and since the private practice of medicine is under attack. One change is a matter of progress, the other of reform. Reform involves fiercer emotions, and moves faster. It is entirely possible that before the last covered bridge is gone from Painter's Creek or the Little Miami River, the medical profession will be altered beyond all foreseeing, physicians will be civil-service bureaucrats, and memories of The Doctor as a person whom one knew and trusted for a lifetime will have become fables of the good old days to tell the children.

12. *There Were Fences*

THERE were fences in the old days when we were children. Across the front of a yard and down the side, they were iron, either spiked along the top or arched in half circles. Alley fences were made of solid boards higher than one's head, but not so high as the golden glow in a corner or the hollyhocks that grew in a line against them. Side fences were hidden beneath lilacs and hundred-leaf roses; front fences were covered with Virginia creeper or trumpet vines or honeysuckle. Square cornerposts and gateposts were an openwork pattern of cast-iron foliage; they were topped by steeples complete in every detail: high-pitched roof, pinnacle, and narrow gable. On these posts the gates swung open with a squeak and shut with a metallic clang.

The only extended view possible to anyone less tall than the fences was that obtained from an upper bough of the apple tree. The primary quality of that view seems, now, to have been its quietness, but that cannot at the time have impressed us. What one actually remembers is its greenness. From high in the tree, the whole block lay within range of the eye, but the ground was almost nowhere visible. One looked down on a sea of leaves, a breaking wave of flower. Every path from back door to barn was covered by a grape arbor, and every yard had its fruit trees. In the center of any open space remaining, our grandfathers had planted syringa and sweet shrub, snowball, rose of Sharon and balm of Gilead. From above one could only occasionally catch a glimpse of life on the floor of this green sea: a neighbor's gingham skirt flashing into sight for an instant on the path beneath her grape arbor, or the movement of hands above a clothesline and the flutter of garments hung there, halfway down the block.

That was one epoch: the apple-tree epoch. Another had ended before it began. Time is a queer thing and memory a queerer; the tricks that time plays with memory and memory with time are queerest of all. From maturity one looks back at the succession of years, counts them and makes them many, yet cannot feel *length* in the number, however large. In a stream that turns a mill wheel there is a lot of water; the millpond is quiet, its surface dark and shadowed, and there does not seem to be much water in it. Time in the sum is nothing. And yet, a year to a child is an eternity, and in the memory that phase of one's being—a certain mental landscape—will seem to have endured without beginning and without end. The part of the mind that preserves dates and events may remonstrate, "It could have been like that for only a little while"; but true memory does not count nor add: it holds fast to things that were and they are outside of time.

Once, then—for how many years or how few does not matter—my world was bound round by fences, when I was too small to reach the apple-tree bough, to twist my knee over it and pull myself up. That world was in scale with my own smallness. I have no picture in my mind of the garden as a whole—that I could not see—but certain aspects of certain corners linger in the memory: wind-blown, frost-bitten, white chrysanthemums beneath a window, with their brittle brown leaves and their sharp scent of November; ripe pears lying in long grass, to be turned over by a dusty-slippered foot, cautiously, lest bees still worked in the ragged, brown-edged holes; hot-colored verbenas in the corner between the dining-room wall and the side porch, where we passed on our way to the pump with the half-gourd tied to it as a cup by my grandmother for our childish pleasure in drinking from it.

It was mother who planted the verbenas. I think that my grandmother was not an impassioned gardener: she was too indulgent a lover of dogs and grandchildren. My great-grandmother, I have been told, made her garden her great pride; she cherished rare and delicate plants like oleanders in tubs and wallflowers and lemon verbenas in pots that had to be wintered in the cellar; she filled the waste spots of the yard with common things like the garden heliotrope in a corner by the woodshed, and the plaintain lilies along the west side of the house. These my grandmother left in their places (they are still there, more persistent and longer-lived than the generations of man) and planted others like them, that flourished without careful tending. Three of these only were protected from us by stern commandment: the roses, whose petals might not be collected until they had fallen, to be made into perfume or rose tea to drink; the peonies, whose tight sticky buds would be blighted by the laying on of a finger, although they were not apparently harmed by the ants that crawled over them; and the poppies. I have more than once sat cross-legged in the grass through a long summer morning and watched without touching while a poppy bud higher than my head slowly but visibly pushed off its cap, unfolded, and shook out like a banner in the sun its flaming vermilion petals. Other flowers we might gather as we pleased: myrtle and white violets from beneath the lilacs; the lilacs themselves, that bloomed so prodigally but for the most part beyond our reach; snowballs; hollyhock blossoms that, turned upside down, made pink-petticoated ladies; and the little, dark-blue larkspur that scattered its seed everywhere.

More potent a charm to bring back that time of life than this record of a few pictures and a few remembered facts would be a catalogue of the minutiae which are of the very stuff of the mind, intrinsic, because they were known in the beginning not by the eye alone but by the hand that held them. Flowers, stones, and small creatures, living and dead. Pale-yellow snap-dragons that by pinching could be made to bite; seed pods of the balsams that snapped like firecrackers at a touch; red-and-yellow columbines whose roundtipped spurs were picked off and eaten for the honey in them; morning-glory buds which could be so grasped and squeezed that they burst like a blown-up paper bag; bright flowers from the trumpet vine that made "gloves" on the ends of ten waggling fingers. Fuzzy caterpillars, snails with their sensitive horns, struggling grasshoppers held by their long hind legs and commanded to "spit tobacco, spit." Dead fledgling birds, their squashed-looking nakedness, and the odor of decay that clung to the hand when they had been buried in our graveyard in front of the purple flags. And the cast shell of a locust, straw-colored and transparent, weighing nothing, fragile but entire, with eyes like bubbles and a gaping slit down its back. Every morning early, in the summer, we searched the trunks of the trees as high as we could reach for the locust shells, carefully de-tached their hooked claws from the bark where they hung, and stabled them, a weird faery herd, in an angle between the high roots of the tulip tree, where no grass grew in the dense shade. . . . We collected "lucky stones"—all the creamy translucent pebbles, worn smooth and round, that we could find in the drive-way. When these had been pocketed, we could still spend a morning cracking open other pebbles for our delight in seeing how much prettier they were inside than their dull exteriors in-dicated. We showed them to each other and said, "Would you have guessed . . . ?" Squatting on our haunches beside the flat stone we broke them on, we were safe behind the high closed gates at the end of the drive: safe from interruption and the ob-servation and possible amusement of the passers-by. Thus shielded, we played many foolish games in comfortable unself-consciousness; even when the fences became a part of the game —when a vine-embowered gatepost was the Sleeping Beauty's enchanted castle, or when Rapunzel let down her golden hair from beneath the crocketed spire—even then we paid little heed to those who went by on the path outside.

We enjoyed a paradoxical freedom when we were still too

young for school. In the heat of the summer, the garden solitudes were ours alone; our elders stayed in the dark house or sat fanning on the front porch. They never troubled themselves about us while we were playing, because the fence formed such a definite boundary and "Don't go outside the gate" was a command so impossible of misinterpretation. We were not, however, entirely unacquainted with the varying aspects of the street. We were forbidden to swing on the gates, lest they sag on their hinges in a poor-white-trash way, but we could stand on them, when they were latched, rest our chins on the top, and stare and stare, committing to memory, quite unintentionally, all the details that lay before our eyes.

The street that is full now of traffic and parked cars, then and for many years, drowsed on an August afternoon in the shade of the curbside trees, and silence was a weight, almost palpable, in the air. Every slight sound that rose against that pressure fell away again, crushed beneath it. A hay wagon moved slowly along the gutter, the top of it swept by the low boughs of the maple trees, and loose straws were left hanging tangled among the leaves. A wheel squeaked on a hub, was still, and squeaked again. If a child watched its progress, he whispered, "Hay, hay, load of hay—make a wish and turn away," and then stared rigidly in the opposite direction until the sound of the horses' feet returned no more. When the hay wagon had gone, and an interval passed, a huckster's cart might turn the corner. The horse walked, the reins were slack, the huckster rode with bowed shoulders, his forearms across his knees. Sleepily, as if half-reluctant to break the silence, he lifted his voice: "Rhu-beb-ni-ice fresh rhu-*beb* today!" The lazy singsong was spaced in time like the drone of a bumblebee. No one seemed to hear him, no one heeded. The horse plodded on, and he repeated his call. It became so monotonous as to seem a part of the quietness. After his passage, the street was empty again. The sun moved slantwise across the sky and down; the trees' shadows circled from street to sidewalk, from sidewalk to lawn. At four-o'clock, or four-thirty, the coming of the newsboy marked the end of the day; he tossed a paper toward every front door, and housewives came down to their steps to pick them up and read what their neighbors had been doing.

The streets of any county town were like this on any sunshiny afternoon in summer; they were like this fifty-odd years ago, and yesterday. But the fences were still in place fifty-odd years ago, and when we stood on the gate to look over, the sidewalk under our eyes was not cement but two rows of paving stones with grass between and on both sides. The curb was a line of stone laid edgewise in the dirt and tilted this way and that by frost in the ground or the roots of trees. Opposite every gate was a hitching post or a stone carriage step, set with a rusty iron ring for tying a horse. The street was unpaved and rose steeply toward the center; it was mud in wet weather and dust, ankle-deep, in dry, and could be crossed only at the corner where there were stepping stones. It had a bucolic atmosphere that it has lost long since. The hoofmarks of cattle and the prints of bare feet in the mud or in the dust were as numerous as the traces of shod horses. Cows were kept in back-yard barns, boys were hired to drive them to and from the pasture on the edge of town, and familiar to the ear, morning and evening, were the boys' coaxing voices, the thud of hooves, and the thwack of a stick on cowhide.

The huckster's song was not the only one we were used to hearing. Almost daily we saw the junkman's decrepit horse and rickety wagon and mimicked his "Any old rags, any iron, any bottles today?" Frequently the umbrella-mender came our way, and the scissors-grinder with his wheel and bell, and far back in the dim recesses of memory echoes the tinker's "Any pots, any pans, any tinware to mend?" These three haughty craftsmen passed outside the gates with their summons; we watched them go, or were sent chasing after them for the sake of a broken-ribbed umbrella or a leaky saucepan. Needier peddlers invaded the yard and took their stand on our doorstep. Every spring a bedraggled woman with muddy petticoats offered for sale a basket of watercress or "fresh greens": dandelion, mustard, and poke; another like her came with little bundles of reddish sassafras bark tied round with black thread. They or their successors still ring our bell, year after year, and so do the more welcome farmers' wives who, in the winter, after the hogs have been butchered, sell from door to door the pork they do not need at home: backstrap and pickled pigs' feet and "loose" sausage, redolent of sage. Other merchants who carried their wares from house to house were expected and depended upon; they have been supplanted and forgotten long ago. The "coal-oil man" made periodic visits. His wagon was a tank which held kerosene in one side and gasoline in the other; under the proper spigot he filled the household coal-oil can—odorous, greasy, and huge, with its disproportionate spout small enough to fit the opening in the lamp bowl. We children were not much interested in him, but we watched for the baker, and when we heard his bell far off down the street we carried into the house the news of his approach. He was a round little German with a round head and drooping mustaches; he drove a high cart with a window in front from which the reins fell steeply to the horse's neck. His crackers should have made his fortune: they were thick and hard, stamped with his name in tiny letters, and eaten preferably two by two, with butter spread so lavishly between that it curled over the edge at every bite. We bought bread from him the year round, and at Thanksgiving and Christmas sent our turkeys to be roasted in his oven.

On Saturday mornings the butterwoman came to the door with butter in a yellow crock. She did not ring the bell but walked in and called "Yoo-hoo" in the dark front hall, and my grandmother went from the kitchen to meet her with last week's crock, clean and empty, to be exchanged for the full one. This was covered with paper turned down over the side and tied about with string; under the paper the convex surface of the butter was embossed with a design of grape leaves and rimed with salt.

Most of the hucksters were men: one sold the first strawberries, another the best asparagus, and another the finest cantaloupes; but there were three women who drove their horses along the curb summer day after summer day. One was the maiden aunt of a boy we knew; as meticulously dressed as for a parlor visit, she sat perched on the front seat of her surrey, among her potted plants. Rows of shelves were hung along each side from the supports that carried the surrey's fringed top, and on them were flowering geraniums and fuchsias, primroses, begonias, and bright calceolarias, all nodding and bobbing as the wheels jerked over rut and rock. Another was the berry woman who came in the middle of the summer when the air of the street was sweet and heavy with the fragrance of boiling jam; she would appear on the step outside the kitchen door, flushed and panting with the weight of a crate of raspberries. The vegetable woman came on alternate mornings all summer long. She, too, circled the house to knock at the back door; when admitted, she sat down for a comfortable gossip in the rocking chair beside the coal range. She was gnarled and little and shriveled; she looked like a Dunkard in her gray calico dress and black sunbonnet, but was in fact a Bavarian and a devout Roman Catholic. It was not until she had said all she wanted to say, in her broken English, about the weather, the crops, the domestic affairs of her married sons, and the trials of a widow woman on a farm, that she and my grandmother went out to her wagon to look over the vegetables. The end of the summer came for her, at our house, when she sold us cabbages for the winter's sauerkraut and spent a day in our kitchen helping the women make it.

When I started in the first grade, and was considered old enough to be sent on errands, my boundaries were enlarged; I came to know minutely the three routes by which I could vary the walk to school, and the three different ways which led to the library, and the five or six blocks on which my friends lived. The streets, viewed for the first time without a grownup looming in the corner of an eye, were for a while new to me, but other yards where I went to play I soon found differed from our own only in their contents. Benny's mother had a yellow rosebush that spread like a fountain from the center of the grass; it bloomed in the spring, and Benny was a lord among us when he distributed largesse in the shape of short-stemmed fragile roses. Mary's aunt had a sweet shrub, and we went there with Mary on her errands that we might be rewarded with one of the maroon flowers to crush in a twisted handkerchief and sniff and sniff. I discovered that ours was the only tulip tree inside the town limits and in its season of bloom brought home my favorite friends and with them ascended to the porch roof, whence we could reach the yellow flowers.

A list of games played on the way to school and of treasures collected in their proper months has the power to give again into the hands, almost as something that can be held, immutable, the very essence of the seasons spring and fall. Summer will forever be best remembered by thinking of the street as it looked from the gate, and of the yard inside the fence; winter can be recalled only as a stage setting for the holidays that crowned the year, but to think of spring and autumn as they once were is to think of walking to school again, and home from school. Yellow roses and sweet shrub flowers, even only in the mind, bring back the feeling of late spring and warm days and school-almost-out. With them belongs the locust tree in flower, the cream-colored tapering clusters hanging in a fall like water through its branches. The locust bloom was cool and sweet in the hand, sweeter on the tongue. . . . I cannot remember that we ever asked anyone's permission to pick the flowers, but locusts were common in our streets, and the trees rose so high without branching that they could not be climbed except by those boys who could shinny up a bare trunk. Because of this difficulty of access, the locust was particularly precious in our eyes, but we did not scorn the weeds that grew at our feet. We crossed two pins in a green apple the size of a pea, dropped one of the pins into the end of a dandelion stem, and by blowing through it bounced the apple up and down; sometimes the apple went whirling into the air and—less often—was caught in the stem again when it came down. Dandelion stems had other uses. Split and sucked, they made false curls: you hung them over your ears, against your cheeks, and spat out with a wry face the bitter taste left in your mouth. Or a very large one—a giant among the other stalks growing in a vacant lot—could be blown like a trumpet with but one profound, bass note. Nature was prodigal of wind instruments. A young leaf held tight over the mouth could be popped like a rubber balloon, and a blade of grass stretched between the thumbs could be made to wail like a banshee. Most effective of all was a maple seed: you broke off the thick end, put the wing on your tongue, thick edge toward the gullet, lifted it to the roof of the mouth and breathed against it. . . . This could be done in school to up-set procedure and annoy the teacher, because without the least contortion of your face beyond a slight parting of the lips a whole range of noises could be produced, from the merest sug-gestion of a sibilant whisper to a most appalling squawk.

When we were children, all the streets of our town were old streets, and among the trees that shaded them, among the ma-ples, were a few that were older than the street, survivors of the forgotten forest. These we knew individually, as if they had been persons, and knew their flowers and the fruits they dropped at our feet. In the spring we left the blossoms on the buckeyes, that their nuts might ripen. With a pocketknife almost anything could be made of them—tiny baskets, earrings hung on string, dolls stuck together with twigs—but they were principally treas-ured for their inherent qualities: rich color, silkiness, and polish, and for the satisfaction they gave to the hand that held them. The rough balls of the buttonwood were merely an oddity. Hick-ory trees and walnuts and persimmons all grew along our curbs in those days: the nuts we picked up from the pavement when they fell, but persimmons the boys got—they knocked them from the boughs with sticks more accurately aimed than ours, and then sold them to us for various favors. . . . Nuts and persimmons both spell autumn still, early autumn and late. The nuts were ripe first: they belonged to those days when there seemed to be a sudden blaze of golden sunshine, intensified in the air by the leaves golden on the trees and bright on the grass that had been shaded in the summer; when goldenrod and ironweed and wild sunflowers filled every waste spot, and earth turned the corner of the year wearing her most imperial colors, defiant, magnificent. . . . It was not until all the leaves had fallen, the sunlight grown pallid, and the last flowers gone to seed or frozen on their stalks that the persimmons were fit to eat. They are connected in the mind, inseparably, with drifts of leaves piling up, lemon-yellow and gold, bronze, russet, and brown, to mask the gutter and hide the sidewalk—with their acrid scent if they rotted in the damp and were crushed beneath passing feet, with the noise they made if they were crisp and dry, and shifted, whirled, and turned in the wind. In those last brief weeks or days before the rains came, and winter, and ruined them, we gave up our other games after school to play in the leaves. We heaped them up and ran and jumped in them, or turned somersaults, or buried each other and were resurrected with leaf crumbs in our hair and mouths. We spread them out and raked them into lines, and had each of us a house after his own plan, with leaves for walls and for floors the vivid young grass of late fall combed flat by the rake. Finally we burned them, and the smoke of bonfires made a haze in the amethystine dusk. Bonfires were lighted in the gutters before the streets were paved; we danced about them like pagans and made burnt offerings of potatoes. When the leaves were burned and smoke no longer scented the evening air, even when the first snows fell, still there could be seen, here and there, a mottled dark persimmon hanging in a naked tree.

Winter, from Halloween to Washington's Birthday, was a succession of holidays; frosts, thaws, and blizzards are remembered as the background of ecstasies of anticipation, most intense before Christmas, and thereafter declining by degrees. When the end of February came there was nothing left but spring to look forward to, and we began to imagine that we could smell it coming. March was spring in our eyes, however grim its aspect. In the slush, in the rain, in the wind, our hearts rejoiced and sang, and we rebelled against winter coats and heavy underwear. After the last of the snow had been washed away, when the sun was warm in its brief intervals of shining, when the leaf buds of the lilacs began to show the narrowest point of green, when the rich, thick, oozing March mud not only covered one's feet but caked one's stockings to the knees, crusted the edges of petticoats, and somehow spread in streaks up jacket sleeves, across the face, and even into the hair—it was then that the gutters ran with water like rivers in full flood, pouring in turbulent rapids down a trampled place where a horse had been hitched, widening behind the root of a tree, eddying around a debris of twigs and straw. We followed one river or another home from school, floating chips on the current, or sometimes a boat made of a bit of shingle with a cork nailed to it; we engineered a way for them to go safely—dredged the bottom, built dams, straightened the channel, scraped and patted the mud along the side into something like a levee. . . .

In this as in other games we were so engrossed as not to notice whether there were grown-up people anywhere about. The fences were a shield when we were outside as well as when we were inside them. Within, we were safe from the eyes of our neighbors going past; without, from the eyes of those who stayed at home and sat behind their windows. Not that we ever felt it necessary to tell ourselves this; we were simply oblivious of the fact that there might be anyone watching. That the fences helped us to this unself-consciousness is surely true, since after they were taken down, a certain feeling of nakedness could not be overcome. On the pavement we walked primly, with sidelong glances at the windows, or were driven by a sense of supervision to the opposite extreme and behaved like hoodlums. In our own yard we were circumspect. We couldn't stoop over without pulling at a skirt to make sure it was decently down; we couldn't do anything a tramp or a peddler or a caller or an aunt would consider silly, because any one of them might at any time take a short cut across the grass and be at our backs unsuspected. The approach of a visitor was no longer heralded by the squeak and clang of an iron gate.

The sudden if intermittent development of an awareness of our elders was not wholly due to the loss of the fences. We were growing up. By a coincidence, the streets had all been made over in the new fashion by the time we crossed the line between "little" and "big." This line was drawn, definite as the equator, between the fifth and sixth grades. It was not one of those imaginary divisions that fade into nothing when they draw near. Once in the sixth grade we were Big. We no longer collected lucky stones or floated chips in the gutter. We made no more dandelion curls, juggled no more green apples. We were in the fourth grade when Market Street was paved. The school was on that street, and on our way back and forth, we stopped to watch the workmen pouring hot tar between the bricks; behind their backs we gouged out chunks of it, still soft, to chew: we told each other it was good for our teeth, and we liked its hot, antiseptic taste. The paving of the central parts of town long before this had not much altered them, since there were few houses there, and no yards or fences. But Market Street was changed. When concrete gutters were put in, and cement sidewalks laid, most of the householders had their fences dug up and carried away. Afterwards, other streets were paved, one by one: Church and King, our street and Spring Hill. It did not occur to us to regret these alterations. We were forbidden to make bonfires in the gutters, but cement sidewalks, uniform for blocks, gave us superb roller skating. . . . And the town did not look so very different, to the casual attention, because the trees still filled the eye to the exclusion of all else. Here and there one died—a wild thing choked to death by bricks—but on the whole they seemed the same, and still do, except for the blighted elms. They are green, their branches mingle overhead, and their leaves will, in the autumn, pile curb-high in the gutter. Only if you knew the streets as a child can you point out among them gaps and replacements: most persimmons are gone, the nut trees are gone; only buckeyes, sycamores, and locusts survive to break the monotony of poplar, maple, and elm. But when they died we sang no elegies for hickory and walnut trees: we were old enough to go to the woods for all the nuts we wanted, burlap sacks full of them.

Slowly, after the streets had been paved, the fences came down. Lawns lay an uninterrupted sheet of green from corner to corner; house fronts, trim and shabby, humble and imposing, were alike exposed to the curious eye. This openness, this candor, helped us to outgrow our childish shyness of the adult world.

We had reached an age, too, which found more pleasures in the riotous games of a crowd than in the quieter and more imaginative fun of one child or two or three. Sunk in the anonymity of the mob, we became positively bold. On spring evenings we assembled on the corner to choose sides for run-sheep-run, or to count out for hide-and-seek; the whole neighborhood, from the lumber hard and sawmill on the uptown corner to the seminary precincts two blocks below us, lay open to our pounding triumphant feet. There was no barrier to impede our flight or keep us out of any back yard. Sometimes you felt a little guilty—perhaps you shouldn't go charging into other people's shrubbery —but before the thought was acknowledged, you were through and away.

This too-jubilant advantage taken of our freedom—the tumult and the shouting—was partly the result, I suppose, of our having always been used to fences. They were down, and where there was nothing to keep us out, surely we were permitted to go.

And it was not long before we had forgotten that there had ever been fences to confine us. We had grown used to a larger world than the yard within the fence and the street that passed the gate. The whole town was ours: courthouse and library and Opera House, the streets of shops and the streets of houses, and ours too were the fields that lay just beyond the paving's end, woods and country roads, streams and the covered bridges that crossed them. But from those deepest buried memories of childhood comes the conviction that only that rare moment will be saved from oblivion that is held in the mind as if suspended in unflawed amber—and that for yesterday's children there were many moments of that sort, in a garden, peaceful and safe, when an iron gate could not be opened without a sufficient warning from its hinges.

13. Four Corners

Most towns that grew up around the right-angled intersection of two roads have kept for generations to the pattern of a cross, however lopsided and misshapen. Lesser streets that parallel the original two were never quite so long, and at the outermost intersections, close to the courthouse square, were four corners of pasture and meadow land. Now every town has expanded to fill those empty spaces, but housing projects spread first and farthest along those two main streets, and so the cross is after a fashion preserved. But the open country has been pushed back—too far, perhaps, for the children of the town to reach it on foot. Once—and not too long ago—in June, when alfalfa and the tall yellow melilot bloom and are cut and lie in windrows in the hayfields, then—as the smell of the sea blows inland—the sweetness of clover pervaded the air of our streets, and even indifferent and abstracted adults remembered how close the country was. Children never forgot it; for them one delight of life in a town the size of ours was the ease with which they could leave it and go to walk in the woods.

In our time, the closest of the four corners, and the one we

knew first, was where the Robertses' land filled the angle between Church and Detroit streets, just a block from the courthouse. A high iron fence shielded the Villa grounds; on Church
Street this fence ran along the edge of the sidewalk for several
blocks, ending on the east at the lane that led to the town pasture. When we were in a hurry to reach the woods we went by
way of that lane, taking a beeline from the spot where it dwindled and disappeared in the grass to the trees that blurred the
horizon, crossing the long sloping meadow and the tilled fields
in the early spring when the wheat was just tall enough for its
blades to tangle round our ankles and an unwary step might disturb nesting killdeer or meadow lark.

The other line of the Robertses' fence was separated from Detroit Street, and hidden, by the railroad embankment. Each of
our four country corners has its section of railroad line, but this
one that follows Detroit Street into and through the center of
town is the most easily reached, and no child grows up in the
town without knowing its ties and cinders familiarly, at least as
far as to where the north fork of Shawnee dives into the tunnel
that leads it under the railroad and street. However, we walked
oftener—often enough to have worn a path in the grass—in the
depression between embankment and iron fence, savoring a
child's delight in being sheltered from adult eyes.

The fence stopped where the swamp began. A thicket of box-
elder trees grew at the edge of the marshy ground; once beyond
that we were safe from the Robertses' hired man, who would not
allow us to enter that part of his domain that lay behind the iron
fences. Under the box elders we sometimes found, when April
was propitiously warm and wet, those sponge mushrooms so
valued by our elders. Other times we might see in the underbrush a nest of burlap sacks and an empty bottle or two, but we
never stumbled on a tramp. Besides us no one walked there,
except old Dr. Harper of the Seminary, and Miss McElwain
with her field glasses, looking for birds.

North of the box elders and closer to the railroad, in the midst
of a circle of trees—sycamores and tall maples—a spring oozed
out of the ground, its water bright and clear between the leaves

of water cress. On the way to the creek it lost itself, widely dispersed through marsh grass and the cattails where red-winged blackbirds congregated. Remembering all this, you know how small you were when first—and best—you knew the swamp: you are in the midst of a wilderness of cattails, crashing through them, and they stand far higher than your head. You are small enough to be intimately acquainted with what lies beneath your feet, too small to look far beyond them. And under your feet are thick unstable tussocks of grass, liquid mud that gurgles as you move, and sometimes a quick green snake flicking away. Cattails in the spring were last year's crop, winter-killed and brittle, and you snapped them off and carried them away for your own purposes. They became spears, or javelins for throwing in mock battle; soaked in coal oil they made torches for burning in our play parades.

In the water of the marsh lived the bullfrogs, which the boys hunted with long sticks, nail-spiked at the end. In the creek itself, darting over the pebbly shallows, hiding at the edge of the bank where the long grass hung down, were minnows and tadpoles. But you could not reach the creek by crossing the swamp: the farther you pushed your way among the cattails, the harder it became to find any safe footing, and you repeated to each other the legend known to generations of children: that strayed cows had been swallowed up in the marsh, sinking to their horns. If you wanted minnows or tadpoles, you came to the creek safely by way of the railroad embankment, or, if you were in search of wild flowers, by skirting the edge of the swamp until you reached the bank of the stream east of the low ground. You knew the spot taken over for their own by the marsh marigolds, and you stopped there: you found it by keeping the box elders on your right hand until they gave way to sumac, then striking off at an angle through the cattails until you came to a solider ring of ground thickly walled around by alder and willow scrub. The bright flowers grew scattered in clumps all through the swamp, among the cattails, but you left them there almost unnoticed, since you remembered from a previous spring what awaited you beyond the alder screen. When you had fought your way through the brush, you looked down upon a saucer-shaped depression perhaps thirty feet wide, and your heart leaped up like Wordsworth's when he saw the rainbow, because the saucer was full to the brim of marsh marigolds, a burning gold in the bright sun. They grew in deep watery ooze, fed by a spring; no one could have gathered the flowers had the boards not been there—always, so far as we remembered; who had brought them no one of us knew. They lay, black and waterlogged, at the edge of the saucer; you walked to the end of one, laid the other down ahead of you, stepped on it, picked up the first one and thrust it forward: you were never satisfied with any but the very central and most inaccessible blooms. When you had pulled all the marsh marigolds you could hold, you withdrew, hauling the boards back to the outer bank with you. You knew better than to carry the flowers on to the woods; you hid them where their stems would be wet, and went on empty-handed. They were never left to be plucked on the return trip: absurdly you feared there would be none left for you if you did not take them before someone else came along. You believed this even about the violets, which grew prodigally everywhere: pale and long-stemmed in the swamp; a solid mat of purple on the banks of the creek, where they were shorter-stemmed and deeper-colored; darkest of all in the woods. A score of children, or a hundred, could hardly have picked all those that flowered beside the creek, but when you reached there you fell upon them, starved and insatiable; you gathered them on both banks, crossing back and forth on stepping stones, or jumping over at the narrow places where the roots of a willow tree, or its branches, offered a handhold on the other side. You picked violets until you could no longer hold them; you tied them up, then—with string if you had remembered to bring some, otherwise with the tape out of your undershirt. You carried them with you to the spot where a field drain emptied into the creek, and there you concealed them as far within the pipe as arm could reach, where it was cool and their stems lay in the trickling water. When your booty was thus secure, you continued on your way to the woods, empty of hand and light of heart.

There were two patches of woodland beyond the Robertses' pastures and tilled fields; you could follow the creek bank almost all the way there. The first wood was perhaps a couple of miles from town. Here in their season bloomed all kinds of violets: yellow, white, and purple; and anemones, May apples, Jacob's ladder, wild geranium, Dutchman's breeches, white and red trillium—in and under and among the saplings and bramblebushes that made an almost impenetrable underbrush beneath the tall high-branched trees. To enter and take what you desired of the flowers you had only to scramble over a snake fence, silvery gray with age and weather, smooth as silk to the finger tips. There was not always time to go on to the second, farther woods, but if there were, you found it even more beautiful than the first, and if you saw it in the one brief perfect hour of spring, you hung transfixed on the top rail of the fence. In that hour the redbuds were past their prime, paler than in their first brightest flowering, but the dogwood boughs lay like thin level clouds, white as snow, across the tender green of young-leaved trees, and all the ground below, as far as you could see, was carpeted with wild phlox—lavender, lavender-rose, lavender-blue—everywhere airy and delicate, with the faintest breath of fragrance. After a pause astride the fence, while you looked, taking it in, you climbed down to gather what you wanted of the phlox. You never touched redbud or dogwood, but you might as well have, for all those trees were cut down long ago.

When suppertime drew near you turned back on your way to pick up the violets from the drainpipe and the marsh marigolds from where you had hidden them. The sun would be low in the west, the spring wind fresh and cold in your face, the sky an ineffable blue, the high white clouds piling up, sailing away. Once out of the woods and over the fence, facing homeward across the rolling fields, you could see the clustered leafing treetops of the town; below them the darker roofs and chimneys; and above, its tiled peak brilliant against the sky, the courthouse tower and the town clock. This scene in its essentials—trees, roofs, chimneys, and tower—has been remembered and transmuted by so many poets that you are forever having it brought to

mind, whether in your high-school English class you are learning "Towers and battlements it sees/Bosomed high in tufted
trees," or farther away and long long after, you are reading Hous-
man's "The farms of home lie lost in even,/I see far off the
steeple stand."

After we were grown, when the last of the Robertses had died
and the estate was broken up, a public-minded citizen bought
the swamp, which his children had haunted in our company, and
gave it to the town for a park. A pond was dug and the marsh
drained; now there are acres of green grass under tall trees; there
is a winding lagoon, with weeping willows leaning over it,
where the cattails used to grow and the red-winged blackbirds fly.
There are stone bridges over the creek, and against a background
of the tallest trees—a slippery elm, sycamores, and maples—
stands the pavilion for dances and band concerts and summer
Sunday-evening union-church services. Children skate on the
lagoon in winter and fish in it for tadpoles and "minnies"
in the spring; perhaps they enjoy it as much as we did the
swamp. As for my generation—no one whose childhood was
happy likes in his heart to have the places that he knew altered
from what they were: each landmark destroyed means a part of
the evidence of that happy past lost and gone forever. But however much some of us may have sighed over Robertses', we are
grateful for the park: had it not been given to the town it
would surely have become building lots. The Villa grounds behind Church Street, the pastures behind the library, were solidly
built up thirty years ago; now the fields and orchards far beyond
that have been cut by winding roads and drives faced by low
modern houses, all shining brick and glass, lying in wide but
generally treeless lawns.

The other three corners of unbuilt-on ground that used to angle in between our streets were farther from the courthouse, and
were not so soon made a part of the city. Children who preferred
the freedom of an untouched waste to the restrictions of a park
could until a few years ago still go to "Dick's." Dick's was the
northwest corner, so called because it had once been a part of
old Cap'n Dick Galloway's farm; it lay between the dead end of

West Street and the Fairgrounds road, away off to the north. Now West Street has been extended to the Fairgrounds road; houses line the new section, and so the view from what was once the top of Dick's hill is blocked out and hidden. But from those new back-yard fences the ground must still slope precipitously to the bed of the stream; Shawnee creek must still flow from behind the old ropewalk where its two forks join, and meander along between narrow flat pastures and scattered groups of trees, in a slow curve, changing its direction from north to west, with the railroad close beside it. And the hills too still curve, following the creek. Along the ridge that carries the Fairgrounds road there used to be farmhouses, their barns and chicken runs and beehives dropping down the slope behind them, under the maple trees, locusts, and elms. Now the Fairgrounds road is just another outlying residential street, the farm dwellings gone or converted to modernity by the removal of their porches and the insertion of picture windows.

But however hidden and diminished Dick's hill may be, there must be many who remember and cherish the memory of it as it once was. The hill before it turns, behind Galloway Street, was always bare and steep, with deep gullies washed by the rains. It was reached in our time by way of a pasture gate set across the dead end of West Street. We climbed the gate in the autumn when we went nutting; in the winter, when we had sleds dragging behind us, we opened it. West End children played on the hills on the other side of the creek; to reach them they followed the railroad track from the Market Street crossing. Our coasting parties and theirs remained distinct and separate, although sometimes we met, amicably enough, on the icebound creek that lay between us.

Never for more than a fortnight or so in the winter was there snow enough to fill the gullies and cover the rocks. While the weather held, suspended were all family rules which ordinarily kept us home on school nights. No matter how low the thermometer dropped, we went coasting. On a zero night, when "the stars looked very cold about the sky," and the crusted packed snow was frozen hard as iron, we built a roaring fire well back on the hilltop, and by its light soared hallooing down the slope, companionably crowded on homemade bobsleds and store toboggans, or singly, belly-buster, on small sleds. And however many of us were flashing down the hill or trudging up, there was still a changing circle of boys and girls around the fire, standing, or sitting on sleds, drying snowy mittens and warming ungloved hands, biting into the apples we had filled our pockets with—crisp red Winesaps whose juice was cold as the air itself, and made our teeth ache.

As we never walked in the swamp except in spring, so we never came here except in fall and winter. On golden autumnal Saturdays we passed by Dick's on the way to gather nuts; with burlap sacks slung over our shoulders we followed the creek to the spot where the hills came close together and were thickly wooded, and among the trees were walnuts and shagbark hickories. The burlap sacks were easily filled to the limit we could carry. In those days woodshed roofs all over town were covered in October with green-hulled walnuts spread out to dry, and we despised just a little anyone whose hands were not brown to the wrists with stain. Sometimes we turned back home—back along the creek bank, up Dick's hill and over the West Street gate—when we had all the nuts we wanted; sometimes we left the sacks to be picked up later, and went on over the hills and down their long westward slope to the road and a country schoolhouse in whose yard we could build a fire and cook bacon or wieners.

Hardly longer ago than yesterday, winter evenings still echoed to the shouts of children coasting on Dick's hill; on a bright afternoon in October pasture and stream were just as they had always been. You climbed the gate and slanted down across the hill through the skeletons of ironweed and goldenrod. Ahead of you the grasshoppers jumped out of your way and tumbled—*spt-spt*—into the long dry grass. Off to the north, half-hidden by scarlet maple and golden elm, outbuildings and barnyards sprawled down the hill. Beyond the creek the western height rose almost to the sun, and its slope was in shadow, but over the rest of the scene lay the gentle old-gold light of the season and the hour.

Dick's would not have changed if man had not changed it. The last time I walked there a score of years ago it was just as it had always been. Below the curve of the creek, where the sherry-colored water ran between and over the flat tiptilted slabs of limestone, two boys were playing at dam-building. The loose stones had always been there, and the dam was made and unmade no one knows how many times, according to the whims of boyhood. On the other side of the stream, cows lay in the shade of the western hill, under a row of elm trees. The elms were vivid yellow against the rusty grasses of the slope, but a little way along a group of tall maples still held their summer color; under them the grass was damp and fine. A white horse tethered to one of the trees turned to watch me as I went by; except for that he did not move, but there were muddy hoofprints cut deep in the turf to show how long he had stood there. This corner, so richly green, was close beneath the hill and deep in shade; only the tops of the maples were lighted by the sun.

On my own side of the creek I came to a row of willow trees. One of them—very old, its trunk four feet at least in diameter —had fallen or blown crashing to the ground; its trunk was so hollow that although it held its shape, little but bark was left of it. I wondered as I passed why the willow has from immemorial time been the symbol of desolation and the end of love—"My mother had a maid called Barbara . . . she had a song of willow"—for all things that draw life from the earth and air, water and sunshine of our landscape, the willow comes closest to being immortal. Up from the shell of that fallen tree, all along the top of its trunk, rose tall green shoots: it was not dead; it was starting life anew. Along here the creek was wide and shallow, the water slow-moving, and its surface was silvered over with a thousand, thousand willow leaves fallen from the thick-boled trees that grew aslant above it. Beyond this line of trees the hills came close, a log made a bridge over the stream, and just below the crossing rose the woods, the walnuts and shagbark hickories, climbing the slope on either hand.

When I turned back I was feeling comforted, reassured in some deep region of the mind where I had not known there was need of reassurance. Unwarranted, unnecessary, had been my resigned acceptance of general mutability: the willow trees, the white horse under the maples, the boys playing in the water were elements of the timeless, identical dream the past has become in all our minds—that past, that dream that is the inalienable common heritage of us who have grown up with a lifelong knowledge of the slope of a certain hill beneath the feet, of the sun-gilded mass of a certain tree against the sky, of the tawny color, like wine, of a particular creek.

The third corner, to the southwest, gave to our feet knowledge in the ditch beside it. Yet we walked that way often, spring and fall, because once past the outskirts of town, we came to land that was pleasant to the eye: land that had been tended and cared for and loved long enough to have lost its roughness and the look that so much half-tamed American farming country has of waiting only until everyone's back is turned to go back to wilderness.

These comfortable fields lay between the roads to Spring Valley and Bellbrook; to reach them you passed a few West End blocks to where the railroad swung out of town; then you followed the tracks in their wide curve from west to south. A long triangle of woodland filled the point between the pike and the railway, sloping gently down from the hill, which the road followed, to a thin little stream filling the ditch by the railway embankment. The tract was not "woods," really: it was a sugar-maple grove. There was no underbrush, but only a carpet of May apples. The trees were widely spaced and magnificently tall, with unlopped boughs that swept out and down to the ground. In the autumn they flamed scarlet and yellow until they seemed the heart of the fire of earth, its center of light; later, when the leaves fell to the ground, the light lay there on the slope, and the trunks and branches of the trees were dark against it. All winter, until snow fell, color persisted on that ground, russet and amber, the very last that earth remembered of the warmth of summer.

Spring or fall, you passed the sugar grove by, and followed the railroad track around the curve, where it came out in open country. On your left hand the ground fell away in a wide valley. Overhead the blue sky arched in a full bow, horizon to horizon. Here but a few miles away and there infinitely remote, the meeting of earth and sky was everywhere screened by trees. Where a stream crossed the valley, its course was traced by willows and sycamores; the willows were green in the spring while the sycamores were still gaunt white-boned ghosts of trees, but in the fall the sycamores let go of their leaves later and more reluctantly; even in November the dry brown foliage clung to the boughs. Other patches of woodland were more varied than the streamside trees: nearby stands were brilliantly multicolored in the fall, and in the spring more delicately so; the line along the horizon was amethystine in October and April, indigo in the light of midsummer. In the autumn, fields were faintly powdered with the green of sprouting wheat, or alfalfa-carpeted in a thick mat of emerald. Pastures were russet and stubble fields a rosy brown, and on every hand stood the wigwams of the corn, diminishing in size toward the horizon, the lines wheeling past you from their distant vanishing point.

On the right the railroad track was paralleled by a country road that lazily followed the contours of the ground, but was never more distant than the width of two or three fields. The farmhouses that faced it were most of them hidden in clusters of trees, but barns and barnyards were plain to see; the pastures that came down to the railroad were hedged with tall Osage-orange trees and shaded by an occasional elm, but otherwise lay full in the sun. In the spring, corners of these pastures were alive with young animals, and you hung over the wire fences to love and admire them. First-born were the lambs, in the cold of early March, when sheep still huddled close to the sheltered barnyard; then the calves appeared, and finally the colts. Pigs could come at any time, seemingly, and were always endearing, all pink and clean under their sparse bristles, squealing fussily around a recumbent sow in a fence corner, then, moved by a sudden whim, galloping off across the field in single file and as suddenly galloping back again.

Early in the spring you thought newborn lambs were the most

enchanting of living creatures, so impetuous and ungainly were they, so rough with the ewes that suckled them, so irrepressible in their games with each other, charging, bucking, leaping with all four feet in the air. But in May the colts appeared (and here and there a baby mule)—velvet-coated, wistful-eyed, at once curious and timid, so that they peered at you around a mare's haunch, from a safe place behind her. Then you forgot the lambs in the pleasure you felt in watching the colts make acquaintance with spring and the world, running with the wind to the far side of the field, trying their heels in sudden wheels and plunges, smelling the sky, nuzzling their mothers.

When you had seen enough of these delights and your feet had wearied of ties and cinders, you crawled through a barbed-wire fence into the first empty field you came to, and crossed to the road. You came out near the farm where a schoolmate lived, dropped in there for a glass of water and a turn in the rope swing hung from the side-yard oak tree, then took the road home and scuffed through the dust with lagging steps.

Such an extent of the town's shabby outskirts had to be traversed before you reached your own gate that the landscape you had seen might have been blotted from your memory. It never was. Far away and, as it then seemed, a long while afterwards, reading Theocritus in college, I saw in my mind those familiar fields. "Lo, Sparta is wide, and wide is Elis . . . and Arcadia, rich in sheep." I did not reveal my eccentric response to those lines, because in those years it was laughable to claim any beauty or any virtue for the Middle West; nevertheless, I stubbornly cherished my pleasure in the belief that however unlike Arcadia my country was in all other aspects, still, if you held your eyes to the sheep and the foolish bleating lambs and the green pastures they moved in, there was no difference to distinguish this place and this time from Greece two thousand years ago.

No one could even pretend today to see any resemblance between that stretch of land and Theocritus' Greece. The fields between railroad and road have been set aside for new industries. The house of my schoolmate that was once well out in the country now faces a new little factory across the road. There are other small factories and large warehouses filling that space—they are modern, clean of line, circled by green lawns. But any child would have a long, long walk on the railroad ties before he came to a country where in the spring he could see lambs gamboling in the fields.

To reach the last of our four corners, that to the southeast, you walked east four blocks and then turned right, up and over the viaduct. Beyond the viaduct you could go straight across Orient Hill to the Wilmington pike; on the hill were several of the roomiest houses in town, built there in the 1870's and 80's by families who needed floor and front-yard space for ten or a dozen sons and daughters. They were square, verandaed houses with rough lawns shaded by oak trees. In our time, in the second generation, there were still five or six children to a house, and you could easily be persuaded by them to give up your walk and join their games under the oaks.

Or, at the top of the viaduct, you could turn to the left and follow the street there, and the country road it soon became. On either hand for a long way the snake fences were lined with wild roses and blackberry vines. On the left, inside the fence, a row of young trees cut off the view. The trees did not impress you unless you passed them in the right week in May; then you saw that they were locusts, hung thick with the honey-sweet bloom that scented the quiet air of the road. Beyond the locusts you came to a grove of oak trees on the other side of the road, sloping gently down and away from you, the grass a rich green, the trees very tall before they branched. It was rather a somber grove, where the wind never seemed to blow, and the light fell strangely across the soft grass late in the afternoon, slanting obliquely down the slope between the trunks.

You did not often walk so far: ordinarily the viaduct itself was your goal. At first, at an early age, you came to watch the trains. To the west of the high bridge lies the railroad station, encircled by a multiplicity of tracks, where freight cars once stood on sidings and switch engines fretted and fumed back and forth. Under the viaduct and off to the eastward runs the double track that goes eventually to New York. Standing there you could see a train pull out of the station. You awaited its coming, did not flinch when its engine disappeared roaring beneath your feet, and were rewarded by explosions of smoke between the boards of the floor that sent your skirts billowing. When you had blinked the soot out of your eyes, you dodged under the wires that braced the struts of the bridge and crossed to the other side, whence you could look down on the tops of Pullman cars as they were drawn out from beneath you. Entranced, you stood listening and watching while the rumble of the train died away, until you heard the engine whistle for the Jasper-pike crossing. You did these things once upon a time, when the viaduct still had a board floor and its railings were low enough to hook your elbows over, but you did not realize how the smell of coal smoke had become a part of your life. It was only later that you knew it, when, coming home from travels east or west, you reached Pittsburgh from one direction or St. Louis from the other, and with the first breath of the familiar nostalgic scent and savor of their smoke there came to your mind the viaduct and its trains, the railroad station, and streets in the winter dusk with smoke pouring from domestic chimneys.

As we grew older we went to the viaduct less frequently to see the trains, more often, in the winter, for coasting. An inch of snow would make its boards slick as glass, while on Dick's hill the weeds would not be covered. The hill was steeper, but our sleds went down the viaduct with enough momentum to carry us across Third Street and halfway up the hill beyond, toward Second Street and the many-chimneyed Kinney house, high on its corner. In those days the few automobiles that townspeople possessed were put up for the winter, and owners of fast horses raced their sleighs only on Second Street; so we were perfectly safe when we shot out past the corner houses and across Third Street. At any rate, safety was not a consideration in our minds when we were coasting, or hitching on behind sleighs and careening all over town, around corners and into and out of drifts, snow in our faces from the runners and horses' hooves.

Children coasting on the viaduct gave to the sport the concentration it deserved. The view which lay spread before them was uncritically accepted for what it was: the town, familiar and homely. That on the one hand it was all taken in by eyes and mind, that on the other it was not consciously observed, as woods and fields were observed, and that no critical judgments were arrived at, I know, for when I went there not long ago to look at it, I was surprised both by its familiarity and by its ugliness.

In the winter the bare tops of trees lace the sky in the always beautiful pattern—but trunk and lower boughs screen nothing. At the foot of the viaduct, right and left, lie the back premises of Third Street houses, their latticed kitchen entries with washtubs hung beside them, their sheds and garbage cans exposed nakedly to the eye. Farther to the right, the East End on its hill is all the drearier in its winter grime because cabin and cottage were brightly painted once, turquoise, rose, or pale green, and have been subdued by sun and rain to one dinginess. Straight ahead, where the farther streets are higher than Third, the square roofs of big houses block the sky, with their three double chimneys to a side. To the left, where those streets drop downhill, a jumble of ridgepoles, gables, and chimneys leads the eye to the courthouse, its tower and clock. The tiled roof of the tower stands above the nearer blight of soiled roof and chimney; bright against a gray sky, its red is the only patch of unsullied color that you see. All else is shabby, worn, and unpicturesque. Once, when everyone in town burned coal and the dun-colored smoke drifted across every roof and down into the street, this view must have been even gloomier in the winter than it is today. Yet that scene, so unconsciously accepted, had its value for us.

Children who grow up in a town the size of ours have as compensation for city advantages the accessibility to them of open country. At first hand they know the local earth and all that thereon lives and grows. Wandering free as the wind, left to their own devices, they are neither led nor hindered by the consciousness of being overseen. There is engendered in them by small things, like the knowledge their fingers have of violet stems, that instinctive, untutored passion for a country that is the beginning of patriotism. As they grow older the specific and particular which they have learned for themselves slip into place in relation to the general and universal. Before they read poetry they have found the stuff of which it is made, and they come to its pages at last with a fine sense of recognition—recognition of those truths that are based on evidence long and familiarly known. They accept the poet's testimony as to an "always": always the firmament of stars by night, the arched bow of the sky by day, and the line of a hill against it, trees and growing fields, wild flowers, streams and the cattle that go down to them to drink, lambs and colts and the birds that fly: these in the verses of the Psalmist, in Theocritus and Horace, in Milton and Wordsworth, are the same as in the days and nights, so many centuries later, when they first saw and noted them. They accept also therefore such philosophies—such conceptions of God and man—as are based by the poets on this immutability.

But town children have also this compensation for the freedom and all the delights of growing up on a farm: when they look down from a height and see, one after another, the many houses that are familiar, there is stored away in their minds a knowledge of the inexhaustible richness and complication of ordinary daily life. They may be unaware of this knowledge, but it will be of value to them in the day when they awaken from the assumption that their own lives are to be brilliantly out of the ordinary.

It was not until I looked from the viaduct again and realized how well I knew the scene before me that I came at last to a full perception of all the meaning it held for us. Children are not aesthetically blind; we could not have thought that view beautiful. Yet I am convinced that we must have resented any criticism of it. It was home: the same, day by day, year after year— eternally, we should have liked to believe. That it was ugly did not matter. Paradoxically, there is a good in its ugliness. The town has had no high moment of beauty and perfection to lay an obligation on us to preserve it as a museum. It encourages no glamorous illusion that life once was wholly fair; it is a background that makes no demands on its children; it does not sustain in them any extravagant hope. In these streets, under these roofs, they are free to dream their dreams in peace; they are free also to forget them when they must, without bitterness, and to accept instead the humdrum daily life of the generations of mankind, the same life—unchanged in its essentials as earth and sky since the days of Theocritus—that has given to the scene that weight and density which even children busy with their sleds have apprehended in it.

And as I stood there on the viaduct staring at ridgepoles and chimneys, I was moved by a further revelation that came like a warmth about my heart. The outward changes that have come in my time—new streets, new houses, the many new people— these are minor and unimportant; it is not because of them that the town is immeasurably richer than when I was a child. It is the added years that make it so, the years lived out in its houses, its streets: the town is richer by the life of a generation. Since I last stood here with a sled rope in my hand there has been that accretion: the roofs of the town have sheltered an added half-century of birth, of childhood, of growing up and falling in love —of growing old and dying: all the hard, sometimes bitter but always rewarding experience of being men and women.